THE COOPERATIVE MOVEMENT

Corporate Social Responsibility Series

Series Editor:
Professor David Crowther, De Montfort University, UK

This series aims to provide high quality research books on all aspects of corporate social responsibility including: business ethics, corporate governance and accountability, globalization, civil protests, regulation, responsible marketing and social reporting.

The series is interdisciplinary in scope and global in application and is an essential forum for everyone with an interest in this area.

Also in the series

The Employment Contract and the Changed World of Work
Stella Vettori
ISBN 978-0-7546-4754-6

Capitalist Networks and Social Power in Australia and New Zealand
Georgina Murray
ISBN 978-0-7546-4708-9

Stories, Visions and Values in Voluntary Organisations
Christina Schwabenland
ISBN 978-0-7546-4462-0

Whistleblowing and Organizational Social Responsibility: A Global Assessment
Wim Vandekerckhove
ISBN 978-0-7546-4750-8

Repoliticizing Management: A Theory of Corporate Legitimacy
Conor Cradden
ISBN 978-0-7546-4497-2

Making Ecopreneurs: Developing Sustainable Entrepreneurship
Edited by Michael Schaper
ISBN 978-0-7546-4491-0

Corporate Social Responsibility in the Mining Industries
Natalia Yakovleva
ISBN 978-0-7546-4268-8

The Cooperative Movement
Globalization from Below

RICHARD C. WILLIAMS
Regis University, USA

with Preface by George Cheney

Routledge
Taylor & Francis Group

LONDON AND NEW YORK

First published in paperback 2024

First published 2007 by Ashgate Publishing

Published 2016 by Routledge
4 Park Square, Milton Park, Abingdon, Oxon OX14 4RN

and by Routledge
605 Third Avenue, New York, NY 10158

Routledge is an imprint of the Taylor & Francis Group, an informa business

British Library Cataloguing in Publication Data
Williams, Richard C.
    The cooperative movement : globalization from below. -
    (Corporate social responsibility series)
    1. Cooperative societies 2. Cooperative societies - History
    I. Title
    334

Library of Congress Cataloging-in-Publication Data
Williams, Richard C.
    The cooperative movement : globalization from below / by Richard C. Williams.
        p. cm. -- (Corporate social responsibility series)
    Includes Index.
    ISBN: 978-0-7546-7038-4 1. Cooperation--History. 2. Cooperation--
Case studies. I. Title.

    HD2956 .W55 2007
    334--dc22

                                                                        2006034024

ISBN 13: 978-0-7546-7038-4 (hbk)
ISBN 13: 978-1-03-283798-7 (pbk)
ISBN 13: 978-1-315-61502-8 (ebk)

DOI: 10.4324/9781315615028

Globalization From Below

A Haiku Ode to Cooperatives
with apologies to the Sphinx and Basque Sheep

Trade might shrink the world
But who dares to extract the
Essence of the thing?

Ideas so grand
Poets strain to compress
Life into sound bytes

We catch early break:
Five syllables found in
"Globalization"

Gross domination:
Mega-multinationals
Quash competition

Rich getting richer
And the poor getting poorer
Can it ever change?

Powerless people
Feel hunger, violence of
The widening chasm

Powerless masses
Return the violence, pressed
Past human limits

The little guy is
Not the enemy, and the
West isn't the Best

We shrivel and die
When competition alone
Is our way of life

We must bridge the chasm
The prophets remind us that
We're in the same boat

We make lots of bread
Off the sweat of the poorest
Then toss crumbs their way

No room at the inn
The Hilton and the five-stars
Have naught to offer

The Spirit can ignite
The potential in us all
To create justice

Development! not
Just a dam, nuclear plant,
And more Mickey D's

A supply-focused
Economy means basic
Needs cannot be met

But demand focus
Allows room for creative
Response to felt need

We need a new view
A view from the other side
Where there is enough

Cooperation
Not hyper-competition
Can it work today?

Individuals
Can work together to be
Truly creative

Not a collective
Controlled by a corrupt state
But something better

How will the co-op
Endure as alternative
To exploitation?

Some folks cry "commies!"
But people of faith and hope
Hear the prophet call:

Let justice roll down
Like a river, righteousness
Like a mighty stream!

The world traveler
Finds myriad miracles
Of cooperation

But only if she
Moves behind the veil of glitz
To the birth of hope

Coffee growers sell
To local co-op, avoid
Coyotes' rip-off

"Untouchables" tap
Source of self-empowerment
Microfinancing

Vision of Agus
Indonesian People's Bank
Open up new doors

Jakartan Mennos
Sing and echo prophet's song:
Justice for the poor

If we don't sing out,
Then who? the Sphinx? the
Shaggy Arrasate sheep?

O God, when shall all
The weary earth cease sighing
And ring out its mirth?

– Brian Ladd
– Bruce Fast

This book is dedicated to the members of the Boulder Mennonite Community, Boulder, Colorado, USA, for their diligence in living and walking a simple and cooperative life-style modeled so ably by their sixteenth century Anabaptist progenitors.

Contents

List of Figures   *ix*
List of Tables   *x*
Foreword   *xi*
Preface by George Cheney   *xiii*
Acknowledgments   *xxi*

Introduction   1

PART I   **HISTORY AND THEORY OF COOPERATION**

Chapter 1   History and Theory of the Cooperative Movement   9

Chapter 2   Comparing Cooperation, Competition, and Individual Effort   37

Chapter 3   The Standard Economic Model and Globalization   57

PART II   **COOPERATIVE CASE STUDIES**

Chapter 4   Cooperation and Microfinance in Southeast Asia and Oceania   83

Chapter 5   The Cooperative Movement in India   95

Chapter 6   Mondragón: The Basque Cooperative Experience   113

Chapter 7   Cooperatives in Latin America   125

Chapter 8   Puerto Rico's Cooperative Effort   139

PART III   **ANALYSIS AND IMPLICATIONS FOR THE FUTURE**

Chapter 9   What Makes a Cooperative Work?   151

Chapter 10   The Blueprint: Globalization from Below   165

APPENDICES

Appendix A Credit Union Statistics						185

Appendix B Measuring Effect Size						207

Appendix C The IMF "Merged Model"						213

Appendix D Interviews: Protocol and Summary Data				215

Index									*223*

List of Figures

Figure 1.1   Number of Credit Unions   26
Figure 1.2   Number of Credit Union Members (in millions)   27
Figure 1.3   Total Assets of Credit Unions (in $millions)   28

Figure 3.1   World Poverty and Income Inequality After Free Trade   65

Figure 5.1   ASP Organizational Chart   102

Figure 6.1   Basic Mondragón Cooperative Organizational Chart   117
Figure 6.2   Four Legs of the Inter-cooperative Structure   118

Figure A.1   Number of US Credit Unions, 1939-2004   194
Figure A.2   Number of Members at US Credit Unions, 1939-2004   195
Figure A.3   Membership Growth at US Credit Unions, 1940-2004   196
Figure A.4   Assets at US Credit Unions (in $millions), 1939-2004   197
Figure A.5   Asset Growth at US Credit Unions, 1940-2004   198
Figure A.6   Savings Growth at US Credit Unions, 1940-2004   199
Figure A.7   Loan Growth at US Credit Unions, 1940-2004   200
Figure A.8   Loans to Savings Ratio at US Credit Unions, 1939-2004   201
Figure A.9   Savings to Assets at US Credit Unions, 1939-2004   202
Figure A.10   Reserves to Assets at US Credit Unions, 1939-2004   203
Figure A.11   Loans to Assets at US Credit Unions, 1939-2004   204
Figure A.12   Dollar Asset Growth at US Credit Unions (in $millions),
              1940-2004   205

Figure B.1   The Standard Normal Distribution   209

List of Tables

Table 1.1   Agricultural Cooperatives' Shares of US Farm Market—
            Selected Commodity Groups   25
Table 1.2   Energy Cooperatives in the United States Selected Utility Data
            by Ownership, US, 2000   30

Table 2.1   Impact of Cooperative, Competitive, and Individualistic Efforts
            on Productivity/Achievement   43
Table 2.2   Cognitive or Moral Reasoning   46
Table 2.3   Mean Effect Sizes for Types of Tasks   48
Table 2.4   Mean Effect Sizes for Quality of Study   50

Table 3.1   World's Real Per Capita Income Distribution, 1988-1993   62
Table 3.2   World Population and Total World Poor (in billions)   63
Table 3.3   Countries Ranked By Percent of Population in Poverty
            (OECD Nations Only)   76

Table 4.1   Sixteen Decisions   86

Table A.1   United States State Credit Union Statistics   185
Table A.2   United States Federal Credit Union Statistics   188
Table A.3   United States Credit Union Statistics   191

Foreword

When I was working on a project with the Mayan people in the highlands of the state of Chiapas, Mexico, I learned of the severely negative effects of the North American Free Trade Agreement (NAFTA) on the native peoples and especially on the coffee growers of that area. Their traditional economic mode for generations had been cooperative, but the provisions of NAFTA that require producing/trading units to be privately owned were forcing their cooperative coffee growers out of business. Before NAFTA, they were able to realize 25 pesos per kilo for their coffee; after NAFTA they could scarcely get 6 pesos for the same partially processed kilos. Competition from the US-subsidized coffee corporations in Vietnam simply nailed the lid on the cooperative coffin in Chiapas. Direct trade lines with similar cooperatives in the US and Europe, created in the late 1990s, promise salvation for the coffee cooperatives in Chiapas.

The current practice of "free market capitalism" is based on a curious set of assumptions. The first of those assumptions has always puzzled me in the light of my experience in administering non-profit groups and in my teaching career: The idea that unfettered competition is necessary to provide balance and equity within the society and within the economy. Something about that assumption drove me to a rational analysis of the research comparing cooperation with competition. To me the results of that research is as clear as the observation that the earth is not flat but spherical and as definitive as the more recent conclusion that smoking is not a healthy activity. Cooperation is much more productive than competition in virtually every conceivable setting.

Still another series of events have claimed my attention: the recent publicity about the ethical lapses of transnational corporations like Enron and Exxon-Mobil. The impression is that these events are mere tips of a much larger iceberg of corporate social responsibility. The decline and fall of the Roman Empire was scarcely noticeable to the ordinary citizen in the fifth century CE; so it is today with the empire being driven by the transnationals that spring from western culture and western "free" market capitalism. The neo-colonial empire of today is showing unmistakable signs of collapse.

What can be done about all of this? I have never been one to rely for long on negative complaints and criticisms. There must be some positive solution to these economic, political, and social problems. This question has driven me back to the idea of cooperative economics. Is it enough to inject our modern conglomerates and transnational corporations with more internal and external collaboration? Is it enough to increase employee participation and loyalty by slightly stretching the limits on employee owned shares or even a bit more input into decision making? It seems that everyone is ignoring what is happening today in the world-wide cooperative movement.

Driven to secure more information on the cooperative movement for my colleagues, my students, and myself, I began searching the literature. Expecting to find a vast literature on the subject, I was disappointed to discover little helpful material. Certainly nothing has been published since the 1970s, except a few low-level manuals on how to start a small retail cooperative and one valuable reference dictionary by Jack Shaffer. Hence, I offer this book. I hope that it is at least a start in filling a very important gap in our understanding of the cooperative movement and its importance to current global economics.

Richard C. Williams, Ph.D.
Boulder, Colorado, USA
September 2006

Preface

George Cheney

From the standpoint of neo-liberal economics, which now holds sway in North America, Europe, and many other parts of the world, the best assurance of democratic political institutions is unrestrained free trade. This position is often credited to Adam Smith (1776/1986), even though Smith himself never envisioned an economy without major roles for "moral sentiments" such as compassion, or where commerce was disconnected from social bonds (see Werhane, 1991). In this way, a particular form of corporate-consumer capitalism is *de facto* equated with the democratization of states and societies (see the analysis of this and related arguments in Almond, 1991).

The neo-liberal position is only one perspective, of course, however dominant it may be on the world stage today and however much it may rely upon a mythic portrayal of industrialization of nations that denies the real protectionism and state sponsorship that occurred in perhaps every case (Korten, 1995). Moreover, as the author of this book, Richard Williams, observes, there is an ambivalent stance toward competition within contemporary corporate capitalism. Competition is championed when convenient and in the official discourses of most world leaders yet it is also restricted when it is in the interest of transnational corporations to do so (compare Aune, 2001). Thus, it is crucial to understand the powerful but ambiguous symbols of democracy and capitalism and examine their dynamics more closely.

In fact, we should reconsider what "democracy" and "participation" mean—or can mean—within the organization (corporation or other) as it responds to and itself fashions processes of globalization, including the trumpeted privilege of the consumer. That is, given market globalization, what can we expect, or hope for, in terms of democracy inside the firm—for the employees at all levels of the organization? At the same time, we should consider the *external* impact of any organization that claims to be democratic. That is, we must ask about how any organization, regardless of sector, contributes to or detracts from an authentically democratic society. These are reasonable assessments to make, especially given the assertion of contemporary neo-liberal advocates that a globalized market is the best route to collective participation as well as prosperity.

However, we are by now accustomed to treating globalization as *something that happens to* people, businesses, and communities—unless of course, we are focusing on the largest of multinationals and transnational governmental organizations. But, this passive stance cedes power a priori to the already dominant players on the world stage and all but ensures the continuance of business as usual. This is precisely why I like to interrogate managers and administrators who insist that "The market made us do it" with questions such as "So, who or what is the market?" "Aren't you part of the market?" And, "how do your policies and choices contribute to that thing we call The Market?" (see, e.g., Cheney, 2004).

The perspective embodied in this book, and being advocated elsewhere, has been called "globalization from below" (see, e.g., Brecher, Costello, and Smith, 2000). This term gives a label to a diverse set of movements, organizations and groups that are attempting to reconfigure the economy in socially just terms while connecting with one another across regional and national boundaries. Richard Williams' wide-ranging and comprehensive study of contemporary cooperatives adopts this frame not only because of current economic reality but also because of the unfulfilled promise of global "cooperativism." That is to say, the motley collection of organizations which call themselves cooperatives differ in origin, structure, governance, degree of participation, ultimate objectives, and of course economic focus. Yet they tend to share allegiance to certain principles that would make commercial enterprise truly democratic.

Under this umbrella we find producer co-ops, value-added co-ops, distribution co-ops, service co-ops, consumer co-ops, worker co-ops, housing co-ops, and financial co-ops. Many of these organizations consciously pursue "A Third Way" between rigidly centralized socialism and unruly and often inhumane capitalism. Some examples, such as many consumer and financial co-ops, are only weakly associated with social commitments: that is, members may be relatively unaware of or unconcerned with the dedication of the organization to positive social change (if in fact it is). To the degree that there is a family resemblance among organizations which call themselves cooperatives, we may say that they share these aspects: 1) some commitment to *collective if not necessarily equal ownership* by members, 2) some commitment to *democratic decision making* by members, and 3) and a belief in *the viability* of like experiments outside of their own experience. To this list, Williams would add, following the famous "Rochdale Principles," the idea of freedom from outside interference, both governmental and private. And, that is a crucial point, both organizationally and economically speaking, as I revisit below.

The cooperative movement—if we may call it that—traces its inspiration and examples to the so-called Utopian communities of Britain and the United States during the nineteenth century, and especially to the enterprises of Scottish industrialist Robert Owen. This lineage is important not only because of the values that are invoked (such as collective ownership at the level of the firm) but also because it makes clear the complexities of any particular case. That is, despite the celebrated autonomy of the cooperatives founded by Owen and his allies, these worker co-ops were neither autonomous with respect to the financial vicissitudes of the market nor with regard to the individual employee being relatively free of over-the-shoulder monitoring at work (see Wren, 1987). Thus, even in the history and mythos of cooperativism, we find important tensions and contradictions that are still being debated today.

On the practical level, scholars, activists, and practitioners identify a broad movement of "cooperativism," which features worker-owned-and-managed cooperatives alongside producer and consumer co-ops. In fact, there is a global association dedicated to these ideals and practices, called the International Cooperative Alliance (1996), along with a number of similarly dedicated national-level and regional associations. Yet, there has been no recent assessment of the strength and promise of cooperativism across diverse types and locales.

With this book, Williams has given us the charge to probe deeply into some of the most prominent examples of cooperatives around the world today. His analysis moves us beyond both broad philosophical statements and abstract economic models, on the one hand, and isolated case narratives on the other. Based on his extensive travels, Williams offers an in-depth look at major cooperatives in Europe, Asia, and Latin America, including some of the most celebrated (yet little understood) cases of economic democracy today. Simultaneously, he considers the roles of several different types of cooperatives in the North American experience, and helps to explain why some took root while others withered away.

A multitude of reviews can be found on the subject of the historical and contemporary forms of organizational democracy (see references in Cheney, 1999, 2006). These studies represent the disciplines of sociology, political science, management, economics, communication, and anthropology. The most famous formulation of participation at work in relation to broader democratic ideals remains Carole Pateman's (1970) *Participation and Democratic Theory*, in which she argues that in the cases of both organizational and national-level participation it is important to get concrete about what is practiced and what is possible, lest myth overpower analysis. Pateman's broad-ranging examination of democracy at work relied upon systems then in place in Yugoslavia for primary examples, and her study became the touchstone for further work on efforts to democratize work.

Much has changed since the late 1960s and early 1970s when Pateman made her observations. Yugoslavia no longer exists as such, and most avowedly communist states have fallen. At the same time, we find a greater degree of concentration in industries ranging from energy to media and that the very structure of many economies has moved away from governmental ownership of key services, regulation of private industry, and assurances to individual citizens. The welfare state has even undergone significant challenges in Western Europe, its bastion. At the transnational level, the World Bank and the International Monetary Fund have become chief arbiters of economic globalization, yet the results of their efforts in the area of development are mixed (e.g., Stiglitz, 2002). Finally, the World Trade Organization, as a distinctive, corporate-governmental partnership operating outside the bounds of national and transnational jurisdictions, has come to epitomize globalization for many people and has therefore been the target of the so-called anti-globalization movement since 1999.

As we speak of change and globalization, we must also place in clear view the transformation of the citizen into the consumer, in the West and beyond. "Consumerism was the twentieth century's winning 'ism'" (Gopnik, 1997, 80). With this bold and deliberately ironic statement, a writer for *The New Yorker* magazine made the point that whatever other movements rose and fell in the past 100 years or so, the force of consumerism is indeed with us. Indeed, it is now so common to speak of "consumer society," to substitute the term "consumer" for "citizen," and to speak of nations like China as "emerging markets of consumer power," that in everyday talk consumption has ceased to be an object of attention. It is as taken for granted as breathing. For people in industrialized societies, regardless of their position on the political spectrum, *consumption is not just a means to live but a way of life* (Miles, 1998; Schor, 2004). Nowhere is this truer than in the contemporary United States, where the "gimme" form of consumerism has swamped the politically responsible form—at least so far (Cheney, 2005). On the face of it, this shift supports large-scale economic globalization and the institution of marketing (in all its facets) which makes an apparently democratic promise to "give people what they want." Against this cultural-economic backdrop, organizations that would organize and style themselves around social values in order to engage people as political actors as well as purchasers have an uphill battle, to say the least.

Williams' comparative study of cooperatives today strikes a necessary balance between unrestrained idealism and the kind of realism which leaves individuals and organizations with little else to do but swim with the tides of change or be swamped by them (or so the metaphor of pro free market advocates goes). In fact, Williams synthesizes the promises, failures, and hopes of cooperatives to develop a blueprint for a more just, more cooperative economy. Several undeniable facts work in Williams' favor here, making such a call seem more firmly grounded today than it would have been 30 years ago. These are the known effects of over-consumption, environmental degradation, and increasing disparities in wealth (Hamilton, 2003). Combine these with the mounting evidence that advanced consumer capitalism, for all its grandiose claims about being "the one best way," is not making people happier. In fact, the contrary may well be the case (Lane, 2000). In this way, Williams does have contemporary history on his side when he argues for a return to the commons, limits on corporate power, the implementation of democratic principles at work, the strengthening of regional economies, and an honest approach to efficiency that accounts for all the costs of doing business (compare Hawken, 1993).

In my own decade-long study of the Mondragón worker cooperatives in the Basque Country, Spain (Cheney, 1995, 1999, 2006), I was led from an initial focus on the internal workings of these firms—including their old and new forms of employee participation—to a broader perspective that saw them as embedded within social, cultural and economic change. In the end, what was most interesting for me was how managers within the co-ops were refashioning the organizations in the image of what they saw as necessary forms of market globalization (compare Goll, 1991). That is, I learned that globalization wasn't "just happening to" the co-ops; rather, they were understanding, translating, and implementing it in particular ways that were sometimes at odds with long-standing democratic principles and, as I argued, sometimes unnecessary.

Here again is where the consumer at Mondragón played an enormous role. As people in Basque and Spanish societies began to think and talk like consumers, they became more accepting of the reconfiguration of work as well as other domains around consumer pursuits—and their attendant pressures. In the communities, this meant greater access to an array of consumer goods and services but also a faster pace of life and a loss of an appreciation of sacrifice, as one founder of the Mondragón co-ops told me plaintively. One "socio" or employee-owner of one of the largest co-ops captured well the relationship between his consumer role and his worker role: "When I'm at the shopping mall, I'm king; when I'm at work, I'm serving the king."

Clearly, there is a great challenge to those like us who would re-envision and refigure the economy along humane, cooperative, and what we believe are more deeply democratic principles. I would put the matter this way: how do we "sell" a vision of a new economic order that is neither state socialism nor unrestrained capitalism, reinvigorate commerce with a new sense of moral purpose, and encourage citizens to reconsider their own consumption practices in ways that do not feel like a loss to them? These are among the most pressing challenges we face, made all the more urgent by global inequalities and threats to the planet's continuance as we know it.

For cooperative and alternative organizations themselves, obviously they cannot have a social impact without sheer economic survival. This is the type of "realism" typically addressed at those who start up worker and other kinds of co-ops. The obverse of this question, though, is equally important: of what good is "prosperity" if it does not include a broader commitment to workers, the community, and the environment? Examining of the case of Mondragón but also looking more widely, I concluded that the following ingredients were necessary for combined economic and social success.

Fostering a Consensus around Certain Values

Maintaining core value commitments is difficult not only because times change or even that the organization changes but also because the people change. Thus, the value commitments of the founding generation of cooperative employee-members may come to be seen as outdated by younger recruits. In fact, this is part of what has happened at Mondragón, where more individualistic conceptions of the career have arisen among 40-, 30- and 20-somethings.

Maintaining a Simultaneously Open and Closed System

For a cooperative or any organization to maintain its core values and practices, some self-protection is necessary. This much was clear from the experiences of the Owenite cooperatives and communities whose distinctiveness was lost once they became dependent upon outside capital and therefore absentee ownership. The zone of protection for a cooperative can include buffering from the vicissitudes of the market (as in the case of an internal banking system); a training and educational system that runs at least somewhat counter to popular, outside views of how to do business; and/or a kind of autonomy that allows the cooperative to shift its production and service emphases so as to preserve itself.

Seeking (and Finding) Leadership and Inspiration

Inspired, even charismatic leadership is perhaps essential to the founding and maintenance of value-based organizations such as cooperatives. While I would have stated this position a bit less strongly during my studies at Mondragón in the 1990s, I would now take a more certain position that reflects the empirical realities of cases throughout the world in the arena of "alternative organizations." Very few succeed with a purely group form of leadership, as can be seen in the record of socially responsible businesses and social movement organizations, in addition to cooperatives. The problem harks back to Weber's (1978) discussion of the "routinization of charisma:" how best to preserve charisma institutionally after the founder is gone (see also Grant, 2004; Roper & Cheney, 2005). The option of simply watching and waiting for the new organizational messiah, as some of the older socios are still doing at Mondragón, is not a hopeful sign for the revival of democratic practice.

Conserving a Common Mission

For any cooperative or other type of alternative organization to keep going with a degree of organizational integrity, values must be revisited—in terms of labels, practices, and preferences of the majority or the whole. For example, an ambiguous but emotionally charged value such as "solidarity" should be considered periodically for what it means in terms of current policies and practices (Cheney, 1997). As the contemporary situation is compared with the founding context, members should ask, how much deviation from the path can be allowed? In part this depends on what the organizational members see as the *constitutive or defining values* of the firm and therefore how much adaptation or modification is deemed permissible.

Recognizing the Interdependence of the Social and the Economic

I would stress that very few managers in any type of organizations appreciate fully just how much these two sets of motivations work together. The typical position on democratic and enlightened human resource practices in tough financial times is "not now." Ironically, a common position on the social side of enterprise during flush times is "not needed." The fact is that socio-symbolic aspects of employment continue to be relegated to a lesser role than the one deserved, despite the accumulated evidence that employees crave genuine autonomy and opportunities for participation in the direction of their own work and the firm's (compare Weisbord, 1991).

Enacting Democracy as a Process

No one can presume an omniscient position to decide what "real" democracy or employee participation is. What we can do is urge any committed organization to engage employee-members in a systematic consideration of their own system of participation (Mygind, 1992), to recognize the practical limitations associated with any system, and to revisit the functioning of participative programs in light of their own goals and new information.

Being Mindful of the Market

I mean this caution not only in the sense of awareness of market forces but also such that the organization consciously adopts a point of view with respect to its market. No value-based organization should consider itself as completely passive in the face of market forces, if only because decisions about product and service specializations or niches may allow the firm more flexibility than initially presumed. To surrender completely to The Market is in effect to renounce innovation, creativity, and the possibilities for localized difference. This strategy also makes for a self-fulfilling prophecy. Such exercises in autonomy, in turn, may allow the organization to establish and maintain the very types of participatory practices that it finds ideal and consistent with core value commitments.

In the global market, Mondragón and the other cases Williams assesses remain a beacon of creativity and hope within the cooperative "movement," alongside feminist collectives, local economies, alternative trade organizations, decentralized action networks, multi-union "corporate campaigns," people's alliances across class and national boundaries, and resistance by the poor against the privatization of water. As breaks continue to develop in what had appeared until 1999 to be an unstoppable tide of "free trade," these various forms of social and economic experimentation should be better understood, nurtured, and sustained. The contest over the meanings and practices of democracy vis-à-vis the market will continue in multiple ways and in multiple sites.

Of all the pithy and provocative ideas about democracy that I could quote or paraphrase here, this one jumps to mind: that the ancient Greeks had absolutely no doubt as to the possibility of democracy, yet they questioned its ultimate worth because of their ongoing reflection about multiple options in political organization. By contrast, "we" have no doubt whatsoever of the ultimate worth of democracy, yet we remain unsure of its practical possibility (Corcoran, 1983). In other words, we are unshaken in holding out a certain vision of democracy as a point of orientation, but we are less sure of how to get there. It is time to realize democracy in that sphere of our lives we call the economy (Dahl, 1985).

George Cheney
University of Utah
September, 2006

References

Almond, G. (1991). "Capitalism and Democracy." *Political Science and Politics*, 24, 467-474.

Aune, J.A. (2001). *Selling the Free Market*. New York: Guilford.

Brecher, J., Costello, T., and Smith, B. (2000). *Globalization from Below: The Power of Solidarity*. Cambridge, MA: South End Press.

Cheney, G. (1995). "Democracy in the Workplace: Theory and Practice from the Perspective of Communication." *Journal of Applied Communication Research*, 23, 167-200.

Cheney, G. (1997). "The Many Meanings of 'Solidarity:' The Negotiation of Values in the Mondragón Worker-Cooperative Complex Under Pressure." In B.D. Sypher (ed.), *Case Studies in Organizational Communication: 2* (pp. 68-83). New York: Guilford.

Cheney, G. (1999, 2002). *Values at Work: Employee Participation Meets Market Pressure at Mondragón*. Ithaca and London: Cornell University Press.

Cheney, G. (2004). "Arguing about the Place of Values and Ethics in Market-Oriented Discourses of Today." In P. Sullivan and S. Goldzwig (eds), *New Approaches to Rhetoric* (pp. 61-88). Thousand Oaks, CA: Sage.

Cheney, G. (2005, March 22). *The United Consumers of America. Or, Is There a Citizen in the House?* Second annual Lecture in the Humanities, University of Utah.

Cheney, G. (2006). "Democracy at Work Within the Market: Reconsidering the Potential." In V. Smith (ed.), *Research in the Sociology of Work, Vol. 16.* London: Elsevier.

Corcoran, P. (1983). "The Limits of Democratic Theory." In G. Duncan (ed.), *Democratic Theory and Practice* (pp. 13-24). Cambridge: Cambridge University Press.

Dahl, R. (1985). *A Preface to Economic Democracy.* Berkeley: University of California Press.

Gopnik, A. (1997, 4 August). "Trouble at the Tower." *The New Yorker*, p. 80.

Goll, I. (1991). "Environment, Corporate Ideology, and Employee Involvement Programs." *Industrial Relations*, 30, 138-149.

Grant, S. (2004). *The Body Shop: A Study of Narrative and Identity.* Unpublished dissertation, The University of Waikato, Hamilton, New Zealand.

Hamilton, C. (2003). *Growth Fetish.* London: Pluto Press.

Hawken, P. (1993). *The Ecology of Commerce.* New York: HarperCollins.

International Cooperative Alliance. (1996). *Statement of Cooperative Identity.* Madrid: ICA.

Korten, D.C. (1995). *When Corporations Rule the World.* San Francisco: Berrett-Koehler.

Lane, R.E. (2000). *The Loss of Happiness in Market Democracies.* New Haven, CT: Yale University Press.

Miles, S. (1998). *Consumerism as a Way of Life.* London: Sage.

Mygind, N. (1992). "The Choice of Ownership Structure." *Economic and Industrial Democracy*, 13, 359-99.

Pateman. C. (1970). *Participation and Democratic Theory.* Cambridge: Cambridge University Press.

Roper, J., & Cheney, G. (2005). "The Meanings of Social Entrepreneurship." *Corporate Governance*, 5, 95-104.

Rothschild, J., and Whitt, J.A. (1986). *The Cooperative Workplace.* Cambridge: Cambridge University Press.

Schor, J. (2004). *Born to Buy: The Commercialized Child and the New Consumer Culture.* New York: Scribners.

Smith, A. (1986). *The Wealth of Nations.* London: Penguin. (Originally published, 1776.)

Stiglitz, J.E. (2002). *Globalization and its Discontents.* New York: Norton.

Weber, M. (1978). *Economy and Society, 2 vols.* Berkeley: University of California Press.

Weisbord, M. (1991). *Productive Workplaces.* San Francisco: Jossey-Bass.

Werhane, P. (1991). *Adam Smith's The Wealth of Nations and Its Legacy for Modern Capitalism.* Cambridge: Cambridge University Press.

Wren, D. (1987). *The Evolution of Management Thought, 3rd ed.* New York: Wiley.

Acknowledgments

No worthwhile project has ever been accomplished in complete isolation, and this book is no exception. Hundreds of people have had input at some point in its formulation—a fitting process on a research project on cooperation. A special note of appreciation should go to the people who inspired the study, the Maya of Chiapas Highlands in southern Mexico. We learned of their plight during three different delegations as members of Christian Peacemaker Teams (CPT). We are also indebted to the tireless efforts of the *dalits* of south-central India, the poorest farmers in the river valley of Bangladesh, the diligent cooperators in the state of Tlascala, Mexico, introduced to us on an EPIC tour led by Profs Paul and Mary McKay of Boulder, Colorado, who continually inspire and support us in our cooperative endeavors. It will never cease to amaze us how hospitable and generous of their time and energy the most oppressed and down-trodden people of the world can be when they know you are trying to get their story out to brothers and sisters in the rest of the world.

While it is not possible to thank everyone individually and by name, several people stand out: Peter Stevens and Cornelia Dragusin, who introduced us to the vast holdings of the Australian National Library and to the Cooperative Bookshop in Canberra; our Indonesian friends and hosts, Agus Rachmadi and Natassa Sandriana, who guided us in our understanding of micro-finance in the Indonesian People's Bank; the Mennonite Central Committee workers in Maijdee, Bangladesh, Roger and Dawn Lewis Sydney and their family, who introduced us to the work of the Grameen Bank and of the Taize Community cooperatives in the countryside. We thank Fazley Rabbi, Principal Officer, and Nurjahan Begum, General Officer, of the Grameen Bank for spending hours educating us about the dreams and work of Muhammad Yunus among the poor of Bangladesh, and now of the entire world.

Our Indian friends in Hyderabad, Secunderabad, and Trivandrum, India, were tireless in their work with us during our weeks among them: Jyothi Neelaiah, the CEO of Ankuram-Sangamam-Poram (ASP) cooperatives in the state of Andra Pradesh; our host in Secunderabad, Mr Raju; Dr Vithal Rajan, formerly of the London School of Economics, now Chairman of the Advisory Board of ASP; Dr Kurian Katticaren, Chairman of the Board of Directors for his guidance in Hyderabad, Kerala, and the cooperative dairy and fishing communities of Kerala and Tamil Nadu; all the staff and board members of the ASP general office and the board members of the Kandukur MACS of ASP; D. Isaac Prabhakar, district judge in Hyderabad, and family; all the members of the Mennonite Brethren Church of Hyderabad; and Anita Deshmukh of Mumbai for her guidance through the fishing villages in Kerala and Tamil Nadu only one month after their destruction by the December 2004 tsunami and for her facilitation of discussions with displaced fishing families.

Thanks to James Wheeler and Linda Herr, country representatives in the Cairo office of the Mennonite Central Committee, for their suggestions about our visit in Egypt.

Thanks go to Dr Sharryn Kasmir of Hostra University, Hempstead, NY, and to Dr George Cheney, University of Utah in Salt Lake City, veteran scholars of the Mondragón Cooperative Corporation in Spain. Special thanks go to George Cheney's friend Mikel Lezamiz of Mondragón, Spain, who spent most of a day with us at the offices of the cooperative, furnished us with reams of information, and pointed us to people and experiences that enlarged our knowledge and understanding of that great cooperative.

Two people in Rio Piedras, Puerto Rico, were particularly helpful to us in our study of the new Cooperative Development Administration of the Commonwealth of Puerto Rico. Ezequiel Mateo and Carmen Lydia Morales spent hours leading us through the complex legal and historical background of this unique project. A local inspiration has come to us from fellow members of the Boulder Cooperative Food Store near our home.

Words are inadequate to thank the staff, students, and my colleagues at Regis University School of Professional Studies for their patience and encouragement through this project. I am sure they have often been mystified by their "absent-minded professor" colleague, when his head has been in the clouds of cooperativism. I especially thank my fellow members of Regis' committee on Ethics in Economics and Business for their constructive comments and suggestions.

Thanks go to our friend, Chris Weeber, and our daughter-in-law, Amy Palmer-Williams, for their hours in proof reading and correcting faulty grammar, obtuse phrases, spelling, and typos.

We extend a special thanks to the authors of the *haiku* epic on the frontispiece, Brian Ladd and Bruce Fast, members of the Mennonite Community in Boulder, Colorado, USA. They were inspired to write this epic by a power-point presentation on cooperation. Appropriate verses of this *haiku* epic have also been included in the chapter headings to sound a poetic fanfare for the chapter theme.

Last, but certainly not least, my gratitude goes to Gretchen, my partner and wife, without whose support and participation in this project, this book never would have come to completion. Her warm relationships with our new global co-op friends have opened up numerous human aspects of the cooperative experience, and her complete notes during our field visits have proven invaluable. All of the above, and too many more to name, have enhanced the content and concepts of this book.

Introduction

The idea of cooperative economic activity is certainly not a new one. Societies from prehistoric times have evidenced interest in furthering cooperation as a way of cultural and economic advancement. It is not the purpose of this book to provide an encyclopedic account of the history and theory of cooperativism throughout all time. Neither does it pretend to serve as a complete compendium of events and ideas but only to provide a summary description of the modern movement since its acknowledged origin in recent times, around 1750. It is important in this regard to distinguish between two general kinds of cooperative activity: the strictly *economic cooperative*, and the *cooperative community*. Examples of the latter grew largely out of the utopian dreams of the early nineteenth century. The utopian ideas of cooperative community, such as those envisioned and tried by the English socialist leaders, Robert Owen and William Thompson and by Buchez, Cabet and Fourier of France, inspired a great deal of hope in those looking for a brighter and more democratic future. That hope has lingered in spite of the universal failure of nineteenth century experimental communities founded on those utopian dreams. It is also not the purpose of this book to review these communities or try to understand why they failed.

There is also a tendency to confuse the concept of "cooperation" with the much discussed idea of "collaboration." Collaboration can refer to group activity within any corporate conglomerate or subsidiary activity and can easily be little more than assent to authority according to a feudalistic, hierarchical organizational system. Cooperation, on the other hand, is rooted in a highly democratic, participatory, and group-directed process. Cooperation demands a move away from a mere collaborative attitude within a typical corporate command chain.

Theory and History

Of the plethora of nineteenth century theorists only Charles Gide produced a significant literature on successful consumer cooperatives in the UK, worker-owned production cooperatives in France, and credit cooperatives in Germany. It was upon the principles of the well-known Rochdale Society in the UK, "where by 1830 more than 300 cooperative societies had been formed" (Shaffer, 1999, 40) and the writings of Charles Gide, in France, that mature twentieth century cooperative theory was formulated. By the beginning of the twentieth century, cooperative societies had been initiated in more than 26 countries. The pace accelerated in the first quarter of the century so that by 1925, 74 countries had thriving cooperatives, by 1950, there were 134, and by 1984, there were cooperative societies in at least 165 countries. In an additional 22 countries, cooperatives existed, but it is impossible to ascertain their exact date of origin. For more detail on this expansion of cooperatives, see Shaffer's list (Shaffer, 1999, Appendix I).

The overall significance of such a rapid expansion can be measured by two kinds of indices, the *penetration index* and the *market percentage*. The penetration index is simply the proportion of the working age population of a country who are members of at least one cooperative. For instance, Shaffer (1999) gives the percentage of cooperative penetration in North America as more than 60 percent (Shaffer, 1999, Appendix III). Penetration in Latin America is reported as less than 5 percent. In most cases the market percentage commanded by cooperatives is a more useful measure. For example, according to a 2002 report of the US Department of Agriculture, the share of the market for milk and milk products in the United States had reached 86 percent, and the market share for all commodities 30 percent (see Chapter 1 of this book, Table 1.1).

It is important to recognize the differences between the origins of cooperatives in the developed world and cooperatives in the developing world. Cooperatives have originated, survived and thrived under totally different social and economic circumstances in those two parts of the world. Historical and theoretical materials are much more available for the cooperatives in the developed world than for cooperatives in the developing world, and a sketch of these materials is provided in this book. On the other hand, cooperatives have played a much more active role in the practical development of economies in the so-called two-thirds world, especially in India and Southeast Asia. Cooperatives offer a truly participatory and democratic model for people emerging from colonial domination. The standard capitalist model espoused by the IMF and World Bank seemed to many—not all, certainly not to the elites of these countries—to be nothing but an extension of their former national colonial models. For these reasons, the bulk of this book, after the first three historical/theoretical chapters, concentrates more heavily on cooperation in the developing countries, or the two-thirds world, than it does on cooperative activity in the developed countries. Empirical data on the cooperative movement in several developing countries was collected during personal field visits in early 2005.

The differences between the cooperative experiences in *developed* and *developing* countries are mostly historical and cultural. Motivations for forming cooperative enterprises vary, but cooperatives in the developed world appear to offer a viable alternative to the overwhelmingly dominant "standard" model. The cooperatives in the developing world are motivated more by the desire to create a viable and sustainable new economy which succeeds where the IMF and World Bank have failed in raising the poor, by ownership and participation, into a more equitable life situation. Each cooperative matrix will be discussed in turn.

Cooperatives in the Developed World

The cooperative movement in the developed world, as most of us understand it, arose as one of two major reactions to negative side effects of the industrial revolution. The other major movement, more adequately treated in other sources and therefore not a major topic of this study, was the rise of the labor movement. While the labor movement found its power in confrontation with management, the cooperative movement focused its energy and found its power in providing a more democratic alternative to increasingly hierarchical free market capitalism.

Part I, in three chapters, sketches out the historical and theoretical formation of the cooperative movement in the developed world. Chapter 1 summarizes major events together with theoretical and legal developments in cooperation since the middle of the eighteenth century. Chapters 2 and 3 examine the theoretical foundations of cooperation and competition as they impinge upon each other in the modern economically developed world.

The idea that competition is a healthy human activity and helps to ensure equity in the distribution of scarce resources is a relatively modern concept and has little or no empirical data to support it. The imagined "invisible hand" that is supposed to be present in fair competition is borrowed from Adam Smith, who used the term to refer to the divine creator. Smith's thought was actually that God would bless a properly and morally structured free market. A refresher course on Adam Smith's thought should reveal that God's invisible hand is at work in society only if several conditions are met:

- There exists a free and open exchange of goods, as in a public auction.
- People all have free and open access to complete information about goods and services offered in such an auction.
- An adequate and fair division of labor obtains in the production and distribution of all goods and services.
- The entire exchange process is governed by moral norms.
- All contracts are enforceable.
- The rule of law holds, especially in preventing fraud and misinformation.

(Adam Smith, 1904)

The theoretical foundation of this book is the idea that cooperation, rather than competition, provides these optimum conditions for a free and fair marketplace. The idea that competition itself generates the "invisible hand" is not assumed under this theory. Rather the assumption here is that human beings are created essentially as cooperative beings and that it is within a cooperative social context, with consensus decision-making, that the divine "invisible hand" can provide equitable exchanges of goods and services. Unlike the assumptions surrounding a competitive system, there are substantial empirical facts to support the cooperative theory. Chapter 2 surveys the experimental results of comparing cooperation and competition in a wide variety of settings. Chapter 3 provides a discussion of "The Standard Economic Model" based on competition, maximized profits and minimized costs.

It is intended that readers will weigh the historical and theoretical materials presented in the first three chapters and evaluate them in the light of their own experience and research. One of my top priorities is to ensure that adequate documentation and references are provided for further and more detailed reading on these important theoretical and historical topics.

Cooperatives in the Developing World

The cooperative experience in the developing world is based on the need for creativity and inventiveness, rather than on reacting appropriately to the push and shove of economic concepts that originated in reaction to the industrial revolution. It is obvious to citizens of the two-thirds world, if not to those in the developed countries, that progress through all the stages experienced by the West may not be necessary in order to achieve a system that is equitable and sustainable. Questions are raised by them whether a capitalism evolving out of a corporate industrial economy is, in fact, the best route to environmental sustainability and social inclusiveness or even economic equity. The *dalit* caste in India, for example, might never have been included in a standard capitalist economy, and indeed never was! Peasants and working class people in the developing world can comprehend quite well that Western capitalism has not been very successful in including their own working class and family farmers in the "free market" dream.

The three chapters in Part I are intended to introduce the reader to the history and theory of cooperatives. The legal matrix within which cooperatives in the developed world have functioned for the last century is exemplified by a discussion of the two major acts in the United States, the Sherman Antitrust Act of 1890 and the Capper-Volstead Act of 1922. These two milestones are reflected by similar legal frameworks throughout the developed world. The two theoretical approaches of competition and cooperation are examined in somewhat more detail in order to provide the reader with sufficient material to understand the current dialogue in global economics.

Part II, a series of five chapters, describes the cooperative movement in three major areas of the world, in Asia, Europe, and Latin America. While the cooperative movement in the developed world sprang up in reaction to the industrial revolution in the eighteenth and nineteenth centuries, the movement in the developing countries was a response to rapid decolonialization during the second half of the twentieth century. This is not to say that cooperatives were unknown earlier, especially in what we might call more primitive cultures, but the nation-wide popularity of credit unions in Southeast Asia and the attraction to agricultural cooperatives in India, for example, began to flourish noticeably during the democratic impulses following independence from European and North-American colonial domination. The cooperative model provided a much more democratic system for peoples used to autocratic domination than did the standard model of capitalist globalization, which tended to exploit labor as a "commodity" and resources or any other economic advantages of "doing business" in the developing world.

In early 2005, sixteen site visits were conducted in Bangladesh, Indonesia, Australia, and two states in southwest and south-central India. The Mondragón Cooperatives in Spain, also visited in 2005, were chosen as the best-known representatives of the movement in the European Union. Gaviotas, in Eastern Colombia; Mexican cooperatives in the states of Guerrero, Chiapas, and Tlaxcala; and the Puerto Rican cooperative experience represent Latin American cooperative development.

Chapter 4 presents the story of different types of cooperatives in Bangladesh, Indonesia, and Australia. The use of microfinance to promote capital for various kinds of production and marketing co-ops distinguishes the movement in Bangladesh and Indonesia. Australia's extensive University Cooperative Bookstore is unique among co-ops of the world.

Chapter 5 introduces the remarkable story of how the cooperative idea, using the concepts of microfinance developed in Bangladesh, has lifted the lowest castes of India out of abject poverty. This chapter deals with agricultural cooperatives in the state of Andhra Pradesh in south central India; dairy co-ops in the state of Kerala on the southwestern coast; and a large fishing cooperative in the states of Kerala, Tamil Nadu, and Karnatka on the southern tip of the subcontinent.

Chapter 6 tells the story of how the large, 50-community, cooperative enterprise centered in Mondragón, northern Spain met a crisis of identity and purpose in the 1990s, and how it has begun to spread around the world in the twenty-first century. To some extent Mondragón is a special case for European cooperativism, but it is an inspiring example of what can be done when cooperation is taken seriously.

Chapter 7 begins by describing a well-known self-sustaining "near cooperative," Gaviotas, in the eastern Pampas of Colombia. The Mayan peoples have begun new coffee cooperatives in Chiapas, southern Mexico. The silver artisans in Taxco, Guerrero, and the farmers of Vicente Guerrero, in the state of Tlaxcala also provide excellent examples of the cooperative struggle in Mexico.

Chapter 8, the final chapter in Part II, tells of a unique linkage between government and cooperatives in the Commonwealth of Puerto Rico. It shows how the ancient native Taíno collective economy has been revived and incorporated into a strong government-sponsored cooperative movement in Puerto Rico.

Plans for the Future

So what makes a cooperative work, and how do we move toward a more cooperative economy? There has been a lot of experience within the last three centuries with the cooperative model. Yet, curiously, the literature is particularly devoid of any kind of careful distillation of the data about successful and unsuccessful cooperatives. There is a tradition in social research of collecting and analyzing historical material, results of interviews and focus groups, and economic data. Putting these kinds of researches together in a meaningful way is, for some reason, a rare activity. The overarching tendency in the social sciences is to treat a question either quantitatively or qualitatively; there is statistical research and then there is qualitative participant observation—and "ne'er the twain shall meet."

Knowing that the procedure might be confusing or disappointing both to the quantitative scientist and to the qualitatively oriented observer, I have tried to merge these two usually diverging approaches. My hope is that by doing so, we can approach a bit closer to the best answers to our questions. More than three quarters of a century on this planet has led me to believe that personal "scientific" analysis of human subjects must always be accompanied by a consideration of the subjects' own take on what exactly the problem is. In other words, if you want to know how and why someone thinks and behaves the way they do, why not just ask them? Certainly centuries of philosophical and scientific enlightenment should have taught us to be skeptical of our own observations and interpretations—including what we may think is "scientific." Some of our interpretations of what we see and hear could be accurate, but a significant portion might in reality be simply a cultural gloss. How do we tell the difference?

In the spirit of an alert personal curiosity, an attempt to understand cultural differences, and a respect for honesty, the last two chapters of the book present an analysis of cooperative experiences around the world, by asking the question of all who may care to answer, "What makes a cooperative enterprise work?" Economic, social, cultural, political, and legal aspects of this experience have all been considered, weighed, and offered as cogently as possible. On the basis of these results, a "blueprint" for a more cooperative and democratic economy is offered in an attempt to answer the question, "How then do we get there?"

Finally, understanding that much of the material of socio-economic analysis can be dry as dust, I have tried to make the "dismal science" of economics a little brighter and thus shed more light on the tough problems of the twenty-first century. I have not tried too hard to balance points of view in this book. This is mostly because what I think are "good" ideas and "bad" ideas do not seem to balance very well. I have simply laid out my view of the world, confident that the readers will do the balancing for themselves, keeping in mind that equilibrium points have a way of migrating, and our perception of them tends to change with the addition of new information. I have altered much from when I started writing (about five years ago) until the date of publication. We can think of this book as a journey through time and space, or rather as directional signs along the journey to a more complete or, at least, different understanding of our social and economic world. In any case, it can be hoped that what is read here can provide a way of changing history rather than simply reading or writing about it.

References

Shaffer, Jack (1999). *Historical Dictionary of the Cooperative Movement*, Historical Dictionaries of Religions, Philosophies, and Movements, No. 26. Lanham, MD and London: The Scarecrow Press, Inc.

Smith, Adam (1904). *An Inquiry into the Nature and Causes of the Wealth of Nations*, London: Methuen & Co., Ltd. (5th Edition).

PART I
History and Theory of Cooperation

For more than two centuries the cooperative approach to democratic capitalism has attracted democratically minded people around the world. For the most part, cooperativism has flourished. Serious research has firmly established cooperation as a more productive and efficient approach to almost any task than competition. Yet the primary assumption driving modern global capitalism is the false assumption that the only way to establish an equitable economy is to foster competition—not cooperation. In this part, the two approaches to the "free" market, cooperative and competitive, are summarized and examined in the context of the Standard Economic Model and the cooperative movement as it has thrived in the developed and developing world.

Chapter 1

History and Theory
of the Cooperative Movement

Not a collective
Controlled by a corrupt state
But something better

(Haiku by BL & BF)

The form of association…which if mankind continue to improve, must be expected in the end to predominate, is not that which can exist with capitalist as chief, and workpeople without a voice in the management, but the association of the labourers themselves on terms of equality, collectively owning the capital with which they carry on their operations, and working under managers elected and removable by themselves.

(John Stuart Mills, *Principles of Political Economy*)

The cooperative movement has changed the lives of millions of people around the world. The formation of cooperatives in the Midwestern United States saved thousands of family farms from the banking crisis of the 1980s. New cooperatives in Chiapas, Mexico, saved the economy and culture of thousands of Mayan families in the 1990s. Large cooperatives in India and Southeast Asia, with their emphasis on microfinance, have begun to rescue the lower castes from neo-colonialism and grinding poverty. Recreational Equipment Incorporated (REI), a cooperative in the United States, outfitted the first American team to reach the summit of Mt Everest; REI, with more than 300,000 members, is now one of the largest recreational companies in the United States. Cooperatives provide 86 percent of the dairy market in the United States. Sunkist, Land O'Lakes, and Ocean Spray, all familiar names in food distribution in the United States, are cooperatives. The Co-op Group is the largest convenience store distributor and retailer in the UK. Most communities in the world now contain at least one credit union, a type of cooperative, and at least one cooperative food market. Cooperatives have raised the quality of life of their members and their communities wherever they are. The extraordinary success of cooperatives is one of the world's best kept secrets.

A commonly held myth concerning cooperatives is that they are more likely to fail than standard corporations. Actually, national records show that 60 to 80 percent of corporations in the US fail after their first year in business, and cooperatives fail only at the rate of about 10 percent after their first year (WOCCU, 2003). The initial success of a cooperative most likely arises from the fact that starting a cooperative requires a great deal of support from the community. Many people must be involved for the successful cooperative to file for incorporation or limited liability, so that few are likely to fail within the first few years of operation. Cooperatives are also more likely to survive in the long term. More than 90 percent of cooperatives are still operating while only 3-5 percent of standard corporations remain active after five years.

Origins of the Cooperative Movement

A fire insurance cooperative was organized in the UK in the early 1700s. In France, around 1750, a group of cheesemakers gathered to form a cooperative, undoubtedly the first consumer cooperative in the developed world. During this period, there were some attempts to initiate cooperative banking or credit institutions in Germany. By 1830 there were 300 cooperative societies officially recognized in the UK, and the first Congress of Cooperatives met in the UK in 1831. One of the first known cooperatives in the United States was the Philadelphia Contributorship, a mutual insurance company founded in 1752 by Benjamin Franklin. Contributorships were companies owned in equal shares by a large number of business people, merchants and professionals to indemnify each other in case of fire and other natural catastrophes which had plagued the large cities in Europe and in the New World. For a more detailed and very instructive timeline of early cooperative formation, see Jack Shaffer's, *Historical Dictionary of the Cooperative Movement* (1999, 1-38).

Also in the mid-eighteenth century, a group of French, English, and German social and political activists designed and initiated a number of cooperative communities. Phillipe Buchez, Etienne Cabet, and Francois Marie Charles Fourier in France experimented with cooperative communities founded mostly on utopian principles. Later Robert Owen and William Thompson, social reformers in Britain, both tried their hands at organizing cooperative communities. Hans Crüger in Germany wrote and worked on cooperative ideals with the strong conviction that society ought to be designed not with self-interest as its base but with faith in the "ideal good" in human nature. In 1825 Owen established his ideal utopian community of New Harmony, Indiana, in the US. Even though New Harmony failed, probably due to financial mismanagement, the idea caught on and cooperatives were formed by the thousands.

In 1844, toward the end of the industrial revolution and almost 100 years after the first fire insurance and cheesemaking cooperatives were formed, a group of 28 weavers in the industrial town of Rochdale, England, established a small cooperatively owned store that sold a few necessities and, later, entire shelves of weavers' supplies, food, and agricultural products. Spurred on by having been relieved of their jobs by their local manufacturing company and after an unsuccessful strike, the 28 weavers pooled 140 British pounds and began purchasing oatmeal, sugar, butter, and flour. They codified their experience in the "Rochdale Principles of Cooperation" that have been amended over time and are now the "Principles of the International Cooperative Alliance (ICA)."

At about the same time as the Rochdale experiment in England, the New England Protective Union in the US, also called John Beck's Buying Club, failed because of poor business practices and internal contention. In Rochdale itself, problems arose in 1849. A prominent mill owner and trustee of the Rochdale Bank embezzled funds which nearly forced the cooperative out of business. Then, a much more serious problem, the Rochdale Cooperative threatened to degenerate when, to finance the purchase of a new mill, it took on investors called "investor members." In 1869, these new members outvoted the worker members and began to convert the co-op into a conventional firm. Some years later, however, these new investor members reconsidered and decided to reconstitute the bank and the cooperative under a new name, Rochdale Pioneer Society, with a total of 3,500 members. The Rochdale Pioneer Society then reorganized as a cooperative and continues today under the original Rochdale principles.

The early success and popularity of the Rochdale group led to the increased number of cooperatives on the European continent, notably in Belgium and Germany between 1848 and 1869. By the 1930s, consumer co-ops became some of the largest retail businesses in northern Europe. Following the Second World War, consumer cooperatives in Scandinavian countries continued to grow and now represent over a third of the retail trade there. In Germany, Netherlands, and England consumer cooperatives declined to fewer than 10 percent of the retail trade by the middle of the twentieth century because of opposition from the strong Social-Democratic and Labor movements during those decades.

Some of the first literature on cooperatives and cooperative theory was heralded by the work of Charles Gide, one of the founders, along with Edouard de Boyve and August Fabre, of the Ecole Nimes in France in 1886. He had earlier contributed to *L'Emancipation—Journal d'education cooperative* and in 1883 published *Principles of Political Economy*. In 1900 he published his landmark work, *La Cooperation*, in which he tied his cooperative philosophy to the Rochdale Principles. Popularity of the cooperative principles stimulated a number of academic groups dedicated to teaching those principles and inspiring the formation of more and different kinds of cooperative enterprises in Europe and North America. A "Chair of Cooperation" was founded at the Universidad Nacional in El Salvador, in 1896, and the International Cooperative Alliance was founded and began meeting in the UK in 1898.

Today France, Spain, and Italy see a rising strength of the cooperative movement, where thousands of worker cooperatives employ over 200,000 worker-members. In Italy, cooperatives now account for up to 30 percent of total trade. In France, co-ops are the fastest growing type of business. In Spain, cooperatives lead all other enterprises in national productivity (ICA, 2002). The most impressive cooperatives in Europe are the Mondragón Cooperatives in the Basque Country of northern Spain. Mondragón integrates over 100 firms in high growth and high technology industries and solves the capital formation problem by operating a cooperative bank with more than 50 branches all over Spain (holding over a billion dollars in deposits). Caja Popular Laboral (the co-op bank), co-op universities, a co-op medical system, cooperative housing, and a large portion of all agriculture form a single cooperative network in over 40 communities in northern Spain. The Mondragón Cooperatives will be dealt with in great detail in Part II, Chapter 6.

In Britain, following World War II, there were only 50 cooperatives. In spite of the sharp decline during two or three decades, interest in the cooperative movement accelerated during the 1980s and 1990s, and at the beginning of the twenty-first century, there were over 500 new cooperatives. A new (June, 2004) UK Cooperative Development Agency has made cooperatives a government priority. The new United European parliament is currently considering measures to encourage the formation of cooperatives and worker-owned firms all over Europe.

In the latter part of the twentieth century, there has been a huge increase in cooperative activity in India, building on earlier credit cooperatives founded in 1906 and 1907 and with the passage of the Cooperative Society Law, expanded and amended in 1912. By 1991, India's movement was the largest in the world, reporting 401,139 cooperatives with over 166 million members (nearly 20 percent of the population). In 1989 the Central Committee of the International Cooperative Alliance (ICA) held its first meeting in the developing world in India. India is rapidly becoming an economic leader in the world, and leads all of Asia and Southeast Asia with its commitment to globalization from below.

Cooperative Principles

The seven principles of the Rochdale Cooperative, as adopted by the International Cooperative Alliance (ICA) in 1995, provide that a true cooperative will:

1. offer voluntary and open membership,
2. govern by democratic member participation (one member, one share, one vote),
3. operate by equal and "fair" investment by the members,
4. remain free of intervention from governments or any other outside power (for example, corporations),
5. educate its members and the community about the nature, principles, values, and benefits of the cooperative,
6. encourage cooperation among cooperatives, and
7. protect the environment and contribute to the sustainable development of the community.

The first six of these principles are essentially the original Rochdale principles; the seventh merely clarifies and extends the cooperative's responsibility to the community. These seven principles are now strongly recommended to all cooperatives around the world by the International Cooperative Alliance (ICA). In practice, cooperatives around the world have found it necessary to modify one or more of the seven principles to fit local cultural or legal constraints.

The first principle, voluntary and open membership, has often been circumscribed by law in the United States. While membership, participation, leadership, and benefits have been available regardless of race, creed, gender, sexual orientation, or other social boundaries, the corporate and financial communities have ensured that the benefits of cooperatives are confined to employees of specific corporations, government entities, or neighborhood residents. Every year various corporations and the banking community introduce bills into federal or state legislatures attempting to curtail cooperatives, especially credit unions, claiming that extension of cooperative rights will give them unfair advantages in pricing and market appeal.

The second principle of democratic member control ensures that no member has a greater voice in the operation of the cooperative than any other member. The basic principle is "one share, one member, one vote." This principle is frequently modified in the case of networks of cooperatives where the principle could actually result in inequities. For example, the members of a smaller cooperative may end up with more decision-making power than members of larger cooperatives, or of the umbrella cooperative itself. The specific roles of non-members remain unclear in most cooperatives. Degeneration inevitably follows opening share-owning memberships to outsiders.

The third principle, of "fair investment" of common ownership, often makes the task of generating the necessary equity very difficult. Some cooperatives solve this problem by encouraging large loans with promissory notes of repayment with interest. Such loans are not shares nor do they imply a greater voice in the development or operation of the enterprise. The incentive of wanting the cooperative to succeed because of its value to the community and to individuals often inspires members to provide large interest-free loans. For others, a fair interest rate is a sufficient incentive to individual lenders both inside and outside of the membership. Loans and grants can then help to keep membership fees at reasonable rates so as not to hinder community members with fewer resources.

Like the first principle, the fourth principle of complete autonomy and independence can create legal difficulties, especially in the United States, and often cannot be followed absolutely. Each state of the US provides corporation laws that vary in their limitations on corporate structure. At present the federal government encourages as broad a definition of "cooperative corporation" as possible. Current law defines the cooperative as "a corporation or association organized for the purpose of rendering economic services without gain to itself, to shareholders or members who own and control it" [United States Grocers, Ltd. V. United States, 186F. Supp. 724,733 N.D. Cal. 1960]. A few nation states, mostly in the Near East, have completely outlawed cooperatives, fearing the loss of control and the threat of competition with government sponsored companies, notably state-sponsored or owned airlines and oil extraction companies. Others such as Spain, Sweden, Norway, and India provide much broader legal umbrellas for cooperative corporations than exist in the United States.

The fifth principle of educating members and the community has seen success in some co-ops but not others. One of the challenges of this principle is to avoid setting up a huge "marketing" program under the aegis of "education." At the same time, effective membership must be based on effective education about the mission and values of cooperation. For co-ops to succeed, education ought to extend to youth and to others in the community for a broader understanding of the nature and benefits of cooperation.

The sixth principle is largely self-evident. As cooperatives of various types proliferate within a community, a need arises to link them in some kind of network. People in the community need to know about the existence of cooperatives, and the various cooperatives can often facilitate their educational and marketing efforts much more effectively through a community association of cooperatives than they can by individual efforts. In the United States, the National Cooperative Business Association (NCBA) helps to achieve this function on a national level. The International Cooperative Alliance (ICA) acts on an international level. In addition to those organizations, there are several home pages for the cooperative movement.[1]

---

1   Home pages for a large number of cooperatives, including NCBA and ICA, are operated by a group called ".coop" at their website www.cooperative.org.

The seventh Principle of Cooperation states a concern for the environment and sustainable living. For example, Biodiesel Cooperatives salvage cooking oil from restaurants and fast food outlets and process it into a fuel that can be used in internal combustion engines. These co-ops provide an alternative to the rapidly depleting supply of petroleum. There are also cooperatives for recycling and other forms of conservation.

Notice that there is no mention of member volunteer labor in the international statement of cooperative principles. Some cooperatives cut costs by using volunteer labor (perhaps in exchange for a deeper discount on goods), but the practice is not universal and certainly not essential. Many cooperatives do not use volunteer labor from their members. Also, not all cooperatives attempt to undercut the prices of large competing corporations. Rather, they may elect to charge a bit more to pay workers living wages and/or to purchase higher quality goods and services.

Types of Cooperatives

How can cooperatives be classified? Probably the easiest way is to identify who qualifies for membership. A list of the major categories and subcategories of cooperatives according to who owns membership in them follows. Parentheses enclose a few examples.

Producer Co-ops

- Farms (So. Minnesota Beet Sugar Co-op, Prairieland Producers, Navaho Dairy Products [US])
- Fishing (SIFF in Kerala, Andra Pradesh, and Tamil Nadu in India)
- Manufacturers (Edinburgh Bicycle Co-op [Scotland, Leeds, etc., UK], The Solar Center [San Francisco], Manchester Bio-Diesel [UK], Co-op sugar factories [India], PPRV [France])
- Dairy (Assoc. Milk Producers, Land O' Lakes [US]; Amul, Anand, MILMA [Mumbai and Kerala, India])
- Agricultural Distributors (Sunkist, Ocean Spray [US])

Value-Added Co-ops

- Dairy (Assoc. Milk Producers, Land O'Lakes [US])
- Agricultural Distributors (Sunkist, Ocean Spray [US])

Supply or Distribution Co-ops

- Farm equipment, fertilizers, seeds
- Hardware (ACE, TrueValue, ServiStar, Coast-to-Coast [US])
- Pharmaceuticals (Independent Pharmacists' Cooperative [Madison, Wis., US])
- Wholesale Food (Shurfine, TopCo and 31 regional cooperative suppliers [US])

Service Co-ops

- Shipping (there are more than 100 shipping co-ops)
- Information (Associated Press)
- Communication (Phone Co-op [UK])
- Graphic Design (Oxford, Swindon, and Gloucester [UK])
- Legal (Legaco-op [Italy])
- Power & Utilities (more than 1000 of these include: Sundance Renewables [UK], Northern States Power and Touchstone Energy Co-ops)
- Entertainment (Green Bay Packers [Green Bay, Wisc., US])
- Transportation (Yellow Cab of San Francisco [Calif., US])

Retail/Consumer Co-ops

- Dry Goods (REI)
- Food (Co-op Food [UK], Panhandle Co-op Association, Davis Food Co-op, Puget Consumer's Co-op [US])
- Cooperative Bookstore (Australia)
- Distribution (FEDCO [Hollywood/LA])

Workers Co-ops

- Artisans (Silvercraft [Taxco and Taxco Viejo, Mexico], Weavers [Tlaxcala, Mexico])

Housing Co-ops

- Co-op Housing [NYC]
- Co-op Housing (Solstice Institute, Thistle, Co-Housing [Boulder, Colorado, USA])

Financial Co-ops

- Credit Unions (Co-operative Bank [Manchester, UK], Self-Help [North Carolina], Santa Cruz CCU, and over 10,000 FCUs in US and Credit Unions around the world)
- Cooperative Banks (CoBank, bank especially for agricultural cooperatives [Global])

It is important to keep these different types of cooperatives in mind, because legal systems in most countries treat each type of co-op in a different way. For instance, in the United States, laws are much less restrictive for farm cooperatives than for other producers (manufacturers), distributors, utilities, or credit unions. Farm cooperatives can engage in a limited form of distribution, and sometimes, in direct sales. Manufacturers are bound to distribute their products through other cooperatives such as Ace Hardware or privately owned retail companies like Wal-Mart, Target, and Safeway.

The largest cooperatives in the United States tend to be *value-added* co-ops. They buy raw materials or products from corporations or cooperatives, add value by processing and packaging them, and distribute them to be sold by retailers. The retailers can, of course, be individuals, corporations, or other cooperatives.

Severely restricted by US law is the combining of cooperative enterprises of various types under a single corporate charter, an activity which could be ruled "unfair trade" and actionable under anti-trust laws. In the US, these restrictions do not necessarily apply to the standard corporation, since it is possible for them to gather various kinds of unrelated companies under a single conglomerate umbrella. This restriction has seriously affected the ability of cooperatives to obtain and retain capital. Also a great deal of time and energy is wasted by individual cooperatives in battling the commercial banking and marketing lobbies, who are continually introducing bills in the US congress to curtail cooperative activities. The individual co-ops are strongly supported by the Capper-Volstead Act of 1922, but, although legally allowed, informal community associations of cooperatives continue to be restricted. No such restrictions exist for the standard corporations. There are more details about these technical legal matters in the section on "Legal Framework" in this chapter.

Recent European Cooperative Experiences

The cooperative movement continued to grow for a short time in the developed countries during the years following World War II. Eastern European countries followed the Soviet model of cooperative organization, with a heavy governmental influence—all except Yugoslavia, which declared its independence from the model by encouraging worker self-management as an objective for all its enterprises. Czechoslovakia, Hungary, and Poland each opted for a more diverse organization of cooperatives while still maintaining some governmental supervision at the top (Shaffer, 1999). In Western Europe, cooperatives reorganized themselves very much in conformity with their earlier traditions. They were able to follow the Rochdale principles, including the avoidance of governmental supervision and control, as they set up more cooperative and more locally based companies.

The 1960s and early 1970s were marked by several waves of massive strikes in Western Europe. After the first oil crisis in 1973 and 1974, governments continued to assign high priority to full employment but began to bring unions still further into the center of policy making. This brought about a new political system known as "neocorporatism." This approach to free-market capitalism and increasing enthusiasm for the capitalist dream tended to draw people away from cooperative participation. The number and strength of cooperatives was severely diminished during this period.

Most Western European governments encouraged management and labor to enter three-way discussions to restore full employment through moderate wage demands. This process, combined with inflation caused primarily by flawed government monetary policies, rapidly decreased real pay scales. Unions continued to negotiate, but they tended to confine their influence to issues of unemployment insurance, retirement plans, on the job training, and mechanisms to absorb increasing worker discontent. The second oil "shock" of 1979 served as a wake-up call and heralded fundamental changes in European economic policy.

The flexibility of the workplace required by competitive production innovations of the 1980s and pressure brought by workers to increase their participation in corporate decision making seemed to require more cooperative workplace relations. Also, under persistent unemployment, the general population became disenchanted with the system, and local worker groups began to form cooperative and quasi-cooperative enterprises in order to survive. Although a slow process at first, Western Europeans began to reject the neocorporate trends and restore their confidence in the cooperative model.

During the neocorporate phase of Western European economies, the statistics show a shrinkage in the number of cooperatives of all types between 1950 and 1990, the time of the crumbling of the Berlin wall. During these 40 years, the number of cooperatives dropped from approximately 26,000 to just under 8,000. Most, but not all, of that shrinkage can be accounted for by the consolidation of credit unions as was the US experience. Total membership during that time, however, tended to remain steady (CICOPA, 2005).

The decade after the fall of the Berlin wall, in 1989 and 1990, was very difficult. Western Europe needed to allow for a great deal of economic retooling within and among their eastern neighbors, and many politicians were of the opinion that cooperatives were an inefficient legacy of the communist era. But, contrary to many expectations, it was soon discovered that the cooperative approach to free enterprise offered an ideal model for the strengthening of a new United Europe (EU). Local communities could begin small and develop thriving enterprises in a cooperative mode. As a result, in Germany alone, the total number of cooperatives rose from about 3,100 in 1990 to 5,469 in 2002. Membership rose from 4.4 million to 16.6 million (DGRV, 2006).

The first assembly of the European ICA (International Cooperative Alliance) met in Prague in 1994. Due largely to the work of ICA Europe, business leaders and politicians now realize the validity and importance of cooperatives in the rebuilding of a struggling economy. Lars Hillbom, president of ICA Europe from 1995 remarked at his retirement speech in 2002, "The cooperative difference has proven to be the solution to many of today's problems. People have grown tired of an egoistic approach and want to be responsible for shaping their own future" (ICA, 2002, Oct.).

Probably the most significant recent event for the cooperative movement was the resolution passed by the International Labor Organization (ILO) meeting in Geneva in June, 2002. That resolution, titled "Recommendation 193," was a remarkable extension of an earlier "Recommendation 127." "Recommendation 127" sent the message to workers around the world that cooperatives should be encouraged in the developing countries to accelerate their economic development, reduce poverty and increase economic equity. Now "Recommendation 193" encourages all workers to promote the formation of cooperatives in Europe. The first of such societies was launched in Italy late in 2005. The European Union already has about 300,000 cooperatives active within its member countries, with a total of 83.5 million members.

Cooperatives in Some Individual European Countries

Europe has a rich history of cooperative enterprise. In most countries, the cooperative movement experienced a slowing of growth and, in several cases, an actual shrinking of the movement.

United Kingdom

At the turn of the twentieth century, there were over 2,000 cooperatives representing many sectors of the British economy. Over the century these cooperatives merged with each other until today there are 39 huge multi-sector co-ops with almost 20 million total members, 10 million active, about 35.8 percent of the population of the UK. The gross earnings of these 39 cooperatives was 12.7 billion pounds in 2005, representing a food market share of approximately 5.4 percent and a non-food share of 0.8 percent or about 2.8 percent of the total market. Pharmaceutical, travel agencies, and postal services are the three largest sectors in the UK cooperative economy. The UK recently confirmed a law based on the ILO's "Recommendation 193" that will be in force as of 18 August 2006. Although the cooperative activity in the UK has declined a bit since 2003, the ILO's "Recommendation 193" should give the cooperative movement in the UK a boost. Four prominent cooperatives are worth mention: The Co-op Group, a chain of retail convenience stores; The Cooperative Bank UK; Midlands Co-op, a retailer of food, appliances, furniture, travel, funeral arrangements, plus new and used cars; and Oxford, Swindon, and Gloucester Co-op, a multi-sector fair trade retail co-op. The Co-op Group recently acquired Alldays convenience stores, adding over 600 stores and making the Co-op Group the leading convenience store operator in the UK. The Co-op Group and the Cooperative Bank UK, are only two of the many offshoots of the earlier Northern Cooperative Wholesale Society. Obviously there is no law in the UK (as there is in the US) preventing such large multi-sectored co-ops.

France

As of June 2005, France had over 3,500 agricultural co-ops with approximately 13,500 members. These co-ops are organized under a single apex organization, "Co-op de France." Also notable is "Hlm," a large cooperative housing group that handles 40 percent to 50 percent of all of France's rental housing. Recently "Hlm" has made agreements with Nexity, a for-profit real estate agency, which now carries all of Hlm's listings. The Groupement National de Cooperation has published a Directory of French Cooperators which contains all current data about the French cooperative movement, including its long and colorful history. It is available from Association Nationale de la Copropriété Cooperative at 13 rue Littré—75006 Paris.

Italy

The heart of the cooperative movement in Italy is LEGACOOP. The Cooperative League originated in 1868 in the northern administrative region of Emilia-Romagna, a region regarded as a stronghold of Italian progressives, despite being one of the wealthiest parts of Italy. Its capital is Bologna and is bounded on the east by the Adriatic Sea, on the north by the Po River, and on the south by the Appenine range. It is estimated that 2 out of 3 citizens of the region are members of a co-op, under the administration of either LEGACOOP or the Roman church's Confcooperative. The main theme of the 36th Congress of LEGACOOP held in Rome in November, 2005, was Freedom and Security. This congress followed two violent attacks on officials of LEGACOOP, which were seen as malicious attacks on the cooperative movement. Appeals to the President of Italy brought a security force to bear on the situation, so the cooperatives could go about their business in peace.

Usually the socialists and the communists, as well as the capitalists, oppose the cooperative movement because it is seen as diluting the commitment necessary to win the struggle against the corruption of the old elite order. There are tens of thousands of cooperatives in Emilia-Romagna. It shows that "Capitalism…is not the only way to drive a [free] market" (Lappe, 2006, 1). Socialist theorist Antonio Gramsci was a major influence on Italy's postwar left. Although he was imprisoned by Mussolini in 1926 and died still under house arrest at the age of 46, his ideas took hold. The Roman Church also came to appreciate cooperatives in strengthening family and community (Pope John XXIII's 1961 encyclical). The idea of the cooperative is that, by aiding each other and sharing the results, all gain. And they have. The per capita income in Emilia-Romagna is 50 percent higher than the national average. The success of the cooperative has impressed socialists, communists, the Church, and everyone else! Critiques of the residual communists in Emilia-Romagna even say that those communists are "nice" communists. We shall see in a later chapter that the same phenomenon has occurred in the state of Kerala in India.

One of Confcooperative's enterprises is, again, cheese making—like the cheese makers in France almost three centuries earlier and the Mennonites in Chihuahua, Mexico. On the outskirts of Bologna, visitors can watch the workers, really artists, stirring the fermenting milk, waiting for the right consistency for Parmagiano-Reggiano—Parmesan to us—and later listen to the "prophet" of the Emilia-Romagna cooperatives, Stefano Zamagni, professor of economics in the University of Bologna's economics department (now, 2006, visiting professor at Bologna's affiliate institution, Johns-Hopkins University, Baltimore, Maryland, USA). Ten years ago Zamagni launched a graduate program in civil economies and cooperation in Bologna. So far it has graduated 250 students.

Another important feature of the culture is that beginning in 1991, all social services in Emilia-Romagna and nearby regions have been assigned to cooperatives. For those cooperatives providing services such as job placement, for example, at least 30 percent of the staff must come from the population being served and become members of the cooperative. Italy's enthusiasm for cooperatives has burgeoned since 1990. More and more policy makers and citizens are seeing cooperativism as a viable alternative to "dog-eat-dog capitalism" (Lappe, 2006, 3).

Russia

Cooperatives in Russia go back to the late 1800s. At the time of the revolution there were already 7,000 agricultural cooperatives, 53,000 consumer cooperatives, 16,000 rural credit cooperatives, and 4,000 artisan and service cooperatives. Under Stalin's government, the land was owned by the government, and cooperatives (or collectives) were subsidized and operated under the supervision of the government. Due to strong authoritarian oversight by the government, workers' motivations slackened and cooperatives failed. By the time of Perestroika, in 1988, there were only 8,000 cooperatives in all, most of them agricultural. By April, 1989 there were over 99,000 cooperatives employing 2 million people, and by June, 1990, there were more than 220,000 cooperatives employing nearly 5 million people (Cox, 1993).

Soon the negative reaction of politicians—treating the cooperatives as remnants of communism—began to undermine their successes, and even associated them with the Mafia. Privatization of the land began and all but destroyed the movement. The percentage of profitable farms had decreased from 97 percent to 25 percent by 1996. The movement continues to struggle. In the present Republic of Russia, nearly 57 percent of the rural population lives below the UN poverty line of $1 US per day, and the number of jobless is close to 2 million. Youth are leaving the countryside and flocking to the cities, contributing to the increase of crime and social confusion.

However, the ICA expects that the new policies of the EU will give the movement a boost in Russia. Current leaders in Russia agree "… on the vital role cooperatives can play in improving this situation and contribute to the development of the national economy" (ICA, 2002, Dec.). Whether this resurrection can happen or not remains to be seen. The extreme volatility of the cooperative movement in Russia in response to changes in national policy boggles the mind.

Consumer Cooperatives in the United States

The first consumer cooperative in the United States was the New England Protective Union in Boston, Massachusetts. In 1844, John Kaulback, a tailor, convinced the members of his labor guild to buy household supplies jointly. Their first purchases were a case of soap and half a case of tea. A store opened in 1845 and by 1847 they had expanded to twelve "divisions" and by 1852 to 403 divisions throughout New England. The Protective Union, unfortunately, ignored the Rochdale Principles and was eventually dismantled as a result of mismanagement, dissension, and deteriorating economic conditions leading up to the Civil War (Honigsberg, 1991).

During the 1870s a coalition of the Farmers' Grange Movement and the Knights of Labor organized consumer cooperatives as a part of their member services. These cooperatives adopted the Rochdale principles of cooperation and learned methods of organization from the European cooperative movement. The Grange and the Knights of Labor flourished, mostly led by immigrants, until the early 1920s. Then these organizations rapidly diminished in size and effectiveness as immigration slowed and consumer cooperatives erroneously became associated with the communist movement—particularly in the South and southern Midwest.

Later in the 1920s and early 1930s, cooperatives, especially farm and utility cooperatives, were supported strongly by the Coolidge, Hoover, and F.D. Roosevelt administrations, and became an "American" idea. The largest boost to the cooperative spirit came with the creation of the Rural Electrification Administration (REA) in 1935. To many this was "the day the lights came on."

World War II interrupted much economic development in the United States, and the cooperative movement that had rescued so many from the Depression very nearly disappeared from mainstream America. The boom produced by reconversion following the war made cooperation seem Utopian and unachievable rather than a thriving sector of the economy.

The myths that cooperatives did not work as well as corporations during boom times, and that cooperatives were most successful and useful in bailing out troubled areas in the economy, were prevalent in Middle America. It was a surprise then that an era of abundance in the 1960s was the spur for the next wave of cooperative activity. Out of this decade of dissent, civil rights marches, and anti-war demonstrations came a new energy to find an alternative to the increasing tendency toward a concentration of wealth brought about by the expansion of hierarchical corporate power and the tendency of corporations to go transnational.

The cooperative movement became a new hope for the generation of Americans who looked toward a new economic order to distribute the nation's resources more equitably. New consumer cooperatives most frequently were a symbol of rebellion against technocracy, hierarchical corporations, and "big business as usual."

Consumer cooperatives organized in this era set the pace for a new period of cooperative expansion. During the decade of the 1960s about 7,000 new co-ops were formed comprising about 10 million new members, mostly in food retailing enterprises in the Midwest. According the USDA figures, 2, 638 new marketing co-ops formed between 1960 and 1970 represented about $3 billion new dollars of annual trade.

Worker or Producer Cooperatives in the United States

In 1791, a group of carpenters in Philadelphia formed the first worker cooperative in the United States. Despite the success of this cooperative, it was not until the 1870s and 1880s that production cooperatives of any kind stirred any large-scale interest. During this period nearly 200 worker cooperatives were started by the Knights of Labor, the most influential labor union of that time.

As mentioned above, the power of the Knights of Labor declined sharply after 1886, and by 1920 there were only 39 Knights of Labor producers. The founding of the Olympia Veneer Company in the state of Washington, after the economic doldrums of World War II, stirred a new wave of interest nationwide. Doubtless the Scandinavian heritage of much of the population of Washington made it a fertile ground for new cooperative enterprises, for soon 21 similar co-ops emerged. By 1964 a total of 24 worker-owned plywood cooperatives operated in the United States. Unfortunately, Olympia Veneer itself, the model for all the others, succumbed to degeneration when they began raising capital by redefining ownership by individually sellable stock shares. Under a siege of "capital starvation" and decreasing supplies of lumber, the 23 remaining worker-owners voted to sell to St Paul and Tacoma Lumber, which then merged with St Regis Paper Company and finally closed in 1967. In spite of its failure, Olympia Veneer became the model for future worker-owned plants providing equitable incomes and bonuses for workers and using the superior processes developed and shared by Olympia.

The story of production cooperatives during the 1960s and 1970s was much the same as that of the consumer cooperatives during the same period. Cooperative production began to expand rapidly in the West and northern Midwest. Among this group of new cooperatives, four dairy producers and retail groups stood out: Mid-American Milk, Dairymen, Inc., Associated Milk Products, and the largest, Land O'Lakes, Inc. In a single year, 1968-1969, Mid-American Milk increased production from $200 million to $300 million; Dairymen, Inc., with member-producers in ten states from Texas to Minnesota, in its first year of production grossed $37.5 million; Associated Milk Products, with 25,000 new members, grossed $31.25 million; and Land O'Lakes, Inc., with 100,000 members grossed $369 million (USDA, 2002).

The cooperative spirit began to influence activities in several sectors of the economy. Questions about the large growth of standard corporations, their hierarchical nature, and often their tendency not to be sensitive to the needs of workers or consumers, stimulated a great deal of experimentation with job sharing, elimination of time clocks, formation of quality groups, and worker-owned companies. Workplace alienation was very much a concern, and alternatives to undemocratic approaches to decision making were again becoming popular. As a result of all of this, the cooperative approach to production, as well as distribution, of goods and services began another surge in the marketplace.

Agricultural Production and Distribution in the United States

Today most producer co-ops in the United States are agricultural, ranging in size from very large national co-ops like Sunkist and Ocean Spray to small ones like La Cooperativa Colonia Mexicana Unida in central California. Today Sunkist has over 6,500 grower-members and approximately $1 billion in annual sales, making it the largest vegetable and fruit distributor in the world. Ocean Spray began with three cranberry growers in 1930 and now runs a very close second to Sunkist. Cooperativa Colonia, on the other hand, is owned by 15 families farming 200 acres of state reclamation land. Unlike most farm co-ops that specialize in single seasonal crops, Cooperativa Colonia employs 28 adults year round (Nadeau and Thompson, 1996).

Calavo Growers of California, founded in 1924, is one example of a typical farm cooperative. This group of avocado farmers, seeking to become leaders in this new industry, faced many challenges. At the same time they had to acquire or build facilities and equipment to handle the fruit, they also had to increase public knowledge of the product. Avocados were a product little known by wholesalers, retailers and consumers, so an effective marketing plan was urgently needed. As the first nationwide marketing activity, the farmers promoted a contest for naming the company, originally called the California Avocado Growers Exchange. Out of 3,277 entries, 16 persons suggested the name Calavo, a combination of the words "California" and "avocado."

Calavo's efforts paid off when first year sales totaled 179,680 pounds of 46 different varieties of avocado. The California state agricultural code of 1925 gave the new industry a further boost by including avocados in its list of standards for maturity and defects. This put avocados in the spotlight for state and national wholesalers and retailers, and ensured a high quality and reliable source for the fruit. The first grower-owned packing house was built in 1928. In 1931 Calavo began to diversify into broader product lines including limes, avocado oil, and, later, coconuts, mangos, kiwifruit, persimmons and Asian pears under such brand names as Sunripe, Selecto, Gusto, Bueno, El Dorado, and Fino.

In 1941 Calavo made its first million dollar return for its grower-members. By 1943 there were 31 sales offices nationwide, supported by the original Calavo office in Vernon, California. The farmers met a rapidly growing demand with steady increases in crop production, which forced them to subcontract their packing and distributing facilities. In 1955, construction on a large new packing house began in Santa Paula, used today as the primary packing facility.

In 1962 Calavo expanded its product line by acquiring Frigid Foods of Escondido and began marketing their first successful processed form of avocado, a refrigerated one-pound can of "Avocado Dip (Guacamole)." Earlier, unsuccessful attempts at processing included avocado paste in a tube and plastic-bagged frozen avocado halves and slices.

By its fiftieth anniversary in 1974, annual sales had topped $25 million and Calavo had accomplished significant advances in picking, packing, and distribution. During this period, Calavo evoked record consumer response from its multicolor ad in *Vogue* magazine. In 1977 Calavo's marketing advisory board became the California Avocado Commission, supervising multimedia promotion of California avocados.

The 1980s became a decade of unprecedented growth in membership and production. In 1985 Calavo opened a fully automated packing house in Temecula, California. This facility became a showcase of agricultural production and distribution, and as a result of this additional facility, 1990 gross sales exceeded $150 million. Calavo also became a worldwide leader in avocado exports from its state-of-the-art facility in Uruapan, Mexico. Today it exports its products to Japan, Europe, and Canada and is developing trade relationships with Chile, Mexico, and New Zealand. It also began to import Hass avocados from another grower in Mexico to supplement the off season in California, providing avocados in the United States year round.

Because of the "free trade" restrictions, mostly in the form of high tariffs, on cooperatives operating internationally, Calavo became a for-profit corporation by a 90 percent vote of its members in October, 2001. Under the direction of its CEO, Lee Cole, one of the largest avocado growers in California, the company has turned its back on cooperativism and joined the ranks of the transnationals.

A second example of the rising tide of cooperativism comes from the increasing popularity of agricultural cooperatives in the northern Midwest due to the bank mortgage crisis of the 1980s. Probably the hardest hit by the crisis were the dairy farmers. The dairy industry increasingly requires larger herds, more equipment and wider markets for survival. It became obvious to many dairy farmers that to keep expenses down relative to sales volume, larger pieces of grazing land and more equipment were needed. In order to expand, many dairy farmers had to mortgage their farms for the capital to achieve the economies of scale necessary to make their enterprises work.

At the same time, commercial banks throughout the Midwest began to pressure farmers for payment. Banks foreclosed on many farmers, forcing them to stand aside and watch their farms auctioned off to the highest bidders—mostly large corporations. It is important to remember that the vast majority of Scandinavians immigrating to the United States toward the end of the nineteenth century and early twentieth century settled in the northern Midwest, because the climate, logging opportunities, and dairy farming environment of that region resembled their "old countries" very closely.

Farmers in the northern plains, many of whom were of Scandinavian origin and accustomed to cooperatives, began to join together in co-ops for purchasing equipment, stock, and marketing contracts. Roughly 20 percent of the farmers in the north and almost all farmers in the southern Midwest still distrusted cooperatives, perhaps considering them a communist, or at least socialist, idea. This idea still remains a strong cultural barrier in middle America. For whatever reason, those who resisted joining cooperatives frequently lost their farms.

Today net sales of milk and milk products by cooperatives in the United States totals over $25 billion, representing nearly 90 percent of all milk sales in the United States (see Table 1.1). Other products with increased shares include grain and oilseed up to over 40 percent, cotton and cotton seed at 43 percent, fruits and vegetables at 20 percent, and livestock and wool at 14 percent. The overall share of farm products accounted for by cooperatives rose to over 30 percent by 2000 (USDA, Rural Development Report, 2002).

Financial Co-ops: The International Credit Union Movement

The credit union movement has always been international. Probably as long as anyone can remember there have been organizations directed toward mutual financial aid. There have been at least a thousand beginnings, one for each local community. Mutual aid and wealth-sharing societies have been called different names around the world. In China, they are *lin-hui*; in India, *chit*; in England, *slates*; in Germany, the cradle of cooperative credit, *Genossenschaftsbank*; in Japan, *mujin*; in West Africa and Trinidad, *sou-sou*; in Latin America, *cundina* or *tanda*; in Thailand, *bia huey*; and so on.

For centuries, people all over the world have used these informal savings and lending societies to finance education, weddings or other formal celebrations, and business ventures. These societies had also been used to alleviate poverty or other crises. For the most part, these small, unregulated, and often transitory organizations have met the needs of their members very well. But they were, and are, only temporary arrangements, sometimes lasting only a season or a year, used only when more institutional means were unavailable. These informal financial arrangements still occur.

Only in the last century have credit unions been established as an integral and indispensable part of the global economic system. Commercial banks and other

Table 1.1   Agricultural Cooperatives' Shares of US Farm Market—Selected Commodity Groups

Commodity Group	Cash Receipts %
Milk and Milk Products	86
Grains and Oil Seeds	40
Cotton and Cottonseed	43
Fruits and Vegetables	19
Livestock and Wool	14
All Others	12
Percent of Total Market	**30**

Source: US Department of Agriculture, rural Development Report, 2002.

corporate financial organizations have fought their increasing popularity but, as yet, without significantly hampering their inevitable growth. The primary difference between a commercial bank and a credit union is that members of the credit union own the institution, develop its policy, and hire its staff. It qualifies as a co-op.

In Europe and the United States, credit unions have flourished and attained maturity as a socioeconomic institution. Their beginnings can be traced to the work of two individuals in late eighteenth century Germany. Hermann Schulze-Delitzsch and Friederich Wilhelm Raiffeisen shared a common dream, to make capital available to crafts people, shop owners, and traders, and provide relief for agrarian families displaced to the cities, but they each worked from somewhat different philosophies of organization (MacPherson, 1999).

Schulze-Delitzsch was a remarkable organizer. His philosophy can be thought of as a form of supply-side or "trickle-down" economics. He was convinced that if the wealthy could have ready access to capital, then the workers and the poorer segments of society would also improve through the generation of jobs and opportunities. By the end of his life he had helped start some 1,900 cooperative banks with 466,000 members throughout Germany. In 1871 he introduced legislation on cooperative banking into the Prussian legislature, creating the model for future laws facilitating and regulating the cooperative banks for all of Germany. The structure of his cooperative banks and the superstructure linking them into regional and national banks was largely financed by wealthy urban savers, a financial basis that was lacking in the more rural areas of the country. For this and other reasons, Schulze-Delitzsch convinced his friend Friederich Raiffeisen to start rural credit unions based on a self-help model for providing funds for poorer borrowers.

A deeply religious and conservative man, Friederich Wilhelm Raiffeisen was very concerned by the rise of poverty in the rural areas of the Rhine Valley in the middle of the nineteenth century. His organizational philosophy concerned the empowerment of common people. Therefore he determined to organize credit unions. By the time of his death in 1888, Raiffeisen had started 423 local institutions loosely federated into a type of cooperative regional bank owned by the local co-op banks. Emphasis on self-reliance and self-responsibility made his model very attractive to pragmatic credit union organizers as long as a century after his death. Along with

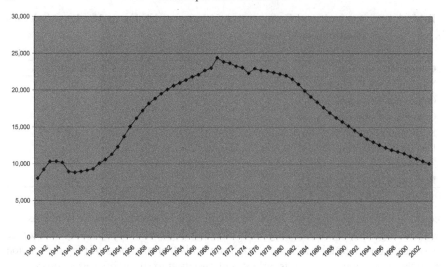

Figure 1.1   Number of Credit Unions
Source: Credit Union National Association (CUNA) data.

his contemporary Schulze-Delitzsch he remains one of the important founders of today's international credit union movement.

The story of the German cooperative banking experience and its success reached the ears of a Canadian government employee, chief stenographer of the Canadian Parliament in Ottawa, during the last decade of the nineteenth century. Alphonse Desjardins immediately saw how the credit union concept could help his family and his neighbors living in the parish (township) of Levis in Quebec.

Alphonse and his wife Dorimene formed the *Levis Caisse Populaire* in their parish of Levis, Quebec. Alphonse's government job took him away from their cooperative bank for weeks at a time. Therefore he appointed his wife Dorimene, a mother of ten, as manager of the bank. Recognizing the vulnerability of the enterprise as a new financial child on the block, Dorimene convinced her husband to introduce legislation in Parliament to secure legal standing for the bank. The first of such laws was passed by the government of Quebec in 1906.

By the time of Alphonse's death in 1920, the Desjardins family had started 175 *caisses* in French-speaking Quebec. In 1908 Alphonse addressed the members of St. Mary's Church parish in Manchester, New Hampshire. As a result of his presentation, the Manchester community organized the first cooperative credit society in the United States. At that same presentation, Alphonse met Pierre Jay, the Banking Commissioner of Massachusetts. Intrigued by Alphonse's presentation and with both of the Desjardins' help, Jay succeeded in persuading the Massachusetts legislature to pass the first credit union law in the United States, allowing such cooperative institutions to be chartered by the commonwealth. This early law laid the ground work for later Federal Law to establish cooperative corporations throughout the US (MacPherson, 1999).

Credit unions began flourishing in the United States when, in the early years of the twentieth century, it became clear to local financiers and common people that the

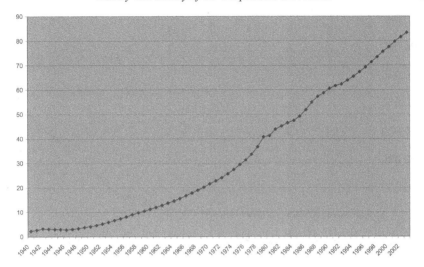

Figure 1.2   Number of Credit Union Members (in millions)
Source: Credit Union National Association (CUNA) data.

commercial banks, with demands for large collateral and high interest rates, were failing to meet the needs of the poor. Boston financier Edward A. Filene became a key figure in the spread of the credit union movement. Committed to serving the needs of working-class men and women, Filene and his brother founded a large specialty store catering specifically to the need for low cost clothing and home furnishings with the innovation of "bargain basement." They had little use for charity; rather they possessed a deep faith in the capacity of working people to improve their lot if they had access to good information and the opportunity to use it effectively. To the Filene's this meant showing how "Yankee ingenuity" could work in the cooperative mode as well as in corporate capitalism.

Working with Pierre Jay of the Massachusetts Bank Commission, Filene succeeded in getting a credit union law enacted. In 1914 he joined other business leaders to form a Massachusetts Credit Union Association and helped to write a statement of credit union principles, defining the credit union idea for Americans and others to this day. Inspired by the work of Jay and Filene, The Rev Dr Moses Coady, notable for his work organizing fishers' co-ops in Nova Scotia, brought the credit union idea to English-speaking Canada in the early 1920s.

In 1939 about 8,000 credit unions were functioning in the United States with a total of over two million members and a total of $190 million in assets. By the year 1968, the number of credit unions had increased to 23,687, with 17,872,270 members and $11.5 billion in total assets. While 1968 remained a peak year for the number of credit unions, the overall number of members continued to increase at an exponential rate. With certain membership restrictions lifted, credit unions began to grow at the rate of about 2 million members a year. Smaller credit unions either disappeared or merged with others to form larger and more economically sound operations (see Figures 1.1 and 1.2).

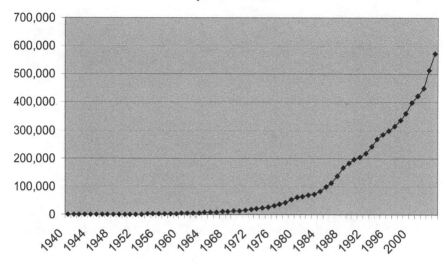

Figure 1.3   Total Assets of Credit Unions (in $millions)
Source: Credit Union National Association (CUNA) data.

By 2002, 10,041 credit unions had a total of 83,345,147 members and total assets of nearly $575 billion. This represents a growth of the credit unions' percentage of all bank accounts from 35.5 percent to 51.1 percent over the sixty-three year period from 1939 and a growth in their share of bank assets from 1.4 percent to 6.8 percent, nearly a five-fold increase in their market share. Figures 1.2 and 1.3 show this growth graphically. (A complete set of United States credit union data appears in Appendix A.)

The National Cooperative Bank in the United States

The National Cooperative Bank (NCB) was chartered by Congress in 1978 and became a member owned cooperative in 1981. Their charter is unique in that it enables them to provide loans to almost any kind of cooperative in the US. They are headquartered in Washington, DC and have offices in Alaska, California, Connecticut, Ohio and New York. NCB currently (2005) has 1,841 members, each with one vote and who qualify as members by being borrowers and by purchasing class B1 stock equal to 1 percent of the value of the loan principle. The cooperative is governed by a board elected by the members at an annual meeting

NCB primarily serves cooperatives and their members in the United States and its territories. These organizations may be legally incorporated as cooperatives or they may embody the cooperative principles. Examples of traditional cooperatives include: housing cooperatives, natural foods cooperatives, purchasing cooperatives and retailer-owned wholesaler cooperatives. Examples of organizations that share in the cooperative principles include: Alaska Native corporations, Employee Stock Ownership Plans (ESOPs), nonprofit healthcare organizations, nonprofit retirement communities, community development corporations and charter schools.

Service Cooperatives in the US: The Day the Lights Went On

During the first four decades of the twentieth century, electricity became available in almost all of the United States—*almost* all. The private utility companies did not see enough profit in stringing wires from farm to farm or through any low-density part of America. A survey conducted by the National Electric Light Association in 1910 claimed that the number of farmers using electricity was negligible. In that year, of 6.5 million farms in the United States, "...the number of farmers with electricity was almost too small to report" (Nadeau and Thompson, 1996, 135). For example in the early 1930s "coal oil" (kerosene) lamps were the preferred utility in rural Southeast Kansas. Only occasionally could one see a gas light, when a private gas well was within convenient piping distance and the farmer could afford the price. Paying the price for electricity was prohibitive.

To help offset the excessive burdens of the depression in rural areas, in 1933 Congress established the Tennessee Valley Authority (TVA), and in 1935, by executive order, President Roosevelt set up the Rural Electrification Administration (REA). A group of residents in Alcorn County, Mississippi, organized a cooperative to work with the TVA to make reasonably priced electricity available in their county. Their cooperative became a model for some 600 electric cooperatives established around the country, and by 1940 approximately 25 percent of farms were served by these co-ops. Today over 800 local rural electric cooperatives (RECs) and 60 regional cooperatives serve some 30 million people in 46 states. In addition to providing electricity at the lowest possible price, these co-ops now attract industry, promote job creation, and provide many other social and economic benefits, such as emancipation from menial tasks with milking machines, separators, and dependable food freezing and refrigeration, in their service areas (Nadeau and Thompson, 1996, 136 ff.).

In early 1990 the citizens of Taos, New Mexico, created a stellar example of an active and successful electric cooperative, the Kit Carson Electric Cooperative. Unlike the co-ops in the Midwest, it has a service area that contains a large Hispanic population and, historically, has experienced a large unemployment problem. The co-op took the leadership role in starting a small business incubator, a group of business professionals organized to help form and support new small businesses. The non-profit incubator corporation that spun off from Kit Carson Co-op built a large facility in the summer of 1996 and now assists more than 15 small businesses to operate successfully and to employ over 500 formerly jobless persons.

In 2000, the Energy Information Administration reported 894 energy cooperatives, approximately 30 percent of the total number of utility companies, with over $20 million in sales to end users. Energy cooperatives produce about 10 percent of the total amount of electric power used in the United States—about 306 million mega-watt-hours (MWH) out of a total of over 3 billion MWH. One of the largest networks of energy co-ops is Touchstone Energy Cooperatives (TEC) comprising more than 550 local co-ops in 39 states with over 16 million members. See Table 1.2 for a comparison of the various types of companies that supply electricity in the United States.

Since their inception in the first half of the twentieth century, electric cooperatives have dramatically expanded their influence, both in bringing electric power to rural

**Table 1.2   Energy Cooperatives in the United States Selected Utility Data
by Ownership, US, 2000**

Data Item	Investor Owned	Publicly Owned	Cooperative	Federal	Total
# of Utilities	240	2,009	894	9	3,152
% of Utilities	7.6	63.7	28.4	0.3	100.00
Revenues (Sales to Ultimate Users)	109,444,470	33,054,956	20,506,101	1,242,031	224,247,558
% of Revenue	75.6	14.7	9.1	0.6	100.00
Sales (1000MWH)	2,437,982	516,681	305,856	49,094	3,309,613
% of Sales	73.7	15.6	9.2	1.5	100.00

Source: Energy Information Administration, Form EIA-861, Calendar Year 2000.

America and in bringing economic power to their members. The pressure increases
steadily on local RECs to sell out to investor-owned utilities and on public utilities to
sell out to large corporate interests or to merge with the large pool of publicly owned
utilities and then be sold out to a private share-holder company.

Other Forms of Group Cooperation

In addition to what we might call "true cooperatives" organized according to the
Rochdale principles, other forms of group cooperation range from livestock grazing
associations that share grazing lands to worker-owned enterprises. Agricultural
producers, for example, have a rich history of cooperation that does not always
conform to all of the seven principles, but solves common problems such as water
use without losing the producers' individual identities. The concept of pooling lands
so that environmentally sensitive land can be preserved is a particularly interesting
project that is essentially cooperative but that also preserves clear lines of private
ownership.

A field of cooperative marketing of environmental amenities has emerged
recently, forming open space and wildlife habitat, to curb the overuse of rural and
public lands. Probably the best examples of this kind of effort are county open space
projects and conservancy trusts. Otherwise land development and conversion would
soon swallow up the small amount of remaining agricultural land in the United
States, either through urban expansion or, more worrisome, large-lot development
(more than one acre per house) in rural areas. Some studies estimate that seventy
percent of agricultural land in the US is located in areas where these kinds of
development are occurring (Carlson, 2003). The open-space projects vary from true
cooperative principles in that they are primarily government (usually county) owned
and administered.

Worker-owned enterprises, such as Peoples and United, manufacturing firms
in the Ohio Employee Ownership Center, and Capital Ownership Group (COG)
have recently arrived on the scene. Formed mostly since 1990, they provide some
experience and guidance in democratizing economic entrepreneurship. Most of these
organizations do not confine stockholding to their members. Rather, they organize

primarily as Employee Stock Ownership Plans (ESOPs). Recent research has shown that companies with more that 20 percent of their stock owned by employees tend to maintain a more equitable distribution of income and are more likely to grow and become more effective businesses (Krimerman, 2001).

Although none of these near-cooperative projects would qualify as true cooperatives under the Rochdale principles, they illustrate the value and necessity of cooperation under several circumstances.

Legal Framework in the United States

From time to time capitalism unconstrained by law or government regulatory agencies shows its natural tendency to form large monopolies and trusts. This was the case when the "Robber Barons" of the last part of the nineteenth century began their march to acquire more and more of the country's wealth.

Advocates of free-market capitalism assume that "healthy" competition will provide a natural check on monopolistic tendencies and establish a natural equilibrium without any kind of outside regulatory activity. This type of equilibrium, however, proves intrinsically unstable, because this notion of equilibrium is based on the twin assumptions that (1) complete market information is available for all players and (2) that all players have equal access to the market for new ideas and products. It is assumed, in other words, that all players have virtually equal strength, resources, and social networks.

If these conditions can ever prevail, certainly neither of them did at the turn of the twentieth century. Consequently powerful corporate forces were so blatantly in violation of fair play that Congress was obliged to step in. It did so with the passage of the Sherman Antitrust Act of 1890. From that time on, the government has played a crucial role in the regulation of markets, and all business concerns including cooperatives have remained subject to strict legal constraints.

The principle of "unintended consequences" prevailed, however, and the antitrust suits that proceeded from the Sherman Act tended to stifle cooperatives by court decisions that cooperative behavior somehow resembled collusion, price-fixing, or other unfair trade. These decisions coincided with a time when the cooperative movement began capturing the imagination of farmers and merchants.

Farmers' associations had been formed in Connecticut as early as 1804 to facilitate the marketing of milk and milk products. Now it seemed that farmers had to curtail those activities. The US Congress had consistently favored the cooperative movement. Yet it was not until the enactment of Section 6 of the Clayton Act of 1914 that the first federal legal protection specifically allowing farmers and agricultural producers to cooperate became available.

Since it covered only some types of agricultural cooperative activity, the Clayton Act soon proved inadequate. During President Harding's administration, "An Act To Authorize Associations of Producers of Agricultural Products (7 U.S.C. 291,292, 1996)" was passed in 1922. Its primary sponsor, Senator Capper, stated that the purpose of the bill "is to give to the farmer the same right to bargain collectively that is already enjoyed by corporations" ([62]Cong. Rec., [2057] 1922). Known today as the Capper-Volstead Act of 1922, sometimes referred to as the "Magna Carta" of cooperatives, had two main sponsors, Senator Capper and Representative Volstead. The act forms the capstone of all law respecting cooperatives.

The Capper-Volstead Act now provides farmers who form cooperatives with specific exemption from the antitrust laws. Such legal protection was, of course, critical to cooperatives. Without this protection federal and state antitrust laws would prevent most of the joint activities required of cooperatives to market, price, and sell their products. At the same time, the Capper-Volstead Act greatly expanded the types of legal activities in which a cooperative organization might properly engage. Also a milestone judicial decision set an important legal precedent with *Olympia Veneer vs. Commissioner of Internal Revenue* in 1926. A federal judge ruled that additional payments and dividends awarded a cooperative's members qualify as legitimate business expenses and are not subject to corporate taxes.

It is just as true now as it was in the 1920s that farmers are continually under pressure from large corporate buyers (called "agribusinesses") either to under-price their products or to sell their land. A large agribusiness might negotiate with individual farmers in this country and abroad so that it has a greater ability to demand the lowest possible prices for the farmers' products. As a consequence, a typical farmer may have only one potential buyer for his product and may be forced to take whatever price the corporate buyer offers. The ability to join together in cooperatives provides farmers with a way to balance the bargaining equation (Barnes and Ondeck, 1997, 2).

Under the Capper-Volstead Act, a farm cooperative cannot be dwarfed as easily by agribusiness as the individual farmer can. Also, a cooperative can resist the agribusiness tactic of delaying negotiations on price until late in season when farmers may need to sell quickly and take an "off-peak" price. Furthermore, a cooperative can optimize the costs of cultivating, seeding, fertilizing, growing, packing, and marketing by aggregating these activities. A cooperative can provide better forecasting and data collection for farmers to use in their negotiations. It can also help to provide a guaranteed outlet for the product, since there may be only a few outlets for certain agricultural products. Without the cooperative a farmer can be forced to accept unfavorable terms of sale and price simply to gain access to the market.

The Capper-Volstead Act provided that only the producers and no one else could be members of the cooperative and receive the Act's protection. Courts have held, however, that some non-producers may be members of a cooperative if they do not have decision-making authority. Later on, processing, preparing for market, handling, and marketing were added to the protection of the Act [7 U.S.C. 291]. The Act also, for the first time, allowed products from non-members to be sold in a co-op. Co-ops can now purchase up to 50 percent of the total value of their products on sale from non-members (Lemon, Citation 44).

Only five Supreme Court decisions have directly interpreted the Capper-Volstead Act, introducing the following interpretations of the Act:

- Cooperative members cannot enter into any agreements that would cause restrained trade with proprietary organizations (US v. Borden, 1939).
- Free association and agreement is permitted between cooperatives.
- The Act forbids any kind of conspiracy with outside corporations.

- Setting prices among members of a cooperative for joint marketing is permitted.
- Merging cooperatives is permitted.
- Proposed mergers of large cooperatives should be judged in the same way as mergers of large corporations (Maryland & Virginia Milk Producers Assoc. v. United States, 1960).

In 1961, members of Congress proposed an amendment to the Capper-Volstead Act. This amendment provided that the Secretary of Agriculture be allowed to approve mergers and acquisitions of cooperatives. The amendment was born of congressional alarm following the 1960 Supreme Court decision giving courts the right to judge the legality of all proposed corporate mergers. This amendment effectively would have stripped away the power of the justice system to make such legal determinations by transferring all the power to the administration. The proposed amendment failed, largely because it gave the Secretary no criteria by which to judge the amendment's effects on overall business competition.

Even though the amendment failed, sympathy for cooperatives in Congress and among the general population ran very high, and mergers generally went unchallenged. The three largest milk cooperatives in the US were formed by a merger of 166 smaller cooperatives between 1968 and 1970. These mergers were never challenged by the Federal Trade Commission or the Department of Justice as a violation of the antitrust laws.

With the passage of the Capper-Volstead Act of 1922 and all the subsequent court decisions in favor of cooperative activity, the cooperative movement again began to grow rapidly. This growth resulted both from an increased social interest in cooperatives and an improved legal atmosphere for them to flourish. By 2002 there were over 4,000 agricultural cooperatives in the United States, with nearly 200,000 employees, combined assets of $45 billion, and a gross income of $120 billion.

Summary and Conclusions

Cooperatives with European roots in the eighteenth and nineteenth centuries have spread throughout the world. Cooperatives differ from other types of corporations in several ways. They require participation of every member under a principle of "one share, one member, one vote," remain relatively free of government and other outside intervention, encourage equitable distribution of resources, generate no profit for individual or group owners, and strive for sustainability with respect to resource and energy use.

Cooperatives exist within several different sectors of the economy. They can be *producers, value-added co-ops, supply or distribution co-ops, service co-ops, retail/ consumer co-ops, worker co-ops, housing co-ops,* or *financial co-ops.* In northern Spain, the Mondragón group can operate in every sector under the same cooperative corporate charter. So far, such an arrangement would still be illegal in the United States because of the constraints imposed by the Sherman Antitrust Act.

The antitrust laws passed in the United States toward the end of the nineteenth century had unintended negative effects on cooperatives, hampering their formation, growth, and development. Realizing this, Congress passed the Capper-Volstead Act ("The Magna Carta of Cooperatives") in 1922, specifically exempting agricultural cooperatives from prosecution under the Sherman Antitrust Act, as long as they remained close to their mission and purpose. Further interpretations of this act would allow associations of cooperatives, but not conglomerate cooperatives.

Cooperatives have proliferated over the world since the 1980s, creating cooperative activity in every sector of the economy and attaining respectable shares of their various markets. In some parts of the world, including the United States, a variety of enterprises in a community or region tend to raise the quality of life of their members and help them to survive monetary crises and economic downturns.

Although essentially local, cooperatives can form legal alliances and networks across regions, nations, and even globally. Since the bottom line of cooperatives is to distribute goods and services more equitably among all its members, not to accumulate wealth for owners and share holders, they represent a more ideal, democratic, and functional globalization than has been experienced so far—a kind of "globalization from below."

The real bottom line is effective service to the common good, and the accomplishment of goals as outlined in the seven principles. These goals remain challenging in the individualistic and competitive matrix of modern monopoly capitalism.

Breaches of the Rochdale principles, particularly the second one, have caused transformations of several successful enterprises. This usually happens by extending memberships, including voting rights, to non worker-members. The Olympia Veneer Company brought itself down by redefining its shares as transferable. Calavo intentionally converted its highly successful cooperative, by member vote, into a powerful transnational corporation.

In spite of all of the legal and cultural barriers (the mythologies about cooperative survival and superiority of competition) and occasional conversion, cooperatives have been surprisingly successful in the United States and other parts of the world. In Western Europe and North America, those firms that have remained co-ops have achieved 30 percent of market share. At both the beginning and the end of the twentieth century, the cooperative movement has shown the way out of economic disaster.

References

Barnes, D.M. and Ondeck, C.E. (1997). *The Capper-Volstead Act: Opportunity Today and Tomorrow.* Washington, DC: Jenkins & Gilchrist.

Carlson, D.L., (2003). "Agricultural Preservation and Development Associations," presentation to Conference on Compensatory Options for Conserving Agricultural Land (Scramento, CA: University of California Agricultural Issues Center). Available from the author at Colorado Department of Agriculture, Denver, CO.

CICOPA (2005). "International Coalition of Production and Artisan Cooperatives. Regional Organisation for Europe." Report <http://www.cicopa.coop>.

Cox, T. (1993). "Cooperative Development in Societ and Post Soviet Society." *Book of Cooperative Enterprise 1993.* London: The Plunkett Foundation.

Credit Union National Association (CUNA). <http://www.cuna.org/download/US_totals.pdf>.

DGRV—Deutscher Genossenschafts und Raiffeisenverband (2006). "German Society of Cooperatives and Credit Unions." Report online <http://www.dgrv.de/>.

Energy Information Administration (2000). Form EIA-861, Calendar Years.

FIDC (2002). *Banking Data, Table CB09.*

Honigsberg, P.J., Kamoroff, B., and Beatty, J. (1991). *We Own It: Starting and Managing Cooperatives and Employee Owned Ventures, Revised and Updated,.* Willits, CA: Bell Springs Publishers.

ICA (2002). "International Cooperative Alliance." Europe Bulletin, Special Issue Oct & Issue No. 15, Dec. Geneva, Switzerland.

Isaacson, Rosenbaum, Woods and Levy, P.C. [Denver law firm] (1996). *Memorandum to the Colorado Department of Agriculture, "Agricultural Lands Project."* Denver, CO.

Krimerman, L. (2001). "Building a Democratic Economy and Culture," Grassroots Economic Organizing (GEO), No. 33 (Fall, 2001).

Lemon, Legal Citation: 44 N.D.L. Rev. 505,510.

MacPherson, I. (1999). *Hands Around the Globe—A History of the International Credit Union Movement and the Role and Development of the World Council of Credit Unions, Inc.* Victoria, B.C., Canada: Hosdal and Schubart Publishers, Ltd.

Maryland and Virginia Milk Producers Assoc. v. United States, Legal Citation: 362 U.S. 458 (1960).

Nadeau, E.G. and Thompson, D.J. (1996). *Cooperation Works! How People Are Using Cooperative Action to Rebuild Communities and Revitalize the Economy,* Rochester, Minnesota: Lone Oak Press, Ltd.

Shaffer, J. (1999). *Historical Dictionary of the Cooperative Movement*; Historical Dictionaries of Religions, Philosophies, and Movements, No. 26. Lanham, MD and London: The Scarecrow Press, Inc.

USDA [United States Department of Agriculture] (2002). *Rural Development Report*, Calendar Years.

WOCCU [World Council of Credit Unions] (2003). *Statistical Data: United States Credit Union Statistics, 1939—2002.* <http://www.woccu.org>.

Chapter 2

Comparing Cooperation, Competition, and Individual Effort

Cooperation
Not hyper-competition
Can it work today?   (Haiku by BL & BF)

Spiro Agnew once pronounced, "A noncompetitive society would represent...a bland experience...a waveless sea of nonachievers...the psychological retreat of a person...into a cocoon of false security and self-satisfied mediocrity" (Johnson and Johnson, 1989, 52).

Do our cultural assumptions about cooperation, competition, and individual effort affect the way we study these processes and do these assumptions affect the results of careful studies within our culture? In our cultural setting, what exactly are the relative values of cooperation, competition, and individual effort?

In the current western capitalist world, classical economists base theories and models on the assumption that competition always keeps prices in balance. Free market forces, if left unchecked by regulatory agencies, will eventually bring equilibrium and equity to all the players, they argue. This assumption has so permeated our entire culture that it is hard to convince ourselves that competition may, in the last analysis, not be good for us at all; in fact, it may be our downfall. The following case history may illustrate the problem.

George and John were brothers, not twins, though they looked alike and were born only one year apart. From the time they were toddlers, John and George competed fiercely with each other. Their mother tried to engage them in cooperative work, but their father encouraged the competition by arguing, "Good, healthy competition never hurt anybody. Besides, their competitiveness will motivate them both to do better." So they continued to fight bitterly for toys, the attention of their parents, and time with their grandparents, who lived nearby.

John was very good at his school work. George struggled. In grammar school, he was passed from third to fourth grade even though his marks did not merit it. In high school, John became very popular with his class mates and attracted the attention of many girls. George also observed how positively the teachers responded to John while George was scarcely noticed. George continued to struggle, but rapidly slipped back. He became quiet and sullen, failing most of his courses.

When George complained to his mother, her response was, "Nonsense! You should observe how polite and helpful your brother is. Why can't you be more like him? You just mope around the house while he is out doing things or studying his lessons."

George had developed a crush on Ruth next door. He began to brighten up some in order to impress her. Just as he had begun to feel like somebody, he came home from school and discovered John and Ruth making love on the living room sofa. Something snapped and, to Ruth's horror, George began beating his brother John with a baseball bat. Ruth screamed at him, but he was so enraged he could not stop. Ruth ran to get help but was too late. George had killed his own brother!

Regrettably, the above story actually occurred. Only the names have been changed. It is certainly an extreme case but serves to point out the shadow side of competition and how ingrained in our culture competition has become.

Three Modes of Achievement

Three major modes of achieving tasks are *competition, cooperation,* and *individual effort.* Competition and cooperation necessitate social interaction while individual effort requires only a single person with acquired knowledge and skill.

Competition

"Competition" is definable in terms of a "game" in which players attempt to accumulate points and "win" by getting more points than others. This kind of game is often called a "zero-sum" game, a game in which there are a fixed number of points so that the accumulation of points by one player (or a subgroup of players) will result in the loss of points by the others. We compete on the tennis court, on the putting green, at the bridge table, in the board room, in the market place, and even on the dance floor. The object of a zero-sum game is for individuals or subgroups to accumulate more points than their opponents. All these cases create a few winners; all the rest, losers. Zero-sum games tend to be individualistic, rule-oriented, and exclusive.

The language of business and economics is filled with "win-lose" terms. You "win" a promotion. You "lose" a negotiation. You "outsmart" the competition. The creed of competition as a virtue is woven deeply into our social fabric. Competition provides the weft of Adam Smith's *Wealth of Nations* and of Herbert Spencer's survival-of-the-fittest interpretation of Darwin's theory of evolution.

Cooperation

"Cooperation" can also be defined as a game, but it is a game in which all players may attempt to accumulate points for the entire group by using their unique capabilities and talents. Cooperation is governed by process orientation rather than rule orientation. This kind of game encourages all the players to develop modes of interaction (cooperation) which will further the common goals of the group. If any points are accumulated at all, no one loses and everyone is a winner. These games are sometimes called "non-zero sum" games or "win-win" games.

Cooperation involves working together to achieve a common goal or the common good. It uses small groups to maximize each other's productivity and achievement. In cooperative situations, individuals perceive that they can reach their goals only if other group members also do so. Their goal attainments are highly correlated and individuals help each other and encourage each to work harder (Deutsch, 1962).

Individual effort

"Individual effort" involves no social interaction at all. Games like solitaire or solving a puzzle require only individual effort. There are scientists and artists who much prefer this solitary mode of approaching a task and, perhaps, would assume that individual effort can be more creative or imaginative than group process. To some the need to devote attention to group processes would impede progress toward the creative effort or toward the solution of a problem.

Cooperative action "... results from perceived positive interdependence resulting in an interaction pattern among participants within which members promote each other's success" (Johnson and Johnson, 1989, 29). In their landmark study, David and Roger Johnson identified 1,325 empirical and quantitative studies comparing cooperation, competition, and individual effort and commenced a meta-analysis of them to synthesize their most significant conclusions.

Studying Cooperation

The literature summarized by the Johnsons formulates a major research question concerning the three modes of activity defined above: cooperation, competition, and individual effort. Which one is the most effective under what circumstances and in what particular types of activity?

Generally, "effectiveness" includes such concepts as productivity, achievement, and cognitive processes such as problem-solving. The above suggests a related research question: "Should cooperation, competition, and individual effort vary with the type of task?" Or put another way: "Might cooperation be called for in certain situations and competition or individual effort in others? Could a mixture of approaches work better in some situations?"

Studies of cooperation, competition, and individual effort focus on several different kinds of outcomes. Some have been primarily interested in productivity measured by output or capital generation and others in individual and group achievement. Some studies have focused on "quality of reasoning" as of prime value in professions and business. Some studies have considered what they call process gain or loss or, in learning situations, transfer of the group gains (or losses) to the individuals in the group.

A series of subsidiary questions have also been posed in the literature: Could the inclusion of persons of very high and very low ability in cooperative groups get in the way of optimal group process and thus hinder performance? Is competition necessary for motivation? Does cooperation encourage malingering and non-participation, thus penalizing the group?

In constructing and reviewing studies of cooperation versus competition or individual effort, several methodological questions arise: Could gender make a difference? Would the size of the group studied affect the results? Should differing academic subject areas, fields, or business objectives call for different research methods? Would socioeconomic class or educational level of the subjects make a difference? How about the age spread of the subjects? And how might the diversity of ethnic or cultural background of subjects affect the results? If we are looking at studies already done, would published studies necessarily be more valid than unpublished ones?

Empirical Studies

Over the last century there have been over one-thousand scientific studies comparing the results of cooperation and competition in a wide variety of fields such as education, business, sports, science, problem solving, motor skills, and psychological counseling. Most of these studies were done within the last thirty years. A smaller set of these studies included analyses of tasks involving individualistic effort.

One large problem with such a massive literature review is the variation in quality of the studies. Part of the Johnsons' solution to this problem was to require every study included in the analysis to meet the following four requirements:

1. The study must involve independent variables, causal factors, and conditions specifically related to social interdependence as defined in the tradition of Morton Deutsch's research in the late 1940s. "Social interdependence exists when the outcomes of individuals are affected by each other's action" (Johnson, 1989, 23). Deutsch defines three types of interdependence: cooperation as coordinated interaction toward mutual outcomes, competition as oppositional action toward mutually exclusive outcomes, and individualistic effort as minimal interaction in achieving personal outcomes. Characteristics of cooperation include sharing a common fate, striving for mutual benefit, operating on a long-term perspective, and maintaining a shared identity (Deutsch, 1949; von Mises, 1949; Johnson, 1989).
2. The study must use quantitative measures of dependent variables, or outcomes, so that effect sizes and z-scores can be calculated. For more detailed discussion of z-score and Effect-size computations and their importance in statistical analysis, see Appendix B.
3. The study must include either reasonably clear controls or pre- and post-test scores.
4. The study must be written in English (only because of the Johnsons' language limitations).

The last requirement definitely hinders the generalization of their results to world-wide applications. Future prospective research in this area should consider the roles of cooperation, competition, and individual effort in more *organic* societies like the Maasai in East Africa, the Maya in Central America, and indigenous societies in South and Southeast Asia. In such societies, cooperation historically has been a more integral and central part of communal life for centuries. In fact, among most peoples like the Maya, competition is considered anathema. In Part II of this book, cooperatives in various parts of the world will be studied in more detail. Such cultural differences could be a key to understanding the role of cooperatives in various regions.

In spite of the language limitation, the research of Johnson and Johnson speaks strongly to the West. It certainly provides a strong basis for further inquiries into this subject and is worthy of our most thoughtful consideration.

Applying their four criteria, the Johnsons' set of studies was reduced to 512. Although analytical methods in this smaller set of studies varied widely, they are of much higher quality. The overall quality of the remaining studies can be defined by a number of factors: better level of randomization, more clarity of control conditions, fewer experimenter or administrator effects (higher reliability), less variable environmental conditions, and more consistent implementation of the treatments (independent variables).

In the final analysis, reliability of the combined set of studies defines their overall quality for the purposes of synthesizing their conclusions. The Johnsons' calculated reliability coefficients for all 512 studies lie between 92-94 percent, high by any standards. This subset of studies is highly appropriate and acceptable for rigorous meta-analysis.

There are several ways of approaching meta-analysis of such a wide variety of studies, performed over such a long time period, with such diverse samples of subjects. We can ask the studies to "vote" on certain common hypotheses; that is, they can be sorted on several outcome categories, for example, favorable, neutral, and unfavorable, and declare the category with a plurality (the mode) as the winner. The obvious problem with this procedure is that we totally ignore sample sizes, strengths of the effects, and overall significance of the results.

If there are enough data presented, as in this case, we can still calculate reliable and valid effect sizes. The method defines "effect size" by the amount that outcome variables change when a causal variable is changed by one standard deviation or, alternatively, the percent of the variability of the dependent variable accounted for by the effect of each independent variable or condition. Also, under the right conditions overall z-scores can be computed. The size of the z-score indicates whether or not the result is significant.

Given the four selection criteria, the 512 studies chosen all meet the requirements for computing effect sizes and z-scores. For a complete list of these 512 studies and their characteristics, see Johnson and Johnson (1989, Appendix). In the Johnson study, the effect sizes were corrected for sample size (Hedges and Olkin, 1986) and for possible bias due to the use of multiple measures in some studies (Bangert-Drowns, 1986). Thus, studies with multiple measures were weighted in inverse proportion to the number of measures used. Effect size is a measure not just of the significance of an effect but of its magnitude in units of standard deviation.

From the effect sizes and z-scores, probabilities, or p-values, can be computed. If the p-value is near 1.00, then the effect sizes and z-scores could have occurred by chance and are therefore not significant. If the p-value is low (below 0.05 or 0.01), the effect sizes and z-scores are high enough to indicate a positive result. See Table 2.1 below for an interpretive example. In comparing cooperation with competition, the results across the studies produced a z-score of 14.98. This means that the overall result for cooperation was nearly 15 standard deviations higher than the result for competition wia probability (p-value) less than 0.0001, about as near certainty as research on human behavior can produce.

A very interesting way of checking the sensitivity of the results to sampling errors is to use these z-scores to estimate how many non-significant or contrary studies would be needed to offset the differences of effectiveness between cooperation and competition, cooperation and individual effort, or competition and individual effort. The last column of Table 2.1, headed NS-Needed, gives this number. The method is quite robust, and the positive results can readily be accepted.

Variables and Measures Used in the Studies

Outcomes, or dependent variables, in the studies were of several kinds, such as productivity/achievement, quality of reasoning, process gain/loss, and transfer of learning. The experimenters used various standardized and non-standardized tests to measure levels of performance, productivity and knowledge retention.

Productivity/Achievement

The assessments of productivity or achievement involve a simple measure of the degree to which goals are attained. In this sense, these two words can be considered synonymous.

Quality of Reasoning

Definitions of "Quality of Reasoning" follows either Piaget's theories of cognitive development (Piaget, 1983) or Kohlberg's refinements in stages of moral development:

- Stage 1: Obey authorities in order to avoid punishment.
- Stage 2: Satisfy one's own needs, such as exchange of "goods," or specific rewards for behaving morally.
- Stage 3: Follow customary moral standards to obtain approval, regard, or liking.
- Stage 4: Obey law and order to preserve social harmony.
- Stage 5: Rely on internalized personal standards of social responsibility.
- Stage 6: Rely on internalized moral principles believed to be universally valid.

(Kohlberg, 1981)

Meta-cognitive strategies

This variation on cognitive quality is defined as using knowledge about one's own cognitive strategies to improve cognitive performance. Persons who engage in meta-cognition demonstrate the ability to evaluate and sharpen their own thinking and reasoning processes. They use meta-cognition when they recognize errors, account for lapses in memory, and make priority judgments about the importance of the material to study or tasks to accomplish. Individuals generally have trouble monitoring their own cognition, but, within a cooperative group, can promote high quality in each other's thinking and reasoning behavior.

Table 2.1   Impact of Cooperative, Competitive, and Individualistic Efforts on Productivity/Achievement

Comparison	Voting Method			Effect Size	z score			NS-Needed
	Neg	NoDif	Pos	ES	z	n	p	
Cooperate/Compete	31	126	214	0.72	14.98	107	<0.0001	8,710
Cooperate/Individual	57	376	474	0.65	21.02	176	<0.0001	28,385
Compete/Individual	25	81	55	0.30	3.14	47	0.0008	123

Neg – Negative result; NoDif – No sig. Diff; Pos – Positive Result; ES – Mean effect size
NS-Needed – Number of studies with non-significant results required to raise overall p-value to 0.05
Source: Johnson and Johnson, 1989, 41.

Process gain/loss

This is a somewhat difficult concept. It is defined in this study as the number of new ideas, solutions, and insights generated by the group process as compared to those generated by working individually. Thus the measure can be either positive or negative. A positive number would indicate a "gain" and a negative one, a "loss" for the cooperative process.

Transfer of learning

Learning transfer is a standard concept in psychology and learning theory. It occurs when individuals, performing within a cooperative group, demonstrate mastery of the material studied, concepts encountered, or skills acquired. Transfer is gauged as either present or absent in a learning situation.

Productivity/Achievement

The data used by the Johnsons generally indicate that cooperation will produce a higher level of productivity and achievement than will either competition or individual effort. Over 50 percent of the findings were strongly in favor of cooperation, while only 10 percent favored either competitive or individual effort. The average person in the cooperative groups performed about 3/5 of a standard deviation above the average person in competitive or individualistic groups. Table 2.1 shows results using all three meta-analysis methods. Remember that high effect sizes, high z-scores, and low *p*-values indicate greater overall differences between groups.

Voting Method refers to a simple comparison of studies that counts the studies the results of which were negative, positive, or zero. For example, a positive result in comparing cooperation with competition represents a conclusion that cooperation is more effective than competition; a negative result represents a conclusion that competition is more effective. No difference indicates that no statistically significant difference was found.

The Voting Method supports the conclusion that cooperation is more effective than competition by a score of 214 to 31. Cooperation also edges out individualism 474 to 57, but the competition vs. individualism election means a tie vote.

By effect sizes, cooperation proves more effective than competition by a rather large margin. The odds are about 1 to 10,000 that such a difference in performance between cooperation and competition could have happened by chance.

The same positive results for the effectiveness of cooperation is shown in comparison to individual effort. While still significant, the difference between competition and individual effort has a much smaller effect size. Referring to the last column of the table, it would take 8,710 more studies with non-significant results to reduce the overall difference in productivity/achievement between cooperation and competition to non-significance (*p*-value greater than 0.05). For cooperation versus individual effort to be reduced to non-significance, by the same definition, 28,385 non-significant studies would have to be added. For competition versus individual effort only 123 additional non-significant studies would be needed to reach a level of non-significance.

Quality of Reasoning

Two isolated studies have suggested that, under rather stringent conditions, cooperation can inhibit the generation of ideas and creative thinking (Hill, 1982; Lamm and Trommsdorff, 1973). Only in these two studies has such a negative result been reported. Participants in the studies were asked to solve a problem with a self-evident yet somewhat elusive solution. Group process would be expected to solve the problem much more quickly than any one individual could. If the probability of solving within a specified time were .05 (5 percent) for one person, then we would expect someone in a group of six persons to come up with the answer six times as quickly—6 times .05 = .30 or 30 percent faster solution. This was called the "truth wins" standard. It is expressed in team solution probabilities as $P = 1-(1-p)^n$.

The psychologically-based studies found that the group process was indeed quicker but seldom reached the level of the "truth wins" standard. This slowness was subjectively attributed to "reduced member motivation" and/or "coordination problems in combining team members' contributions." This kind of result was congruent with psychological studies between 1950 and 1990 reviewed by James H. Davis (Davis, 1992).

When two economists, David Cooper and John Kagel, carefully applied the same "truth wins" criterion to a simple limit pricing game, they obtained quite different results. The teams routinely far exceeded the standard (Cooper and Kagel, 2003a). Now why would psychologically based and economically based research produce such disparate results? Keep in mind that the psychologists were focusing on the performance of individuals and neither accounted for nor defined the group process. The groups were left entirely free to interact in any way they could and were considered as nothing more than an aggregate of individuals. No distinction was made between cooperative and competitive behavior.

The economists, on the other hand, defined teamwork very carefully in their experiments. The team interactions were recorded and analyzed to determine exactly how those interactions were used to solve strategic problems. They found that the teams played consistently more strategically than individuals, generated positive synergies in the more difficult games, beating the demanding "truth wins" norm. The superior performance of teams was particularly striking when rules encouraging competitive behavior were introduced. The teams tried competitive behavior at first but eventually rejected it in favor of the more productive cooperative solutions (Cooper and Kagel 2003b).

The application of probabilities in the construction of the "truth wins" standard contains numerous logical flaws. For example, can we assume that there is a relation between the speed of solution and the number of persons in the group? Assume a group of 40 students, and suppose it would take the brightest student 15 minutes to solve the problem, the formula would imply that someone of the 40 students would come up with the answer in 40 X .05 =200 (200 percent faster = one-third of the total time of 30 minutes) or ten minutes, which would be impossible. By extension of this logic, whatever length of time it would take the brightest student in the group to solve the problem, by adding to the size of the group, we could *always* identify someone brighter than the brightest student—a clear contradiction.

As mentioned above, questions have been raised about the relationship of cooperative models and the quality of reasoning. Both cooperation and competition are essentially social activities and demand at least some attention to interpersonal relationship while attempting problem-solving or other cognitive tasks. "Quality of Reasoning" is a term used by cognitive researchers to indicate ability to generate ideas, assemble thoughts, and focus mental resources on a cognitive task or to use meta-cognitive strategies (defined below).

Three different sets of studies using: (1) levels of cognitive reasoning as defined by Piaget and Kohlberg, (2) meta-cognitive strategies used in situations where information and concepts must be learned, retained, and used to solve problems, and (3) quality of reasoning, as defined by the specific studies, have all indicated that cooperation definitely enhances quality of reasoning.

Studies using Piaget's and Kohlberg's theories of cognitive and moral development have discovered that transitions to higher levels of reasoning are promoted by cooperative activities. In fact, "When persons express differences of opinion, thinking is enhanced" (Johnson and Johnson, 1989, Chapter 6). It was found that *all* persons in the studies were observed to manifest quickened and enriched cognitive function. Taken together these studies indicate that disagreements among members of cooperative groups *can* bring about transitions to higher stages of cognitive and moral reasoning. See Table 2.2.

Meta-Cognitive Strategies

A group of researchers did in fact discover that emphasis on meta-cognitive tasks promoted even higher achievement and productivity in cooperation as compared to individual effort (Spurlin, Dansereau, Larson, and Brooks, 1984).

Table 2.2   Cognitive or Moral Reasoning

Comparison	Mean ES	s.d.	z-score	*p*-value
Cooperation vs. Comp	0.79	0.63	3.25	<0.01
Cooperation vs. Indiv	0.97	1.40	4.66	<0.01
Competition vs. Indiv	0.13	0.00	0.14	< 0.99 NS

An instructive group of studies involved categorization and retrieval (Johnson, Skon, and Johnson, 1980; Skon, Johnson, and Johnson, 1981). First grade students were given 12 nouns in random order, asked to memorize them, and required to perform a series of retrieval tasks the next day. The nouns were in four categories, three fruits, three animals, three items of clothing, and three toys. Eight of the nine cooperative groups discovered and used the categories, and only one subject in each of the competitive and individualistic groups did so. Salatas and Flavell (1976) found that third graders in an individual setting had difficulty with category-search procedures. Surprisingly, even first-grade students were able to use these cognitive strategies if they were organized in cooperative groups.

Process Gain/Loss and Group-to-Individual Transfer

These two components of productivity and achievement are very difficult to assess from the studies available. Some researchers claim to show that cooperative groups perform on some projects at lower levels than persons working individually. This would indicate a "process loss" for those particular projects. Persons in the arts and music point out that for individuals to learn their art, they must put in extraordinary amounts of time in individual practice and study, and that group processes interrupting such practice often keeps the outstanding performer from reaching full potential. The results of Johnson's meta-analysis outlined above would seem to indicate otherwise.

The clear success of group methods like Suzuki classes for teaching violinists and pianists would point to the value of group learning ("process gain" and "group to individual transfer" of skills). Musicians also know that complete competence and facility with an instrument cannot be achieved without some playing in ensembles (group work), yet a case may still be made for the idea that perfection comes only after a great deal of individual effort. Perhaps concepts are transferred from the group to the individual in the ensemble, but the actual skills required are perfected by individual practice. The individual might not know *what* to practice without the group work, and the effectiveness of the skill might have to be retried, after practice, through group work. This particular combination of learning behaviors was not included in the Johnson studies.

Answering Possible Objections

In spite of the strength of cooperative approaches to productivity/achievement, quality of reasoning, process gain, and transfer, there remain a number of possible objections to these positive conclusions about cooperation. These objections can be summarized under seven general topics: (1) motivation, (2) type of task, (3) ability levels of participants, (4) low quality of many studies, (5) use of group vs. individual measures, (6) mixtures of cooperation, competition, and individual effort, and (7) gender differences.

Is Competition Necessary for Motivation?

There is a myth in Western culture that unless there is something or someone to compete against, persons will not be motivated to excel in their tasks. For some reason it is assumed that cooperating with others in a group project reduces the individual's sense of achievement and interferes with the building of self-image and self-definition. The Johnsons ask, "Are any of these assumptions true?"

Motivation in the cooperative setting can be defined as the degree to which persons are committed to achieving goals that are perceived by the group to be worthwhile and will increase their own feelings of pride and satisfaction. Motivation can also be seen as either internally or externally generated. It could be that long term efforts to achieve are most likely to be based on internal factors, qualities inherent in the activity, such as joy of learning and satisfaction from activities which benefit others. Internal motivation also appears to be maintained by meaningful feedback from social interaction, such as expressed appreciation for one's work and ideas.

On the other hand, motivation from a competitive goal structure tends to encourage:

- A monopolistic focus on relative ability
- Forced social comparison on relative ability
- Uncertain subjective probability of success and outcomes (because they depend on relative performance)
- Rewards restricted to only a few winners
- Effort expended to win
- Contingent self-esteem
- Defensive avoidance of future competitions so as not to lose again.

(Johnson and Johnson, 1989, 81)

Competition is difficult and only a few (usually only one) can succeed. It generally results in a perception of ability as hierarchically distributed and a sense that success is always evaluated relative to others. Expectation of success is a primary mediator in motivation, and in competitive structures becomes polarized and results in a monopolistic focus on task-related ability. For example, on a math test expectations for success tends to be based on one's own and others' math ability. Any other ability becomes irrelevant. Self-esteem is focused on a single hierarchical comparison of math ability and is supported only by winning. Winning is not everything, it is the only thing!

Because of the focus on relative ability, "winners" tend to attribute their successes to superior ability (Ames, 1978, 1984) and attribute others' failure on lack of ability (Stephan *et al.*, 1977, 1978). On the other hand, "losers" tend to band together and label the winners as "geeks," "brains," "nerds," "brown-nosers," and "hustlers" just to devalue their apparent superior abilities. Both "losers" and "winners" tend to attribute their own failures to luck.

Table 2.3   Mean Effect Sizes for Types of Tasks

Type of Task	Mean ES	s.d.	n	F-ratio	p-value
Cooperative vs. Competitive					
Verbal	0.59	0.85	66		
Math	0.60	0.81	32		
Procedural	1.39	1.31	17		
Rote/Decoding	0.35	0.71	6	$F(3,117) = 4.06$	<0.01
Cooperative vs. Individualistic					
Verbal	0.65	0.84	109		
Math	0.65	0.77	48		
Procedural	0.69	0.71	15		
Rote/Decoding	-0.21	0.48	5	$F(3,173) = 1.85$	<0.14 NS
Competitive vs. Individualistic					
Verbal	0.35	0.50	16		
Math	0.23	0.50	11		
Procedural	0.30	1.30	10		
Rote/Decoding	0.27	0.39	2	$F(3,35) = 0.05$	<0.98 NS

Source: Johnson and Johnson, 1989, 45.

Of special interest here is that the studies show that winners tend to become overconfident in their innate extrinsic abilities and thus motivation actually diminishes, while losers avoid competition, working, studying, and practicing. Motivation for them, if it ever existed, also rapidly diminishes (Johnson and Johnson, 1989, 82). Either way it seems clear that competition definitely does not produce or maintain motivation. In fact, external motivating factors would appear to be less sustainable both to the winners and to the losers.

Cooperation, however, develops high internal motivation, a high level of probability of success, and a tendency for high expenditures of effort. Cooperators are more likely to attribute success to acquired ability, their own and that of others. Cooperative attitudes toward achievement actually correlate positively with striving to reach goals (Johnson, Johnson, and Anderson, 1978).

Should Cooperation, Competition, and Individual Effort Vary with the Type of Task?

There has been some controversy over applying cooperative structures to all tasks. The questions are (1) whether some tasks are better achieved by cooperative, competitive, or individual effort and (2) whether researchers have biased their results by choosing only tasks that are accomplished better with one or another approach. Table 2.3 shows the effect sizes found in Johnson's study (45) as related to the types of tasks, roughly categorized as verbal, math, procedural, and rote/decoding.

The **F**-ratio in the table is a statistical measure similar to z-scores, representing the relative size of the difference among mean effects of the groups. If the means were all equal, **F** would be zero. If there is a large divergence among the mean **ES** effect size measures, then **F** will be large. See Appendix B for a complete discussion of how these measures are computed and what they mean.

The third part of the table, dealing with competitive versus individual tasks, is probably invalid since one of the categories contains only two subjects. In the comparison of cooperative and competitive structures, there does seem to be a significant difference. Although all tasks appear to be better achieved by cooperative approaches, the Procedural tasks appear to generate an effect size more than twice the size of the others. For rote work and decoding, although still positive, cooperation has a rather low effect size, and given the negative effect size in the second part of the table, the rote tasks appear to favor the use of individual effort.

The results here corroborate the research of Miller and Hamblin (1963). Even if rote tasks may be best performed by individual effort, the strong results presented in the rest of the table should convince us that cooperation must be considered as more effective than competition on the general verbal, math, and procedural tasks.

Can Low Levels of Ability Hinder Performance on Cooperative Tasks?

The studies disagree on whether persons with low and medium abilities can hinder the persons of high abilities in the achievement of goals in a cooperative setting. Some researchers maintain that the mixing of abilities in cooperative groups creates problems. Hill (1982), for instance concludes that low and medium ability cooperators get in the way of achievement that could be better accomplished by high level people in their own group, or even individually. Others state that low ability students in a learning group do not benefit from the ideas and knowledge of high ability students. They are simply told the answers and never learn how to work *on their own* (Slavin, 1984). Note the unconfirmed assumption, that the ultimate test of learning is the ability to achieve by individual effort.

Performance can be considered a composite of three factors: achievement of goals, learning more, and maintaining the working group. When the question of including persons of low ability is asked, it should be addressed to all three of these component factors.

The studies carry strong evidence that persons of varying abilities *learn more* by collaborating with persons of widely variant abilities than by collaborating with persons of the same level of ability (Frick, 1973; Webb, 1977). Most surprising is that high-ability individuals working with low- and medium-ability persons develop higher levels of reasoning than they do working competitively or individually (Johnson and Johnson, 1981). In general the data can be interpreted, even conservatively, as demonstrating that including persons of low and medium levels of ability not only *does not hurt the group process* but "often facilitates the achievement of high-ability individuals, and clearly benefits the achievement of medium- and low-ability individuals" (Johnson and Johnson, 1989, 47).

What About the Potential Corruption from Low Quality Studies?

The methodological shortcomings found within many of the studies included in Johnson's meta-analysis apparently do not reduce the certainty of any of their conclusions. Each of the 512 studies was given a rating between 5 and 16 depending on its methodological quality and then categorized as High, Medium, or Low quality.

Table 2.4   Mean Effect Sizes for Quality of Study

Quality	Mean ES	s.d.	N	F-ratio	p-value
Cooperative vs. Competitive					
High	0.86	1.13	51		
Medium	0.56	0.82	43		
Low	0.49	0.56	34	$F(2,125) = 1.98$	<0.14 NS
Cooperative vs. Individualistic					
High	0.59	0.66	103		
Medium	0.73	1.02	67		
Low	0.42	0.49	12	$F(2,179) = 1.08$	<0.34 NS

Source: Johnson and Johnson (1989), 42.

The inter-rater reliability of this scoring procedure was 94 percent. Again there were too few studies in the low quality category for an adequate comparison between competition and individual effort. Table 2.4 below summarizes the effect sizes for three levels of quality. We can see that the variability in quality of the studies makes no significant difference in the results. Neither F-ratio proves large enough to be statistically significant.

Group vs. Individual Measures

If the purpose of the cooperative group is to maximize individual achievement and productivity, then it might make a difference whether the measures of productivity were taken on the group as a whole or on each individual. Perhaps the cooperative groups did well because, as soon as one person in the group got the answer, everyone in the group received credit for it (Slavin, 1983). If that is so, then studies that used group measures should outperform those that used individual measures of achievement or productivity.

Comparing again for differences between studies with group measures and those with individual measures, we find for Cooperation vs. Competition a t-ratio (two-group statistic similar to the F-ratio for multi-group comparisons; see Appendix B) of 1.29 (p<0.20 NS, Not Significant) and for Cooperation vs. Individual Effort a t-ratio of 1.78 (p<0.08 NS, Not Significant). The t-ratio for the comparison between Competitive vs. Individual Effort was 2.61 (p< 0.01). Here we see that there was no significant difference between using individual and group measures for cooperation vs. competition, nor for cooperation vs. individual effort. The measurement procedure did make a difference in assessing Competition vs. Individual Effort. The results were significantly better, not worse, for Competition than for Individual Effort when measured by individual scores (Johnson and Johnson, 1989, 43).

Productivity from Mixtures of Cooperative, Competitive, and Individual Efforts

There have been a number of studies comparing outcomes from mixtures of cooperation, competition, and individual effort. Some would argue that a mixture of approaches might be best in trying to increase achievement or productivity. When such mixtures are compared with interpersonal competition, an effect size of 0.37 is found for the mixture and 0.70 for the "pure" cooperative approaches with a t-ratio of 1.49 ($p<0.07$), no significant difference. For the cooperative vs. individual comparisons, mixed procedures produced an effect size of 0.42 and "pure" ones showed an effect size of 0.63 with a t-ratio of 0.88 ($p<0.19$), no significant difference. Although both the mixed and "pure" cooperative strategies produced positive effect sizes and the trend is in the upward direction for the "pure" strategies, the difference between them is not statistically significant. This indicates that mixed strategies are not going to produce any better results than cooperation by itself (Johnson and Johnson, 1989, 42-43).

Does Gender Make a Difference in the Comparisons?

An overall analysis concluded that there are no significant differences between the performance of males and females within three types of interdependence. One study, a dissertation by Renee Peterson (1985), randomly assigned science students to three different classes and each taught one of three science units. These three classes were randomly subdivided into three groups each, one group in a cooperative style, another encouraging competition, and a third using only individual effort. The outcome results concluded that there were no long-term differences between the achievements of males and females under these three different conditions regardless of which unit was taught. In the individual efforts group for the first science unit only, the males scored slightly higher than the females. But under the cooperative conditions, males and females achieved similar scores. Curiously, in all groups both males and females scored higher when they were in the minority in a group than when they were in the majority. In general, under ordinary circumstances, it would be correct to conclude that persons of both genders would learn faster, at about the same rate, in a cooperative setting.

Other Issues

One might look for problems of evaluating outcomes from the Johnson's study in other areas:

- Decade in which the study was published;
- Size of groups;
- Academic subject areas;
- Socioeconomic class of subjects;
- Age of subjects;
- Sample size;
- Ethnic or cultural background of subjects;
- Whether studies were published or unpublished;
- Research laboratory vs. field settings.

Statistical analyses of variance found that there were no statistical differences among the studies on any of these factors (Johnson and Johnson, 1989, 47).

When Might Cooperation Fail?

From all of the above it would seem that cooperation cannot fail. A little thought would tell us that cooperation, since it is a group activity, would be prone to the same ills that plague any group process. Any event or attitude that would reduce the sense of personal responsibility, the commitment of members to the goals and life of the group, could bring failure. Anything that would reduce or prevent free personal interaction also would reduce or prevent the frequent and regular group processing necessary to get the job done, and would cause failure.

Regardless of the basic condition of interdependence, cooperation or competition, less able members sometimes tend to let the more able ones shoulder the bulk of the task. This is called the *free rider effect* (Gürerk *et al.*, 2006). This effect also tends to create resentment on the part of the more able members, who then tend to expend less effort in order to avoid the *sucker effect*. High ability members may also take over the important leadership roles in ways that tend to benefit them at the expense of the other members, the *rich-get-richer effect* (Kerr and Bruun, 1983). In fact, it may not necessarily be the most able members who monopolize leadership roles, creating what we could call the *old guard effect*.

In some groups we find a diffusion of responsibility or a dysfunctional division of labor, and an overweening tendency to say or think, "I am the initiator or the creator and you are the drudge." On the other side of that attitude, others may inappropriately defer to authority. Any unhealthy patterns of behavior would undermine group performance.

There are really no data showing clearly that the conditions of cooperation would be more prone to such behavioral effects and patterns than any other condition or mix of conditions. All of these debilitating processes can be found as mediating factors in competitive situations as well. A review of research by James H. Davis, quite independently of Johnsons' meta-analysis, concluded that the preponderance of research shows that achieving a sense of positive interdependence, considerable face-to-face interaction, group skills, and an equitable distribution or flexibility of social roles arise more frequently within a cooperative framework (Davis, 1992).

It is clear that positive attitudes toward personal responsibility, productivity, and achievement are dependent upon clear *values* and goals. Some understanding of the common good must be present to motivate persons to give up a measure of total individual autonomy and social control to reach a social goal which is satisfactory to everyone. After the "rich get richer" and have a taste of a larger and larger share of power, sacrificing that power on behalf of a more equitable distribution of influence and a sense of partnership becomes much more difficult.

Genetic Factors

Some recent research on human values and behavior even suggests that altruism, willingness to sacrifice ones own autonomy in favor of the well-being of others, may be at least partially genetic (Trivers, 1971; Boorman and Levitt, 1980; Boyd and Richerson, 1988). This line of research is quite new and has not yet reached a sufficiently solid conclusion. In any case, the existence of a cooperative genotype is a minor factor compared with the much-researched and stronger socio-cultural forces.

Anthropologists, for example, in primate studies, have suggested possible evolutionary benefits to social cooperation. Several wild baboon populations have been studied for decades. Joan Silk and her co-investigators exploited 16 years of data from a long-term study of baboons in Kenya (Silk, 2003). One of their conclusions was that females who socialize significantly more than their cohorts will produce healthier progeny that are much more likely to survive into adulthood (over 12 months) and begin breeding. These progeny, in turn, socialize with each other and produce healthy progeny. The "socialization" manifested is a typical primate cooperative grooming activity. These cooperative social bonds were "independent of dominance rank, group membership, and environmental conditions... For humans and other primates, sociality has adaptive value" (Silk, 2003, 1231).

Summary and Conclusions

Over 1,000 studies comparing cooperation and competition were performed during the last century, most of them within the last thirty years. In the Johnson and Johnson meta-analytical study, selecting only those with a reasonably high quality methodology produced 512 studies with sufficient reliability and validity to compare their results meaningfully.

Only in a few psychologically based studies did individual effort prove to be more successful than group work in specific settings. These group work settings did not differentiate between cooperation and competition, so it is impossible to compare these two radically different group styles or even to sort out the two factors in comparing group and individual effort. In dealing with groups it is crucial to define group interactions as significantly more than mere aggregates of individuals. The fuzzy results of these few studies demonstrate that varying styles of group interaction must be considered in any setting which purports to compare group and individual behavior.

Of course cooperation can fail when values and goals are unclear or when group process is undermined. Clearly this principle would be just as true in a competitive setting. In fact, independent reviews of cooperation/competition literature by Johnson and Johnson and the individual/group literature by James Davis both conclude that competition can actually become a primary cause of group failure.

Recent genetic research on the hypothesized "altruism gene" or "cooperative gene" is still in its infancy. Even if such a genetic factor exists, it would only be one factor alongside the many and much-researched socio-cultural factors. All of these factors can affect productivity, achievement, quality of reasoning, and learning. But apparently the cooperative approach (versus competition and individual effort) has proven to be highly effective in producing desirable outcomes in a wide variety of task settings.

Comparing z-scores for productivity/achievement, quality of reasoning, process gain/loss, and transfer of learning from group to individual across these 512 studies, demonstrated the clear value of cooperation in generating high levels of productivity and achievement, across a wide range of fields. The probability of reaching this conclusion in error proved to be less than 1 in 10,000 ($p < 0.0001$, nearly 15 standard deviations) with an effect size of 72 percent. Adding a hypothetical 8,710 studies with insignificant results would be required to raise the error probability above 0.05 (a conventional cutoff point for significance). Furthermore, these studies showed that cooperation is also more effective than individual effort ($p < 0.0001$, 21 standard deviations) with an effect size of 65 percent. Competition is also more effective than individual effort ($p < 0.0008$, 3.14 standard deviations), but with an effect size of only 30 percent.

Similar results were obtained with all dependent variables: production/ achievement, quality of reasoning, process gain, and transfer of learning from group to individual. In all cases, cooperation proved to perform better than either competition or individual effort.

These studies also show that competition is not as effective as cooperation in generating motivation or incentive. The results did not vary with the type of task, the ability levels of the subjects, or the inclusion of some low quality studies. Mixtures of cooperative, competitive, and individualistic conditions could not be shown to surpass pure cooperation.

One of the strengths of the Johnsons' study is that studies chosen comprised a wide range of fields, academic areas, research goals, social situations, sports, experimental conditions, and cognitive training. Subjects varied widely in economic status, trade/profession, and ethnicity. Genders were equally represented. Academic areas included language arts, mathematics, science, motor skills, reading comprehension, logic, psychology, drama, geography, and business administration. Variations in social situations included smaller and larger groups, game playing, classroom settings, workplace activities, laboratory testing, and field trips.

Thus the findings of the meta-analysis seem to be fully generalizable, making them applicable to a wide scope of situations. A further strength of the Johnson method of meta-analysis was the computation of z-scores for individual studies and an overall z-score for each condition (cooperation, competition, and individual effort).

The weaknesses of any meta-analytical study include the unavailability of the original raw data for reanalysis, the variability in quality of the sample studies, the lack of control of data collection, and often the long time period over which the data were collected. Researchers can assess the effects of these limitations on the outcomes of meta-analysis with "sensitivity analysis." This procedure involves reanalyzing after removing various articles from the sample or by including other studies perhaps of less methodological quality. The Johnsons employed a way of estimating how many weaker studies would need to be added to make significant changes in their results, offsetting these weaknesses to some degree. Researchers would need to conduct a much larger study, perhaps with thousands of subjects, to completely overcome them.

Still, because of careful design of the analytical process, the Johnsons' study resulted in large effect sizes and z-scores that showed strong positive results across the 512 studies. The large sample of studies included in the analysis and the robustness of their meta-analytical techniques ensured highly dependable results that can be applied very broadly in a large variety of social situations. Since the settings of the experiments were so diverse and the positive results so strong, there is virtually no basis for an argument that competition would be a wise option under any set of circumstances.

References

Bangert-Drowns, R. (1986). "Review of Developments in Meta-Analytic Methods." *Psychological Bulletin*, 99, 388-399.

Boorman, S.A. and P. Levitt (1980). *The Genetics of Altruism.* Academic Press.

Boyd, R. and P.J. Richerson (1988) "The Evolution of Cooperation." *Journal of Theoretical Biology*, 132, 337-356.

Cooper, D.J. and J.H. Kagel (2003a). "Are Two Heads Better Than One? Team Versus Individual Play in Signaling Games." Working Paper Case Western Reserve University/Ohio State University. www.gsb.stanford.edu/facseminars/events/economics/pdfs/teamsD7.1.pdf.

Cooper, D.J. and J.H. Kagel (2003b). "Lessons Learned: Generalizing Learning Across Games." Supplement to "Signaling and Adaptive Learning in an Entry Limit Pricing Game" RAND *Journal of Economics*, Winter 1997, 28(4), 662-83 (a).

Davis, J.H. (1992). "Some Compelling Intuitions Concerning Group Consensus," *Organizational Behavior and Human Decision Processes*, 52 (3), 2-38.

Deutsch, M. (1949). "A Theory of Cooperation and Competition." *Human Relations* 2, 129-152.

Deutsch, M. (1962). "Cooperation and Trust: Some Theoretical Notes." In M.R. Jones (ed.), *Nebraska Symposium on Motivation*, 275-319. Lincoln NE. University of Nebraska Press.

Frick, F. (1973). *Study of Peer Training with the Lincoln Training System (AFATC Report KE 73-116)*. Harrison, MS: Keesler Air Force Base.

Glass G. (1977). "Integrating Findings: The Meta-Analysis of Research." *Review of Research in Education*, 5, 531-379.

Güreck,O, B. Irlenbusch, and B. Rockenbach (2006). "The Competitive Advantage of Sanctioning Institutions." *Science 312 (7 April, 2006)*, pp. 108-11.

Hedges, L. and I. Olkin (1985). *Statistica Methods for Meta-Analysis.* Academic Press.

Hill, G.W. (1982). "Group Versus Individual Performance: Are N+1 Heads Better Than One?" *Psychological Bulletin*, 91, 517-5349.

Johnson, D.W., R.T. Johnson, and D. Anderson (1978). "Relationships Between Student Cooperative, Competitive, and Individualistic Attitudes Toward Schooling." *Journal of Psychology*, 100, 183-199.

Johnson, D.W., L. Skon, and R. Johnson (1980). "Effects of Cooperative, Competitive, and Individual Conditions on Children's Problem Solving Performance." *American Educational Research Journal*, 17(1), 83-94.

Johnson D.W., and R.T. Johnson (1981). "Effects of Cooperation and Individualistic Learning Experiences on Interethnic Interaction." *Journal of Educational Psychology*, 73(3), 454-459.

Johnson, D.W. and R.T. Johnson (1989). *Cooperation and Competition: Theory and Research*, Interaction Book Company, Edina MN.

Kerr, N. and S. Bruun (1983). "The Dispensability of Member Effort and Group Motivation Losses: Free-rider Effects." *Journal of Personality and Social Psychology*, 44, 78-94.

Kohlberg, L. (1981). *The Meaning and Measurement of Moral Development Vol XIII, 1979*, Clark University Heinz Werner Institute (March 1, 1981).

Lamm, H. and G. Trommsdorff (1973). "Group Versus Individual Performance on Tasks Requiring Ideational Proficiency (Brainstorming): A Review." *European Journal of Social Psychology*, 3, 361-388.

Miller, L. and R. Hamblin (1963). "Interdependence, Differential Rewarding, and Productivity." *American Sociological Review*, 28, 768-778.

Piaget, J. (1983). "Piaget's Theory." In P. Mussen (ed.) *Handbook of Child Psychology.* Wiley, NY.

Salatas, H. and J. Flavell (1976). "Retrieval of Recently Learned Information: Development of Strategies and Control Skills." *Child Development*, 47, 941-948.

Silk, J.B., S.C. Alberts, and J. Altmann (2003). "Social Bonds of Female Baboons Enhance Infant Survival." *Science* 302, 1231-1234.

Skon, L, D.W. Johnson, and R.T. Johnson (1981). "Cooperative Peer Interaction Versus Individual Competition and Individual Efforts: Effects on yhe Acquisition of Cognitive Reasoning Strategies." *Journal of Educational Psychology*, 73(1), 83-92.

Slavin, R. (1983). "Meta-Analysis in Education: How has it Been Used?" *Educational Researcher*, 13(8), 6-15.

Spurlin, J., D. Dansereau, C. Larson, and L. Brooks (1984). "Cooperative Learning Strategies Inprocessing Descriptive Text: Effects of Role and Activity Level of the Learner." *Cognition and Instuction*, 1(4), 451-463.

Stephan, C., J. Kennedy, and E. Aronson (1977). "The Effects of Friendship and Task Outcome on Task Attribution." *Sociometry*, 40, 107-112.

Stephan, C., N. Presser, J. Kennedy, and E. Aronson (1978). "Attributions to Success and Failure after Cooperative or Competitive Interaction." *European Journal of Social Psychology*, 8, 269-274.

Trivers, R.L. (1971). "The Evolution of Reciprocal Altruism." *Quarterly Review of Biology*, 46, 35-57.

von Mises, L. (1949). *Human Action: A Treatise on Economics*, Yale University Press, New Haven.

Webb, N. (1977). "Learning in Individual and Small Group Settings" (Tech Report No. 7), Stanford CA: Stanford University, School of Education. Aptitude Research Project.

Chapter 3

The Standard Economic Model and Globalization

We need a new view
A view from the other side
Where there is enough

(Haiku by BL & BF)

In Chapter 2 we established with reasonable certainty that a cooperative approach to almost any problem is preferable to a competitive one. This chapter will consider the difficulty of living with an economic model based not on cooperation but on competition.

The primary purpose of the chapter will be to lay a foundation for understanding the differences between a cooperative, capitalist economic system and a "free market," competitive, capitalism. In order to accomplish this, we must understand the concept of "free market" and how a particular application of the "free market" concept, called "The Standard Economic Model," arose and how it works.

The Free Market

The "free market" model is best conceptualized as a huge open auction where all the bidders are present, have the information they need about the products being auctioned, and enjoy equal opportunities for bidding. The competitive bidding process generates the fairest possible prices and ensures the most equitable distribution of goods. The "free market" economy of the nation is an open auction with a large enough body of buyers and sellers to ensure liquidity at virtually every moment in time. Two essential assumptions are embedded in this conceptual model: (1) There exists free, open, complete, and instantaneous information available to all buyers and sellers of goods and services; and (2) there is equal opportunity for all buyers and sellers to present, exchange, accept, reject, or select bids. That second assumption, in turn, implies that buyers and sellers have sufficient resources for exchange and equal access to the market.

A further, unstated assumption is that a properly operating "free market," uninhibited by external controls, will produce economic growth. There is no empirical evidence for this assumption about the *production* of growth, but that continual growth is an absolutely essential component of the present version of the free market is a fact. This necessary growth process results in a completely unsustainable system, often called "The Standard Economic Model" or the "Washington Consensus" (Dasgupta, 2003; Schumpeter, 1951).

Years of government and international policies based on the standard economic model have promised that the private market is the best solution to inequality and that somehow the world can "grow" its way out of poverty. A booming economy, as measured by a growing GDP, will result in income improvements being spread through the economy. Eventually poverty will shrink and disappear.

It just is not so. Studies of market performance during three periods of recession and recovery over the last 25 years present startling findings. Market improvements during booms have accumulated at the top, flowed somewhat into the top half of income earners, and dried up before reaching the poorest 10 percent. A further frightening statistic is that the share of market improvements have accelerated for the top 10 percent over the last three decades. Their share has increased from 23 percent in the boom of the 1970s to a whopping 37 percent in the 1990s—almost doubling the share of the top 10 percent. These empirical data indicate that the model is not working as claimed (Curry-Stevens, 2002).

There is a huge contradiction between this predominant economic model, sometimes called the "Standard Model" or the "Washington Consensus," and the results of empirical research that clearly shows that competition is much less effective than cooperation in approaching almost any objective in human relations. This contradiction could explain, in part, why the cooperative movement has proven so popular and successful, and why the current market model shows unmistakable signs of failing (Bakan, 2004, Caulfield, 1996, Korten, 1999).

Constructing Models

A model can be a useful simplification of reality. It may consist of a physical representation, like a model railroad, a model airplane, or even a motorized working model of the solar system with varying sizes of spheres representing planets revolving around a glowing sphere representing the sun. A model could also be achieved mathematically as a computer simulation. Or it could be simply a conceptual model like the auction model of "free market" discussed above.

The amount of detail which can be added to a model to make it more realistic can be endless. A mechanical model of the solar system can serve as an example of this. The planetary spheres in a solar system model can be rotating around their own axes, replicating the day and night cycles of each planet. Satellites can be added to the system. Perhaps one could manage to inscribe tiny mountains and valleys on the appropriate planets. In a mathematical model, more equations may be added to express complicated relationships. More complex ideas can always be added to a conceptual model.

Yet as endless as the possibility of adding elements to a model may seem, many details would still prove impossible, or at least impractical, to include. In our solar system model, to maintain an absolutely correct scale would be impractical. If the tiny planet Mercury were within a few inches from a sun the size of a golf ball, the rest of the planets would have to be across the room, down the street, and with Pluto thousands of miles away. The builders of such models have always had to compromise sizes and distances to create a useful model.

Even on the fastest modern computer, it would be impossible to include in a mathematical model of the global economy all of the financial, geographic, environmental, social, cultural, and psychological variables that might be relevant.

The simplest models of large-scale social and economic models could require many pages of related mathematical equations. An exceptionally accurate computer model of a national economy could take until next week to predict tomorrow's market.

No matter what kind of model is constructed, its creator must always balance the desirable with the practical, the possible with the absolutely necessary, in the light of the model's purpose. In defense of the "Standard Economic Model," it has been constructed using the best theory and knowledge of classical economics. The variables and functional relationships have been trimmed to the bare essentials and have been finely tuned over many decades.

Models can have several uses: to explain observable events, to make predictions about possible future events, and to manipulate a system or suggest changes in problematic outcomes of the system. To some extent everyone uses models, perhaps in designing and building a home, setting up and running a business, or simply making daily decisions. Most people use them unconsciously and unquestioningly, basing decisions on experience and reasonable assumptions about how life works. And most realize that, although ideally a decision should be made with total information, most of the time not all of the necessary information is available before the decision must be made.

In the case of building an economic model, three kinds of information are necessary. The first kind is information about the various relevant elements of the model, such as *capital* (the means of production: tools, property, machinery, and money), *resources* (raw materials, labor), *technology* (processes, intellectual property, etc.), and *the market* (supply, demand). The second kind of information concerns the relationships among all the basic elements. The third kind of information defines the objectives of the model.

Attention to the objectives of the model becomes unnecessary when the model is used purely for description or prediction. If, however, the user of the model wishes to achieve certain goals or objectives, those goals and objectives must be clearly defined and must match the variables and relationships contained in the model.

The relevance of the elements and the validity of the relationships among them are established by empirical observations or theories that have had reasonable confirmation through scientific testing. The scientific community that deals with these observations, theories, and models is made up of human beings prone to resisting new or "controversial" ideas (Kuhn, 1996). This human element is too often forgotten by users of models.

A good model can provide useful insights into a complex process, yield valuable predictions, or suggest ways to help social or economic systems serve the common good. Yet it is all too human to become personally invested in a particular model and fail to realize its limitations, that it may not be working properly, or that it is simply wrong for the task.

Ideally the user of a model should always to be ready to modify the model if the descriptions do not match reality very well, if predictions cannot be confirmed, or if the objectives in using the model are not reached. Proper modification of models, of course, requires an open and critical attitude toward them. In the human experience, necessary and prompt modifications of working models seldom happen, especially where governments are involved.

Models are always vulnerable to criticism at three points: (1) the variables or causal factors that have been chosen, (2) the nature of the relationships determined or assumed to exist between the variables, and (3) the match between the model and the goals and objectives claimed for it. The "Standard Economic Model" has been criticized many times on all three of these points. In the sections following, several such criticisms are reviewed.

The Standard Economic Model

The "Standard Economic Model" is essentially a mathematical formula, consisting of a set of economic variables and their relationships with each other. It was constructed by economists in the IMF and World Bank in order to assess economic health and growth of developing countries. A full list of the variables in the IMF/ World Bank formula is given in Appendix C. In summary they include government debt, trade balances, goods consumption, price levels, average wealth, monetary supply, exchange rates, average income, interest rates, wages, tax rates, profits, inflation rates, and government spending on social programs.

The model was originally designed to assist European countries to recover from the ravages of World War II. Application of the model, supplemented by large amounts of money from the allied nations such as the Marshall Plan, was particularly effective in helping continental Europe and the Far East to get back on solid economic ground. This was the primary task assigned to the new international agencies, the IMF and the Bank for Reconstruction and Development (more popularly, World Bank), by international meetings at Bretton Woods, New Hampshire, in 1946.

Using the original formula, given accurate data for a given country, a simulation is generated to show what that country's economy will do if any of the values of causal variables, such as tax rates, energy prices, etc. are changed. These simulated results are used to generate recommendations to the country's leaders and policy makers. Policy makers and leaders must then follow the resulting recommendations in detail before their loan application is approved. This process is called a "Structural Adjustment Program" (SAP) by the IMF.

As the economies of Europe steadily improved after World War II, and the Standard Model demonstrated such resounding success as applied to post-war problems that IMF analysts set their sights on using the successful model for the benefit of the entire developing world. However, in order to apply the model to helping developing countries to bolster their economies and reduce poverty, the IMF had to incorporate in its formula four further and more specific assumptions. The IMF economists refer to this new version of the "Standard Model" as the "Merged Model." These new and more specific assumptions are:

1. Growth as measured by the Gross Domestic Product (GDP) will reduce poverty.
2. Trade between any two countries is fully symmetric and simultaneous.
3. Open global trade ("free trade") generates jobs and raises all incomes.
4. Trade liberalization (reductions or elimination of tariffs and price supports) may cause some temporary distress and even declines in the general welfare

while the national structures are being realigned, but eventually it will bring in large gains and long-term improvements.

The rebuilding of Europe went extremely well, and the application of the model to developing nations, with a totally different set of problems, seemed to be functioning reasonably well during the 1950s and 1960s. Even into the early 1980s, the growing strength of the US economy was loudly proclaimed (especially during the presidential campaign of 1984). The real[1] gross domestic product (GDP) was growing. The dollar was getting stronger against the Swiss franc, the German mark, the French franc, the Italian lira, the British pound, and the Canadian dollar. Through 1984, inflation, measured by the consumer index, rose more slowly than during any year in the 1970s. The official unemployment rate (does not account for part-time workers or workers dropped off the welfare roles) had decreased from 10.7 percent in 1982 to 7.2 percent by the end of 1984.

There were some mildly negative signs in 1984 which were not very troubling at the time. The economy was growing but at a much slower rate than in the 1970s. Unemployment, though lower than in 1982, was gradually beginning to creep back up. Leading indicators behaved uncertainly. The commentators interpreted these signs as good: America was once again on a more long-term growth phase. The "Standard Economic Model" still seemed to be working. War-torn European countries had reentered the global market place, and all but Eastern European countries and the Soviet Union had achieved a high rate of travel and commerce throughout the world. It was commonly assumed that a more liberal global market, exploiting infinite resources, aided the accumulation of wealth all over the world, and that increasing GDP was gradually eliminating poverty. One frequently heard the phrase, "A rising tide lifts all boats."

Critiques of the Stated Assumptions

The Standard Model in its current form grew out of the "free market" by adding the four assumptions listed above: (1) Growth reduces poverty; (2) free trade among countries is symmetric and simultaneous; (3) global free trade generates jobs and raises all incomes; and (4) after some minor distress, trade liberalization will bring large gains and long-term improvements for all participants. Criticisms of the model have centered on these four assumptions plus a growing discomfort with unstated assumptions of "imperialism," the "domination paradigm," "hero mythology," the "vertical paradigm," and the "myth of competition" that the stated assumptions imply.

Does Economic Growth Reduce Poverty?

Gross Domestic Product(GDP) derives from GNP (Gross National Product) by subtracting the foreign spending and investments by a country's citizens from the

---

1   A "real" monetary value, measured over time, is one which is adjusted for inflation and other temporal changes and is pegged to a specific year.

Table 3.1   World's Real Per Capita Income Distribution, 1988-1993

Percentile of Income Distribution	(1) Income in 1988 in US$$/year	(2) Income in 1993 in US$/year	Increase/ Decrease in %
5	277.4	238.1	-14
10	348.3	318.1	-9
15	417.5	372.9	-11
20	486.1	432.1	-11
25	558.3	495.8	-11
30	633.2	586.0	-7
35	714.5	657.7	-8
40	802.7	741.9	-8
45	908.3	883.2	-3
50	1,047.5	1,044.1	0
55	1,314.4	1,164.9	-11
60	1,522.7	1,505.0	-1
65	1,898.9	1,856.8	-2
70	2,698.5	2,326.8	-14
75	3,597.0	3,005.6	-16
80	4,370.0	4,508.1	3
85	5,998.9	6,563.3	9
90	8,044.0	9,109.8	13
95	11,518.0	13,240.7	15
99	20,773.2	24,447.1	18

Source: Branko Milanovic, True World Income Distribution, 1988 and 1993: First Calculation Based on Household Surveys Alone, *World Bank (2000). Lines are drawn at the 20th percentile and the 80th percentile for ease of comparison of the income distribution changes between the top and bottom fifths of the population.*

total monetary value of goods and services produced by the country. Until recently the GDP was not appreciably different from the GNP, so GNP has long served as the best indicator of the size of a country's economy. Since the sharp increases in international activity in the late 1970s, GDP has supplanted the GNP as the best indicator of the individual country's economic strength.

The monetary value of GDP can be determined either by directly summing up the value of all goods and services sold or by summing up all the amounts spent on goods and services within the country. Although money is not the only measure of a nation's economic strength, it is the easiest way to sum up the value of all the apples and oranges, automobiles and computers, football games, medical care, and college classes a country produces in a given year.

The GDP, by itself, turns out to be a particularly inefficient measure of economic health because it includes large amounts of waste, environmental degradation, and ignores the distribution of income and wealth. Social costs, also called "externalities," and poverty are not accounted for by this measure. Also, the measure includes corporate inventory build up and non-realized income from capital investments, neither of which affects household income on the lower level, except to reduce it, for

Table 3.2   World Population and Total World Poor (in billions)

Year	World Population	Percent Population Increase	Total World Poor*	Percent World Poor	Percent Increase
1993	5.614	--	2.661	47.4	--
1996	5.779	3	2.555	44.2	-4
1999	6.034	4	3.145	52.1	23
2002	6.228	3	4.147	66.6	32

*   *"The Poor," as defined by the World Bank are all those persons earning less than $2.16 per day, Purchasing Power Parity, in 1993 US dollars. That is, the amount of goods and services one could purchase for $2.19 in 1993.*
Sources: World Bank and J. E. Stiglitz (2003).

example, by interest rates on loans or consumer debt. Quantitative research by the World Bank itself now shows quite clearly that GDP is not significantly correlated with reduction of poverty (World Bank, 2000; Levinsohn, 2003). A number of alternative indicators have been proposed. The Gund Institute at the University of Vermont recently published estimates of a Genuine Progress Index (GPI) that adjusts for distribution effects, the value of unpaid household work, volunteer community work, pollution, costs of population mobility, and depletion of social and environmental resources (2003).

The case for The Standard Model as used by the IMF and the World Bank is usually based on GDP figures. Very rarely are income or wealth distributions examined by the model's defenders. Table 3.1 shows changes in income distribution in the world in just the five years between 1988 and 1993. This is the first example of calculations based on household surveys that clearly shows the differences in trends between the lower and higher incomes in the world for those five years. The Gross World Product (GWP), simply a sum of all countries GDPs corrected for all the different monetary evaluations, between 1988 and 1993 increased from 31.8 trillion (US$ equivalent) to 35.6 trillion, an increase of a little more than 12 percent.

Notice that real income decreased between 1988 and 1993 for everyone in the distribution up to the eightieth percentile. The only income increases were for the upper 20 percent. Admittedly these were years of recession throughout the world. Unfortunately the same kind of data does not exist for the boom years following 1994 up to 2000. World Bank does have estimates on the total world poor as a percentage of the total world population for those years. These data are presented in Table 3.2 above.

Note that, except for the years between 1993 and 1996, the increases in the number of the world poor far outstripped the increases in population. Across all these years, 1993-2002, the estimated Gross World Product increased from 35.6 trillion to 46.0 trillion (US$ equivalent), an increase for those nine years of nearly 30 percent, while the world's poor increased by 55.8 percent. It would be proper to conclude that growth in the world's material production did not, by any means, reduce poverty. Only the top 20 percent of the world's population enjoyed an increase of income during that period. The first assumption of the Standard Model must be rejected.

Is Trade Between Countries Always Simultaneous and Symmetric?

The idea of simultaneous trade has led the IMF, in particular, to apply its model expecting instant improvement in wealth distribution, forgetting their fourth assumption. The Structural Adjustment Programs are not gradually phased in or negotiated with local leaders, but are put into immediate effect regardless of their impacts on the poor.

Use of the word *symmetric* is another way of affirming a level playing field for all players in world trade. The model does not recognize that trading partners may not all be equally endowed with bidding or negotiating power. It assumes that every country in the world has some comparative advantage it can use in free trade, but in the words of the pig in George Orwell's novel, *Animal Farm*, "... some are more equal than others." For example, Mexico was supposed to have found prosperity following the January 1, 1994, passage of the North American Trade Agreement (NAFTA). Actually, they were forced to devalue the peso late in 1994, and their trade deficit soared from $1.6 billion in 1993 to $32 billion in 2002. Mexico was prevented by the agreement from subsidizing its corn growers, while the US government continued to subsidize corporate corn farms in the United States. Those delicious tortillas in Cuernavaca were not made by hand from local cornmeal but bought from the local Walmart. Trade with Mexico is certainly not symmetric—nor aptly described by any other word intended to mean "fair." This second assumption should be rejected.

Does Open Global Trade Actually Generate More Jobs and Raise All Incomes?

More open trade, as defined in the typical "free" trade agreements (GATT, NAFTA, ALCA, PPP, etc.) were designed by representatives not from among citizens of each country in the consortium but from among the large transnational corporations. US Congress approves trade agreements now without significant debate, in other words, essentially as the large corporations have written them. When these large outside corporations (Costco, Wal-Mart, Exxon-Mobil, etc.) come into another country, they compete with small local companies, dominate the economic landscape, and siphon profits off to the more developed countries. In this way, open trade, as commonly practiced, has actually increased the disparity between incomes of the rich and the poor both nationally and globally (see Figure 3.1).

The lines on the graph of Figure 3.1 represent the number of people in the world below World Bank's poverty line of $2.19 US per day, in this case based on the 1996 US dollar. The two lines, upper for the entire world including China and lower for the world excluding China, help settle the dispute about whether the poverty increases were mostly because of China's unstable economy. We can see that the slopes of both lines are almost identical, indicating that China's economic system has had nothing whatever to do with the increase in poverty since 1996—two years after the initiation of NAFTA and about the time of the beginning of serious discussions about "free trade" in the Pacific Rim.

The sharp upturn in this poverty graph should also settle the question about the effect of global economics on poverty. The old saying used by the defenders of The Standard Model and the neo-imperialist version of free and open trade, "A high tide lifts all boats," should be modified to allow that small boats tied up to the larger ones will be swamped.

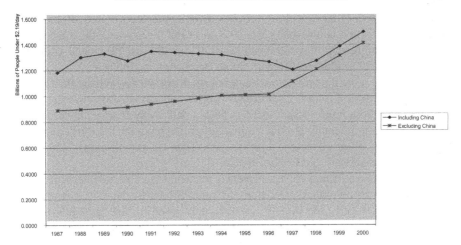

Figure 3.1   World Poverty and Income Inequality After Free Trade
Source: Malinkovic, World Bank, 2000.

The third assumption of the Standard Model should be rejected.

Will Trade Liberalization Bring Large Gains and Long-Term Improvements?

Trade liberalization is supposed to result, at least eventually, in large gains and improvements in the client countries. What is seen from the empirical data is just the opposite (Stiglitz, 2003: World Bank Reports 1996-2002). For 12 to 18 months unemployment and poverty indicators seemed to begin shrinking, but over the following years all indicators of economic health have deteriorated sharply. Strictly applied by the IMF and World Bank, Structural Adjustment Programs (SAP) based on The Standard Model are supposed to put countries on a path to economic health and prosperity. But how are "health" and "prosperity" defined and measured? Targets of these programs are Growth, Capital Reserves, and the Domestic Price Level. The "standard equations" try to tell developing countries that these targets will all increase if they do the following: lower credit to the government, devalue the exchange rate (value of the currency in US dollars), and at the same time reduce government spending on social programs, eliminate product subsidies, and avoid bailouts of failing enterprises. These recommendations form the basis of the SAP mapped out for virtually every situation, a "one-size-fits-all" prescription. The message of real data has so far not upheld this fourth assumption. It should be scrapped as well.

Inequality and Its Causes

Since 1994, inequality on a global scale has continued to increase at an accelerating rate. By the year 2000, the richest 447 billionaires in the world had more wealth than the *poorest half* of humanity (Malinkovic, 2000). In the United States the richest individual person had wealth equal to that of the *poorest 40 percent* of the American people (UNDP, Human Development Report, 2000).

The net worth of the world's 200 richest people increased from $440 billion to more than $1 trillion in just four years 1994 to 1998. The assets of the three richest people were more than the combined GNP of the 48 least developed countries. (UNDP, Human Development Report, 2000; Brecher *et al.*, 2000).

Among the more immediate causes of poorly distributed wealth are the shifts of industry away from hiring less-educated workers and a related downward shift in pay scales at those levels. Also there has been a shift away from goods-producing industries that traditionally provide high-wage employment for low-skilled workers and a shift toward more technical service industries disproportionately employing college graduates (Daly and Cobb, 1994).

Root causes would include the increasing tendency of transnational corporations to move their lower-skilled operations to countries where labor is considerably cheaper. This "race to the bottom" is noticeably lowering the aggregate income of low level workers everywhere—even in US and Europe. Under the "free trade" agreements, the ease of transferring capital to elites in other countries and the expansion of investment abroad have also contributed to the displacement of workers, increasing distress, and poverty of the lower levels of the world's peoples (Daly and Cobb, 1994, Chapter 11, "Free Trade versus Community").

These "trickle-up" effects (transferring wealth and capital to the elites of the world) of our ever more rapidly expanding capitalism are a significant characteristic of the kind of globalization we have experienced lately, particularly in the last decade. The new accelerating factors include more rapid transfer of larger amounts of capital, larger investments in our own enterprises abroad, and the availability of cheap labor in less developed areas of the world. In short, the global disparities in wealth and income have been the necessary fallout of this accelerated expansion (economic imperialism). Kevin Phillips (2002) has argued persuasively that the growing gap between the haves and the have-nots in the United States, and elsewhere in the world, is not only unjust but threatens the foundations of democracy.

Unstated Assumptions Underlying the Model

As early as 1776, in *The Wealth of Nations*, Adam Smith warned of the possible reversion to colonialism as capitalism spread throughout newly industrialized Europe (Smith, 1776, 523-606). Even at that early date, as the United States was just achieving independence from England, the larger nations of Europe were showing the tendency to exploit the resources of the smaller countries of the world. Historians of economics call this period the era of "classical imperialism" (Boulding and Murkejee, 1972).

Economic Imperialism

Country **B** would most likely be part of country **A**'s "empire" if:

1. Country **B** allows country **A**'s capital, interest earnings, or profits to flow in and out of **B**.

2. **A**'s capital invested in **B** is concentrated in low wage interests such as farming or mining.
3. When **A**'s capital is invested in modern industry within **B** it is in **A**-owned firms or branch plants, the higher positions in the hands of **A**'s citizens and/or speaking **A**'s language, espousing **A**'s religion, and supporting **A**'s government during any conflict between **A** and **B** (these people are often called *compradores* by analysts).
4. **A**'s modern technological products have free entry into **B**'s market, with no duties imposed. Reciprocal trade agreements may exist but only for agricultural products or raw materials, never for completely processed or manufactured goods. (See discussion of North American Trade Agreement—NAFTA on 64.)
5. **A** provides substantial assistance to **B**'s military budget, often supplemented by military hardware or training. In an exchange, **A** is permitted bases for its military within **B**'s borders, usually on prime property.
6. **A** has sufficient power to embarrass, subvert, or overthrow **B** when **B**'s government becomes unfriendly.
7. **A** has a tendency to expand its influence over one undeveloped country after another, especially if those countries contain desirable resources including cheap labor.

(Adapted from Bronfenbrenner, 1972)

Between 1919 and 1927, Joseph Schumpeter, a brilliant Austrian economist, began studying the expansionist tendencies of **A**-type countries and suggested that "imperialism" of this early era should be understood by looking at two factors, (1) the habits of aggression developed by the relations of production found in the history of **A**'s (not **B**'s) culture and (2) the perceived needs of **A**'s elite ruling classes.

He illustrates his argument by citing the activities of the Normans in southern Italy as they dominated that region in the early part of the twentieth century. They cannot be explained simply by looking at the relations of production prevailing in Italy at that time or the perceived economic needs of the people living there (Schumpeter, 1951).

One must find the sources of their acquisitive "mentality" in the cultural and economic background from which the Normans came to southern Italy. Indeed the cultural heritage of the Normans had a profound effect on England and France—and subsequently on the United States. For example, we must credit the Normans with the invention of modern bookkeeping along with the concept of the "bottom line" in the early 1000s CE. Before that, merchants and artisans were only dimly aware of the idea of profit and had few tools to assess the accumulation of wealth.

In the 1970s, Boulding and Mukerjee collected a series of articles pointing out the tendency of capitalism to emulate the colonialist policies of the larger European countries during the sixteenth and seventeenth centuries. These studies confirmed the fears expressed by Adam Smith two centuries ago (Boulding and Mukerjee, 1972, 34-59). As early as the late 1800s, economists were realizing that overproduction was the real driving force behind imperialism. Empires could maintain their volume of production only by expanding territory for new sources of raw materials, cheap labor, and extended markets for goods. Recently, economists and policy makers have discovered that acquiring actual land is not necessary as long as economic influence and control is maintained (Hobson, 1972).

The only other way of dealing with overproduction is to form monopolies, or trusts, to control the supply of goods and services and keep the prices up. In the United States, the Sherman antitrust laws prevent a certain amount of this kind of activity. It doesn't matter much, because, sooner or later, even that road would be closed anyway, corporations would need to expand beyond borders to survive, and the United States, would have broken through a conservative policy:

> ...and flung itself into a rapid imperial career for which it possessed neither the material nor the moral equipment, risking the principles and practices of liberty and equality by establishment of militarism and the forcible subjugation of peoples which it could not safely admit to ... American citizenship.   (J.A. Hobson, 1972, 3)

Thus US imperialism perpetuates itself globally by continuing to overproduce, channel its increasing capital to the upper classes everywhere, and expand its military and economic influence all over the world.

Economists of the late twentieth century who have observed the history of "classical imperialism" have concluded that, from a purely rational point of view, imperialism is no longer economically feasible (Boulding, 1972). With the advent of industrialization, imperialism in the classical sense could no longer be supported. (When it became possible to squeeze ten dollars out of nature by production and exchange for every dollar that could be squeezed out of a colony, empire simply ceased to pay.) By the middle of the twentieth century, Sweden had abandoned any external empire and remained at home minding its own business and developed at a much more rapid rate than any other European country. On the other hand, Portugal, the largest, long-lasting, four-hundred-year empire during the classical imperial period was still trying to control its holdings in the middle of the twentieth century. As a result, it had the smallest per capita income in Europe by the 1970s (Boulding, 1972, Intro, xiii).

Kenneth Boulding also reminds us that any attempt at empire in the modern industrial and post-industrial eras is bound to fail. Britain, France, Netherlands, Belgium, Spain, and Portugal all abandoned their bids for world domination strictly for economic reasons. World domination was no longer feasible (1972, Intro. xiv ff.).

The puzzle here is why it seemed to take the rulers and decision-makers of the imperial countries such a long time to find out that, from an economic point of view, imperialism simply does not work. And a further puzzle is why on earth a country like the United States, founded on democratic principles and one of the first rebels against empire, would design such an imperialist model like "The Standard Economic Model" and try to dominate the rest of the world with it.

The work of Robert Heilbroner and Lester Thurow represent another strand of critical economic thinking in the 1970s. As we pondered the effects of the collapse of communism, we also began to understand the fall of US capitalism. Though not as catastrophic, this fall was almost as surprising as the fall of the Soviet economy. At the end of World War II, the US was the leader, an economic powerhouse in the world, and common wisdom thought it would always remain so. But rapidly "...we lost leadership in steel, automobiles, ships, machine tools, electronics, and ladies' fashions." We also lost political leadership, fostering unnecessary wars to regain hegemony. Even the dollar depreciated by almost 50 percent between 1985 and 1989. Our account deficit (trade balance) increased by 3.6 percent of GNP between 1979 and 1987, while during the same period Japan and Germany experienced a trade surplus of 4.4 percent of their own GDPs (Heilbroner and Thurow, 1982, 257).

Apparently economic exigencies alone have not been able to deter the United States from taking its turn in attempting to dominate the world. Some underlying and unquestioned relational assumptions, needs, or fears must have driven this urge to dominate.

The Domination Paradigm

Two telephone company advertisements have recently appeared in the popular press. One by a local telephone company (USWest) pictures a secretary sitting in her office chair on top of a globe simultaneously talking on her telephone and typing on her computer. The other by a long distance company (MCI) shows a telephone receiver resting on the top of a globe. Both ads portray our not so hidden Western cultural image of the globe as an object to be "mastered, managed, and controlled" (Tsing, 2000, note 1, 478).

These familiar advertisements highlight a common assumption in Western society that the world is here for human beings to dominate. Nature is to be subdued, not feared or appeased. Humans are created to conquer and use their environment for the satisfaction of their own needs and comfort. The earth is now not God's footstool but belongs to human beings. This set of assumptions, rarely questioned, can be called the "domination paradigm."

The "domination paradigm," at some point in recent human history, seems to have reached beyond the physical environment to include human beings. Not *all* human beings were created equal, and certainly very few are destined to dominate. A sinister implication of this paradigm leads to the assumption that people from different (non-Western) societies are, after all, a part of the physical environment, and therefore are to be conquered and dominated. That people can be equated with earth-bound resources and commodities has become an essential part of the modern economic model (the Standard Model).

This strange extension of the domination paradigm contains a fatal flaw which has led over the centuries to a *hierarchical* or *vertical* model of social organization, a kind of top-down view of human relationships. To maintain a "proper" domination model among humans, the vast majority of the human family must be relegated to subservient roles, slave labor, or chattel. For a substantial period of history, and even now, those lower classes included women, darker-skinned people, and folks speaking "foreign" languages. This categorization results in a huge waste of human energy and talent, for traditionally, 60 to 80 percent of the population has been shut out of decision making, intellectual pursuits, and even partial development of their full potential.

A corollary to the domination paradigm is a "hero" mythology, illustrated by the myth of the strong and thoughtful leader. The myth that the most efficient government is the benevolent dictatorship probably derives from Plato's idea of philosopher king presented in his classical work, *The Republic*. This myth could lie at the root of the present-day *vertical* model.

There are two kinds of problems with the idea of benevolent dictator; one is logical and the other is empirical. The logical question then: Is it possible to be "benevolent," defined as working for the common good of everyone, and "dictator," a leader with unquestioned power to make decisions and direct others, at the same time? These two concepts appear to be mutually exclusive and contradictory. In order to be benevolent, the dictator would have to be totally open to receiving information from the lower echelons as well as the elite of their society.

Benevolent dictators would have to make decisions solely on the basis of their understanding of the common good, sometimes at their own expense. Soon the dictators could no longer be defined as dictators, but only as ordinary people, perhaps hired by all the other people to be their "decision makers" only as long as their decisions serve the common good. Modern dictators are CEOs of corporations.

The empirical question is: Has a benevolent dictatorship ever existed? If so, for how long, and what came of it in the long run? Did any of the more popular dictators through history truly behave benevolently toward all of their subjects? Even if such a thing were possible, the "efficient" dictatorial government would still be elitist and not participatory. The Prince would have to live as a Pauper a good long while to know what his subjects really needed. The vast majority, called "the masses" by philosophers, would eventually have little, if anything, to say about their own fates.

Vertical and Horizontal Paradigms

The *vertical* society looks much like the familiar organizational chart with people and well-defined institutions in boxes connected by lines of influence and accountability. The people in the boxes are not named as persons but labeled by their individual or institutional status or function in the organization. The *vertical* paradigm is routinely associated with "civilized" societies and the *horizontal* with "primitive" tribes. Of course, these two words, "civilized" and "primitive," have historically meant "advanced" and "retarded" respectively.

In contrast to the *vertical model*, the *horizontal* social organization is one which is built on the common physical, psychological, and spiritual needs of the group. Persons associate with each other according to commonalities of interests, gender, blood lines, tribes or moieties. Persons in a *horizontal* society tend to relate and function along very personal lines of influence and commitment, while *vertical* organizations tend to be hierarchical and mediated by a duly established institution or authority. So pervasive is the *vertical* model in our Western society that many frequently assume that this hierarchical model is the only "natural" one.

Another common assumption claims that, while *horizontal* social organization might be appropriate for smaller human groups, large social systems must by definition be *vertical* in structure and function. Again, as we look at the larger cooperatives in the present European and American contexts, this assumption remains, at least, questionable.

Still a third belief about these two paradigms suggests that no single and well integrated society can have elements of both the *vertical* and the *horizontal*. It requires only a quick glance at our own social surroundings to conclude that this is not correct. Western society, though predominantly *vertical*, is full of examples of *horizontal* social relationships.

Social scientists often refer to marriage and family and religious affiliation as "institutions," that is, well-established *horizontal* relationships embedded in primarily *vertical* society. In spite of a few predictions, for example by some current sociologists (Stark, 2001, Ch. 13), that these horizontal "institutions" would shrivel and die on the *vertical* vine, they appear to be alive and well, albeit struggling for survival, for example the 50 percent divorce rate. It would seem that the cooperative movement can be classed as a horizontal element, if not an institution, within our society, and its popularity and strength within Western capitalist society is rapidly growing.

Just as a symphony orchestra can play in two or more quite different keys at the same time or even no key at all, individuals, groups, and institutions can operate on different theoretical models at the same time. Sometimes the effect is pleasing, or at least interesting; at other times it can be excruciating. There is no apparent reason why the *horizontal* and *vertical* components of social structure cannot exist side by side.

Another possible paradigm is to see these two approaches in a kind of dialectic or "yin-yang" relationship. Corporations are essentially vertical and competitive in the way they produce and market in the economy, but they cooperate via trade associations to further common goals. Recently corporations have been employing cooperative techniques to improve the performance of management and production teams. At the same time, competitiveness exists for recognition of excellence and promotions, with the idea that competition can sometimes produce motivation to excel.

Herman Daly and John Cobb (1994) have made a persuasive case for embedding the entire economy within environmental and humanistic (both horizontal) concerns in order to balance the more vertical goals of pure economic efficiency. They perceive that present economic theory, dominated by competitiveness, requires a new focus to deal with real issues of environmental sustainability and distributive justice. They understand that such a focus would demand an unprecedented amount of cooperation.

These concepts promoted by Daly and Cobb depend on the exhaustive quantitative research of cooperative economist, Jaroslav Vanek (1977). Vanek was one of the first recognized economists to make a convincing case for including the idea of "common good" in a full economic model and maximizing it for laborer income instead of for corporate profit. His work provided a more solid foundation for the expansion of the cooperative movement during the last decades of the twentieth century, by showing that the standard model can include horizontal or cooperative factors as well as vertical or hierarchical ones in the same meaningful and functional model.

The Entrepreneurial Hero

Closely associated with the domination paradigm, at the beginning of the twentieth century several heroes emerged from our competitive capitalist system. Stories about such heroes as Henry Ford, the Rockefellers, Ivar Kreuger, and others certainly reinforce an elitist idea of the superiority and dominance of the upper class.

For example, Ivar Kreuger, a Swedish financier, provided capital support for most of the countries of Europe though World War I by borrowing against his own company's bonds and buying and selling American and other foreign bonds. *The*

Economist reported, "He is no mere gambler on a gigantic scale in the world's bourses, no mere 'promoter' in quest of personal profit...[but] a man of great constructive intelligence and wide vision" (quoted in Barman, 238 and Caufield, 34).

Whenever a country's credits dried up and Europe was starving for money, Kreuger would appear out of nowhere like the Lone Ranger with hundreds of millions of dollars to lend (Caufield, 35). In 1932, he was trying unsuccessfully to raise money in New York and again in Paris when, one evening, he placed a Browning automatic to his heart and pulled the trigger.

Then it was discovered that Kreuger had obtained his wealth in any number of fraudulent ways. A maze of his holding companies turned out to be fictitious businesses, each rich with imaginary assets held by imaginary banks. Actual banks holding $150 million in Italian bonds, ostensibly from his company's treasury and from the Bank of Sweden, discovered that the bonds were all forgeries—and not very good ones at that.

The reason Kreuger could defraud his investors over and over again was that banks never required him to deposit the actual bonds with them. No one ever examined the cash, the bonds, the debt papers, and the equity certificates that Kreuger posted for security. Even after his death, *The Times* of London paid homage to the hero with the words, "Least of all does personal suspicion light on him in his last day" (Barman, Part 1, 57).

Our heroes and legends of today still include stories of great international financiers and noble transnational corporations improving the lives of ordinary people around the world—"Better living through chemistry!" We have forgotten the "robber barons" of the early twentieth century, but now face even more powerful frauds and thieves on a global scale.

Mythology of Competition-based Economic Models

Economists have accepted the assumption that competition is necessary for a healthy free market for at least two centuries, but until the last couple of generations most economic actors have employed it with a good deal of circumspection. When, early in the twentieth century, over 90 percent of the population lived on the farm, and large families were valued highly, the idea of cooperation was instilled in families, especially in farm children. On the farm it was obvious that everyone must pitch in to make the family unit work, relationally as well as economically. Now in an era of smaller families and with individualism on a high pedestal, the value once placed on cooperation has been submerged. Most children are trained, through little league or other sports activities, that "Winning is not everything, it's the only thing!"

The Future of Globalization

The proponents of globalization have promised increasing prosperity for all of the world's people. Workers and communities around the world have effectively been told that if they downsize, deregulate, cut funds for social services, education, and health, and in general become more competitive, the "invisible hand" will stretch out and increase their quality of life. These instructions have been channeled through the United States Treasury to the IMF and, to a lesser extent, the World Bank.

The World Bank recognizes that not all the peoples of the world are prospering under the standard model and has initiated a poverty study to assess the effects of globalization on the poorer and indigenous peoples of the world. This program, adopted in 1999 by both the World Bank and the IMF, was evaluated two and one-half years later. The Poverty Reduction Strategy Paper (PRSP) re-evaluation effort was strictly a *process* evaluation noting that some of the parts of the program were good and should be kept while the bulk of the PRSP should be revamped. The dozens of non-governmental organizations (NGO's) involved in this review pushed for an *outcome* evaluation, a hard-nosed look at what the process actually produced, a request which was largely ignored.

> Neither the Bank nor the outside commentators are asking the hard questions. The right question to ask is the following: Relative to what would have happened absent the adoption of the Poverty Reduction Strategy Paper (PRSP) process, has the implementation of the PRSP process yielded benefits that exceed its considerable administrative costs?
>
> (Jim Levinsohn, 2003)

It was obviously an evaluation from the inside and was heavily biased in favor of the developed nations in control of the World Bank and IMF. All that the PRSP process requires of a developing nation is to write a paper describing what it would do to reduce poverty in its own country. Some of the smallest countries relied on considerable consultation from the IMF and World Bank, who actually ended up writing most of the papers. In addition, all of the papers, regardless of who wrote them, had to be approved by the directors of these two global institutions.

It is important to recognize that the developed countries, especially the United States, have their own agendas in all of these negotiations, that is, to design international trade in such a way as to enrich their own coffers at the expense of the developing countries' resources and cheap labor. This bias has always been justified by the assumption that any accumulation of wealth or increases in GDP of GWP, at whatever level or place in the world economy, would eventually reduce poverty—an assumption already discredited by the facts.

Globalization from Above

This kind of globalization from above, then, was not the result of some insidious plot but was the result of honest decisions carrying unintended consequences. This kind of globalization involves at least the following aspects:

- Increasing production by moving factories to low-wage parts of the world.
- Expanding markets by encouraging international trade.
- Internationalizing capital markets and encouraging international monetary systems such as the Eurodollar.
- Developing new information, communication, and transportation technologies.
- Forming global institutions such as the World Trade Organization (WTO), the International Monetary Fund (IMF), and the World Bank.

- Restructuring corporations to make international business more effective. Strategic alliances, global outsourcing, captive suppliers, and transnational mergers (like Exxon-Mobil) allowed concentrated control.
- Re-commodification of labor, attacking worker rights, barring formation of labor unions, reducing worker benefits, ignoring environmental degradation.
- Spreading monetarism and supply-side economics.
- Limiting governmental or societal regulation.
- Reducing the power of the nation-states, particularly their power to serve their constituents.
- Increasing capital mobility, further reducing the power of the state.
- Increasing mobility of upper-class people and encouraging travel and tourism among the wealthier classes.
- Placing a high value on cultural homogenization, undermining local and indigenous communities.

(Brecher *et al.*, 2000)

The classical imperialism of the eighteenth, nineteenth, and twentieth centuries was driven by the global expansion of nation states. Now, in place of the nation, it is the transnational corporation, operating under a system of free-market "fundamentalism," that drives this new colonial imperialism. Contemporary economists, especially Latin American ones, refer to this new imperialist, free-market political economy as "neo-liberal." The major apologist for the neo-liberal position, Thomas Friedman, sums it up by stating,

> Globalization is not just a trend, not just a phenomenon, not just an economic fad. It is the international system that has replaced the cold-war system ... Globalization means the spread of free-market capitalism to virtually every country of the world.
>
> (Friedman, in *New York Times Magazine*, 1999a)

and,

> Globalization requires a stable power structure ... The hidden hand of the market will never work without a hidden fist ... And the hidden fist that keeps the world safe for Silicon Valley's Technologies to flourish is called the US Army, Air Force, Navy and Marine Corps.   (Friedman, 1999b, 375)

This last statement is set in the context of a tirade against capitalists for ignoring the need for control: "For too many executives there is no geography or geopolitics anymore" (Friedman, 1999, 373). Although transnational corporations appear to be the focus of power in the new colonialism, we should note that this power stems indirectly, but firmly, from the US Treasury Department through the functions of the IMF, World Bank, and G-8. Note that Friedman's "hidden fist" is defined as the US military, not the UN or even NATO forces. These statements confirm the definition of imperialism at the beginning of this chapter.

Globalization from Below

Tyrants have no power without the consent of the people. "The ultimate source of power is not the command of those at the top, but the acquiescence of those at the bottom" (Brecher, 2000, 23). Globalization from above can continue indefinitely in spite of the gross injury to people and damage to the environment as long as ordinary people assume that a wealthy elite is a necessary force in the competitive socio-economic mix and tacitly give it their consent.

Globalization can be a good thing if all people can share in its benefits and if those benefits can be attained without depleting the world's resources and beauty. Fortunately for the future of the world, more and more of its peoples are joining together in healthy forms of globalization—globalizations from below. Gene Sharp in his *Methods of Nonviolent Action* suggests 198 methods of withdrawing consent from the systems of domination (Sharp, 1973b). This withdrawal from the systems of domination is the first step in developing a healthy globalization developed with new models involving the democratic input of the people and considering the common good.

Using combinations of several of Gene Sharp's non-violent methods, social movements through history have overcome serious concentrations of wealth and power. Colonized people from North to South and East to West have overthrown imperial powers that possessed military strength and wealth many times greater than their own. Most often the oppressed peoples had no wealth and used no military power at all; they had only their bodies to place in the way of persistent domination. Popular global movements have eliminated the transatlantic slave system and made huge inroads on racism, such as the tearing down of institutionalized apartheid in South Africa. Popular movements have thrown out autocratic regimes with little more than resolve and global solidarity.

Then why have there not been more such non-violent shifts of power toward the people in recent decades? We can find many reasons for lassitude within our society. Perhaps many even identify with the power structure through loyalty to religion, nation, or career instead of to a people's movement, the welfare of all, or to the eradication of poverty, racism, and militarism. And clearly many people unsatisfied with the *status quo* fear reprisals and punishment from the authorities and refrain from violating social rules, that is the will of the powerful (Gene Sharp, 1973a, 16-24).

During the 1980s the World Bank agreed to suspend the Narmada Dam project in India when 900 organizations in 37 countries pledged a campaign to defund the bank by cashing in shares and refusing to purchase World Bank bonds. The demonstration in Seattle in 1999 was merely a culmination of a series of actions against these groups and against offending transnational corporations. In early 2000, Monsanto was forced to agree to the Cartagena Protocol, a preliminary agreement to limit global distribution of GMO's (genetically modified organisms).

In addition to these examples, there are pockets of grassroots resistance to "business as usual" in the global markets. European distributors refusing to purchase genetically modified corn, students refusing to buy school clothing manufactured in sweatshops, the boycott against Nestle for their indiscriminate marketing of infant formula in the developing world, and the 2003 boycott against Coca-Cola for the company's apparent part in murdering and "disappearing" union leaders and members are all examples of social movements "in the interstices" (Michael Mann,

Table 3.3   Countries Ranked By Percent of Population in Poverty (OECD Nations Only)

Rank	Country	Rank	Country
1	Sweden	10	Japan
2	Norway	11	Italy
3	Finland	12	Canada
4	Netherlands	13	Belgium
5	Denmark	14	Australia
6	Germany	15	United Kingdom
7	Luxembourg	16	Ireland
8	France	17	United States
9	Spain		

NOTE: No further rankings were assigned to OECD nations.
Source: Human Development Report 2003, 248.

1986, Chapter 1). Networks among groups form full-scale global social movements, which in turn have forced large institutions to modify their activities.

> Social movements may lack all the paraphernalia of power: armies, wealth, palaces, temples, and bureaucracies. But by linking from the nooks and crannies, developing a common vision and program, and withdrawing their consent from existing institutions, they can impose norms on states, classes, armies, and other power actors.
>
> (Brecher, 2000, 24)

The globalization movement from below operates on many levels: at the global level, the state level, and most importantly at local levels. Social networks behind grass roots activities continue to grow and strengthen, signaling to the G-8, World Bank, and IMF that their policies will be countered. There is literally now no place for the imperialists to hide from public scrutiny. The current resistance against the World Bank, IMF, and the protests in Seattle and elsewhere against the WTO have demonstrated the effectiveness of the power of nonviolence in making crucial policy changes.

Democratic Free Markets

There is not just one free-market model. There are deep differences among the models used by the United States, Sweden, Netherlands, Canada, and Australia. Several countries with per capita incomes comparable to the United States have significantly better records on income inequality, poverty, violent crimes, retirement benefits, and health. For example, there are 16 developed countries that rank higher than the United States on the United Nations' poverty index, that is, countries that have *less* poverty than the United States. Table 3.3 shows the rankings given in the UN's Human Development Report for 2003.

The usual objection to this information is, "Yes, but the taxes in these countries are much higher than in the United States." To counter that critique, one only needs to add up all the national and local taxes plus out of pocket medical, insurance, and retirement expenses paid in the United States to realize that total payments of US citizens far exceed the amounts people pay directly in taxes for such benefits in other countries. These direct expenses that are paid in the United States do not even cover the social costs of environmental and resource depletion, air and water pollution, and increasing unemployment and underemployment. Furthermore, people in the lower income levels of the United States bear the brunt of these expenses.

The proponents of "globalization from above" sincerely believe that their single-minded pursuit of commercial and financial interests above all else is not simply self interest but is in the *general interest*. In spite of the overwhelming evidence, free-trade and free-market advocates genuinely expect that everyone will eventually benefit from their efforts.

> Many believe this so strongly that they support forcing countries to accept these "reforms," [SAPS] through whatever means they can, even if there is little popular support for such measures.   (Stiglitz, 2003, 216)

The real challenge of these organizations (IMF, World Bank, and WTO) is not so much in their concept, but in their structures and their mind-sets. There is a natural tendency to ignore environmental degradation, poverty, threats to democracy, and fair trade because the entities the international organizations are accountable to are not interested in these issues. "The typical central bank governor begins his day worrying about inflation statistics not poverty statistics..." Similarly entrepreneurs, producers of goods and services, and policy makers, all those in charge of productivity and trade, worry about exports and not about pollution or oil spills (Stiglitz, 2003, 217).

> Although I have made a fortune in the financial markets, I now fear that the untrammeled intensification of laissez-faire capitalism and the spread of market values into all areas of life is endangering our open and democratic society. The main enemy of the open society, I believe, is no longer the communist but the capitalist threat.   (Soros, 1997)

The Cooperative Movement

> One can discern in evolution a repeating pattern in which aggressive competition leads to a threat of extinction, which is then avoided by the formation of cooperative alliances.
> (Sahtouris, 1998)

It is "curiouser and curiouser" that in all the literature criticizing the "Standard Economic Model" there is scarcely any mention of the cooperative movement. Yet it would seem, from all of the history and theory of the movement, that it is a prime candidate for the avoidance of extinction mentioned in the quote above from the writings of the evolutionary biologist, Dr Sahtouris. There is room, at this time, for a proactive public policy to encourage human-scale cooperative enterprises owned by the stake-holders to displace the highly subsidized megacorporations. These subsidies, corporate welfare, have come both in the form of tax advantages and the public payment of social costs (poverty and environmental degradation). There have already been moves toward increases in stake-holder control by increasing worker input and the offering of employee stock ownership plans (ESOPs). But total democratization of the workplace would require a corporate structure built on the one membership/one share/one vote principle of the cooperative.

These corporate reforms must begin on the local scale, perhaps supported by policy and financial support at the national level. The international cooperative movement continually grows and strengthens. United Europe has already entered a new era of cooperation and human-based economic activity.

Conclusions

The three basic assumptions about the "free market" are: (1) Information is freely, equally, and simultaneously available to all bidders; (2) all buyers have equal opportunity to bid in the market; and (3), if uninhibited by government or corporate controls, the market will cause the economy to grow. From the data surveyed, we must conclude that those assumptions are seldom (if ever) satisfied. Supply and demand remain the vehicle of the "free market" model, but the suppliers drive it (not the demanders). The suppliers cleverly market wasteful and unnecessary goods (like SUVs) to expanding markets, treat labor as a commodity to be purchased as cheaply as possible, and ignore social costs, "externalities," such as poverty and environmental degradation.

Fortunately for the future, more and more ordinary struggling people of the world are banding together. There are "free markets" that are more democratic than what the United States, the US controlled IMF (through the Treasury Department), the World Bank, and the WTO have generated. Sweden, Norway, Finland, Netherlands, and Denmark, for example, have far less poverty than the United States, and they have better records on crime, health, and education. Grassroots democratic movements all over the world are including the formation of cooperatives as a part of their strategy. Part II presents in more detail what is happening in the human cooperative enterprises around the world.

One of the huge differences between the Standard Model and the cooperative model of capitalism is that in the Standard Model, labor becomes a commodity to be bought at the lowest possible price. In the cooperative model, workers are also members. They hire the management. Laborers become people again in the cooperative model, and demand is again the driver. Globalization can be good for the world, if it becomes more democratic, serves all of the people, and arrives truly as "globalization from below."

References

Bakan, J. (2004). *The Corporation: The Pathological Pursuit of Profit and Power.* The Free Press, NY.

Barman, T.G. (1932). "Ivar Kreuger: His Life and Work." *Atlantic Monthly*, August, 1932.

Boulding, K.E. and T. Mukerjee (eds) (1972). *Economic Imperialism.* Michigan University Press, Ann Arbor, MI.

Brecher, J., T. Costello, and B. Smith (2000). *Globalization from Below: The Power of Solidarity.* South End Press, Cambridge, MA.

Caufield, C. (1996). *Masters of Illusion: The World Bank and the Poverty of Nations.* Henry Holt and Co., NY.

Curry-Stevens, A. (2002). *When Markets Fail People.* CJS Foundation, Ottawa, Canada.

Daly, H.E. and J.B. Cobb, Jr. (1994). *For the Common Good.* Beacon Press, Boston.

Dasgupta, P. (2003). "World Poverty: Causes and Pathways." In B. Pleskovic and N.H. Stern (eds) *World Bank Conference on Development Economics, 2003.* Washington, DC, World Bank. Available at: www.econ.cam.ac.uk/faculty/dasgupta/worldpov.pdf.

Friedman, T. (1999a). *New York Times Magazine*, March 28.

Friedman, T. (1999b). *The Lexus and the Olive Tree: Understanding Globalization.* Farrar, Strauss and Giroux, NY.

Gund Institute for Ecological Economics (2003). Paper on GPI Draft October, 2003. Available at www.uvm.edu/%7Ejdericks/GPI/GPIpaper.doc.

Heilbroner, R. and L. Thurow (1982). *Economics Explained: Revised and Updated 1994.* Simon and Schuster, A Touchstone Book, NY.

Hobson, J.S. (1972). "The Economic Taproot of Imperialism." In K.E. Boulding and T. Mukerjee (eds) *Economic Imperialism.* Michigan University Press, Ann Arbor, MI.

Korten, D. (1999). *The Post Corporate World: Life After Capitalism.* Bukarian Press, Barret-Koehler Publishers, Inc., San Francisco, CA.

Kresse, J. (2004). "The Changing Form of Business." *Timeline.* The Foundation for Global Community. Palo Alto, CA.

Kuhn, T. (1996). *The Structure of Scientific Revolutions, 3rd Edition.* University of Chicago Press. Chicago, IL.

Levinsohn, J. (2003). *The World Bank's Poverty Reduction Strategy Paper Approach: Good Marketing or Good Policy?* UN G-24 Discussion Paper Series No. 21, April 2003. United Nations.

Malinkovic, B. (2000). *True World Income Distribution, 1988 and 1993: First Calculation Based on Household Surveys Alone.* World Bank.

Mann, M. (1986). "Societies as Organized Power Networks." Chapter 1 in *The Sources of Social Power, Volume 1.* Cambridge University Press, Cambridge, MA.

Phillips, K. (2002). *Wealth and Democracy.* Broadway Books: Random House, NY.

Sahtouris, E. (undated) "The Biology of Globalization." www.ratical.com/LifeWeb.

Schumpeter, J. (1951). *Imperialism and Social Classes* (translated by Heinz Norden), Augustus M. Kelley Publishers, New York.

Sharp, G. (1973a). *Power and Struggle: Part I of The Politics of Non-violent Action.* "Why Do Men Obey." pp. 16-23. Porter Sargent, Boston.

Sharp, G. (1973b). *Methods of Nonviolent Action: Part II of The Politics of Non-violent Action.* Porter Sargent, Boston.

Smith, A. (1776). *An Inquiry into the Causes of The Wealth of Nations.* Available as *The Wealth of Nations*, Random House: Modern Library Edition, NY.

Soros, G. (1997). "The Capitalist Threat." *Atlantic Monthly*, Feb. 1997.

Stark, R. (2001). *Sociology 8ᵗʰ Edition.* Thomson and Wadsworth (internet edition).

Stiglitz, J.E., (2003). *Globalization and Its Discontents.* W.W. Norton, NY.

Tsing, A. (2000). "Anthropology of Globalization." *Cultural Anthropology* 15(3): 327-60.

United Nations Human Development Reports (UNDP) by Year (1996-2003).

United States Census Bureau, *Current Population Surveys 1947-1998. A*vailable online at http://quickfacts.census.gov/qfd/index.html

United States Census Bureau, (June 2000). *The Changing Shape of the Nation's Income Distribution.* Washington, DC.

Vanek, J. (1977). *The Labor-Managed Economy.* Cornell University Press, Ithaca, NY.

World Bank (2000). World Development Reports (WDDR) by Year (1996-2003). New York, NY.

PART II
Cooperative Case Studies

A more detailed review of the successes of cooperatives in the developing world tells a story of participation of all segments of society in a renewing and exciting democratic economic model. How have emerging democratic governments responded, and how have the two-thirds world poor received new hope in an inclusive pursuit of survival and fulfillment of their true potential as social human beings? In more exceptional parts of the developed world, this part also includes a summary of the theory and history of cooperatives in Oceania and the Mondragón cooperatives in Northern Spain.

Chapter 4

Cooperation and Microfinance in Southeast Asia and Oceania

The world traveler
Finds myriad miracles
Of cooperation.

(Haiku by BK & BF)

Muhammad Yunus should be classed with Saul Alinsky (1935) and Paulo Friere (1970) as the most effective change agents of the twentieth century. These three characters in the drama of twentieth century social change pursued similar objectives in many respects, especially in their goals to empower the poor. They differed widely, however, in their approaches. Saul Alinsky, the labor leader's mentor from the first half of the twentieth century, dedicated his life to helping wage laborers receive what was rightfully theirs both in terms of income and the twin safety nets of health care and retirement benefits. His method involved confrontation and face-to-face conflict. Paulo Friere, father of liberation theology during the second half of the century, took a slightly different tack. His method featured transforming the structure of oppression by helping the poor understand that, being in the majority in developing countries, the power for social change always rested with them. Both Alinsky and Friere empowered the poor by convincing them that the elite classes depend on the lower classes for their survival and support. They both demonstrated that the laboring classes always have the power to withhold their consent to enslavement.

Professor Muhammad Yunus followed a still different path to empowering the poor. He had learned from history that strictly confrontational revolutionary movements, once in power, easily became as oppressive as their predecessors. Often the same oppressive governmental institutions and structures were perpetuated. To Yunus, what society needs more than anything else is a participatory process and a financial structure that empowers all of its members. Therefore, he focused on that participatory process now called the Grameen (village) model, a process adopted in some form by nearly every micro-credit effort, both cooperative and commercial. He also addressed the problem of making such a participatory process sustainable.

A key to making a participatory model sustainable is the concept of "critical fit." In a very early study, David Korten (1980) has elaborated this concept, reminding us that what works beautifully within the culture of Bangladesh may not quite fit in Indonesia or central India, and that such a fit is critical to the sustainability of the process. "Critical fit" involves both the specific tasks required for a community to fulfill its function to all of its members and the competence of the community organization to fulfill those tasks. Thus, education or "capacitation" becomes extremely important in achieving an optimal fit of any economic system to a particular society.

A landmark study of the Asian Development Bank (ADB) in 2004 (Charitonenko) detailed the process of micro-credit formation in different countries of Asia, Bangladesh, Indonesia, Philippines, and Sri Lanka. Two of those countries, Bangladesh and Indonesia, provide examples of two entirely different approaches to micro-credit. Bangladesh exemplifies the original Grameen model, which centers on the village and its native tendency for cooperation and self-regulation, maintaining a clear separation between the Bank's commercial operations and the micro-finance opportunities offered to the villages. Indonesia utilizes a portion of the Grameen model but adapts it to the local social dynamics and combines it with a typical commercial model.

Cooperation in Bangladesh

When you have money, it is often easy to get more; money makes money. But if there is no money, nor any access to money, there is virtually no way to increase quality of life, or perhaps even to sustain life at all. One of the poorest areas in the world, India, had long been under the colonial domination of Great Britain. After much suffering and struggle, using a nonviolent approach taught by Mohandas Gandhi, a trained lawyer and Vedic scholar, the people of India finally achieved independence following World War II.

At the same time, the people in the area of India then called East Bengal wanted to separate from India and form their own country. The resulting separation caused much suffering and conflict. Although East Bengal was predominantly Muslim and the greater part of India between the Indus River and Kolkata (Calcutta) was predominantly Hindu, there were people of both groups who had lived peacefully for generations in each area. After a number of years of strife, East Bengal was established as the People's Republic of Bangladesh.

Colonizers from the UK stripped India of its resources and power, especially power over resource distribution, and left the people very poor. Or perhaps we should say that the people of India gave up their resources and power to the colonizers. East Bengal, now Bangladesh, was even poorer. Soon there was no money and no way to make money. It is remarkable then how one of the poorest countries of the world was able to begin an economic revolution through the extending of micro-credit to the poorest of the poor.

Noting the inability of poor people to obtain credit through the traditional financial institutions, Professor Muhammad Yunus first applied the principles of a sustainable credit program for the poor in the village of Chittagong, in the region of Jobra. This experiment proved so successful that it was replicated in a pilot project of the Central Bank in 1976, called the Grameen (village) Bank project. Soon other institutions for micro-credit were formed. Financial Credit for the Poor (PKSF) for example, estimating that the bottom 10 percent of people in extreme poverty were still not being reached, began a crash program in the year 2000.

Now Grameen Bank, PKSF, Bangladesh Rural Agricultural Center (BRAC), and ASA (a Bengali word meaning "hope") have cooperated in helping an estimated 10 million people emerge from the poverty trap. With a total of 50 million persons below the UN poverty line ($1 US per day) in Bangladesh, the Bangladeshi government has set a goal of eliminating at least half of that poverty by 2015. Under the strong encouragement of the Bangladeshi government, commercial banks are also instituting micro-finance programs.

In the Grameen system, a local village group is formed (with five members, typically all women), this group is linked to seven other groups forming a "center," with 50 to 60 centers making up a "branch." The groups must be made up of persons who own practically nothing and have no income. Loans do not require any collateral. The village model of Grameen is not commercial. It is a true cooperative sustained by interest and savings deposits from its own members.

Asma Kathun joined Grameen Bank and took out her first loan of 1,500 taka (US$20) in 1986. "Now I know I can do it," she said two years later. It was for a cow to provide milk, and she always worried that it would get sick and die, leaving her with an unpaid loan and no income. She remembered the early years when her father sacrificed his entire plot of land to pay dowries for his daughters. The family no longer had a proper house to sleep in and they always suffered from colds. The dowry system had reduced them to extreme poverty and ill health, with no means for subsistence.

Both Asma and her husband had attended school through fifth grade. Her husband was quiet and very retiring and could get only occasional work with the government. Asma continued to take out loans, first for a shop at the local bazaar, then for a sewing machine. She put her eldest son of 25 in charge of the tailoring, who soon hired a second tailor, paying him 40 taka per day. Eventually the family qualified for a housing loan of 10,000 taka. They combined that with their savings of about 8,000 taka, for a nice house, a "Chouchala" model, which they keep very neat. Asma showed us around with an air of obvious well-being; she is now 45 years old, strong and prosperous.

"The members of my 'center' are a united lot. When someone gets a housing loan, everyone pitches in and helps to build the house," she explained. As we walked back to her shop near the mission, she continued to chat with us and tell us how she and her "center" all attend the mission church together. To Asma, the Grameen Bank has been her family's salvation. Her husband quietly nodded his assent and smiled. "People now speak well of us. It wasn't always that way."

This socio-economic revolution has been carried out largely by the women of the country. About 95 percent of Grameen Bank's members are currently women. Some women borrowers have been elected as Chairpersons of Union Parishads, Bangladesh's lower echelon of local government. In order to get a housing loan from Grameen Bank, all the family's property ownership must be transferred to the woman's name. Because of their increased financial independence, many women have been able to stop domestic violence in their homes.

Why Such Success?

Professor Yunus applies the Rochdale cooperative principles (see Chapter 1) in setting up his micro-credit system. Each prospective member must begin saving at the rate of 5 takas a day during a seven day training period, called a "long meeting."

Table 4.1   Sixteen Decisions

1. We shall follow the four Grameen principles: Discipline, Unity, Courage, and hard Work.
2. We shall bring prosperity to our families.
3. We shall not live in a dilapidated house.
4. We shall grow vegetables all year around, eat plenty, and sell the rest.
5. During planting season, we shall plant as many seedlings as possible.
6. We shall plan to keep our families small, minimize expenditures, and look after our health.
7. We shall educate our children and ensure that they can earn enough to pay for further education.
8. We shall always keep our children and the environment clean.
9. We shall build and use pit latrines.
10. We shall drink only tubewell water.
11. We shall not take any dowry to our son's wedding or to our daughter's wedding. We shall keep the "center" free from the curse of dowry. We shall not practice child marriage.
12. We shall not inflict any injustice on anyone, nor shall we allow anyone else to do so.
13. For higher income we shall undertake larger collective investments.
14. We shall always be ready to help each other. If anyone is in difficulty, we shall all help.
15. If we come to know of any breach of discipline in any "center," we shall go there and help restore discipline.
16. We shall introduce regular physical exercise in all our "centers."

"Mara, I didn't see your latrine."
"You missed it. It's just behind the house."

"Where is your vegetable garden?"
"I just planted the seeds yesterday."

"Are you going to repair the roof over your porch?"
"My husband has just gone for the materials."
                                         [parts of conversations heard at a "center" meeting.]

As soon as the saver has accumulated 100 takas (about $1.50 US), she gets a share in the Grameen Bank and is initiated into its membership. Also the member can now vote for the group's officers. Thus the one-member one-share one-vote principle is achieved. Through training, group formation, and assent to cooperative principles in the form of the "16 decisions" (see Table 4.1), new members become full cooperators and can apply for small loans to start a business or to purchase a rice plot.

Contributing to the model's success is a strong cultural commitment to work hard in overcoming poverty. Directing the progress of Grameen is a council of 13 members, 9 of which are elected by the members; 3 are appointed by the Bangladeshi government and 1 is strictly *ex officio* from the management. Management and staff are all hired and approved by this 13 member council. Fortunately at this time, at least, the government strongly supports the work of the micro-credit groups and avoids creating obstacles to the organization's growth and achievement. The Council hires and supervises staff now numbering over 15,000 (in 2005), serving a total of 5.44 million member-borrowers through 1,700 bank branches in 58,806 villages.

Challenges

All micro-credit financial institutions still need to create more financial products appropriate to their target group in order to include more people from the bottom 10 percent of the population. To some extent the Grameen group has expanded its activities into the commercial sector by opening up its savings deposits, at a current (January, 2005) 8 percent interest rate, to the general population and to larger businesses. Also Grameen has instituted a Pension Savings Plan for all depositors.

But most importantly, the new plan considerably relaxes all the rules of Grameen Bank for totally destitute members and members experiencing the aftermath of a huge natural disaster such as the recent flooding of Bangladeshi lands. Also Grameen will now offer "venture capital" and partner with its members in their new enterprises. Still there is much to do to enable more persons in the lowest socio-economic level to participate in their program.

The staff at Grameen cite natural disasters as their chief challenge for the future. During the last flood, reserves were sadly depleted. They are still perfecting plans to assure that their goal to completely eliminate poverty by the year 2015 is reached. Global warming has raised the level of the sea, and since all of Bangladesh is now only a few inches above sea level, residents expect even more flooding during future storms.

Cooperation in Indonesia

At the time of independence in 1945, Indonesia's vice president, Mohammad Hatta, strongly recommended the cooperative model for rebuilding Indonesia's economy. Both Sukarno, Indonesia's first president, and Hatta provided strong leadership in the formation of cooperatives, and in the following years giant strides were made in reconstruction following World War II and recovery from the struggle for independence from the Dutch.

From the beginning, then, the Indonesian government played a strong role in encouraging and capitalizing cooperatives. Consequently in 2003 there were 123,181 cooperatives, 93,800 of which are still (in 2005) classed as "active." Of course, in providing such strong funding support, the government felt it had a right to impose itself in most of the decision-making processes. As a result, many cooperatives became heavily dependent on the government to maintain their programs, and most members, very busy maintaining their own financial solvency, were glad to leave the heavy-duty fund-raising to the government. Now one of the major challenges in the cooperative movement is to reduce the amount of government intervention and still maintain the viability of the cooperatives.

Under the auspices of the government Ministry of Cooperatives, there are basically four classes of cooperatives: (1) the village co-ops, mostly agricultural production enterprises; (2) dairy co-ops; (3) consumer co-ops; and (4) savings and loan co-ops. The last class is more complex in that most savings and loan units are part of individual cooperatives in other sectors. For example, there are 1,350 independent savings and loan cooperatives and 35,874 units as part of other cooperatives, bringing the savings and loan sector up to a total of 37,224 savings and loan co-ops, as of 2003. The strongest sectors of the cooperative economy are the dairy farming and the savings and loan cooperatives.

All of these cooperatives follow the Rochdale principle of one member-one share-one vote. A difficulty, however, arises in applying the principle that a cooperative should remain as independent of the government as possible. Once again we see the challenge of capitalizing cooperatives. The Indonesian ministry is currently struggling with defining its proper role. Its own recent studies show that cooperatives that perform best are precisely the ones that have received the least financial support and intervention from the government.

The ministry has created a Deputy Minister of Cooperative Education, one of whose charges is to provide public school curriculum for teaching primary and secondary school students how to form and operate a cooperative. Another task is to suggest strongly that all cooperatives include education as part of their most important community activities.

Along with, perhaps even superseding, the challenge of the proper role for government in encouraging and supporting cooperatives is the external challenge of *globalization*. Transnational corporations, with their penchant for placing money rather than the people on the bottom line, commodifying workers, and ignoring the common good, are threatening to out-compete the cooperatives. As a response to this challenge, the members of the cooperative movement, backed by the Ministry of Cooperatives, are waging their own form of globalization. They are beginning to form international alliances and meetings for global planning and education, hoping to bring to the world an economy for, of, and by the people.

Primary Public School Teachers Cooperative

One of the largest single cooperatives in Indonesia is the Koperasi Keluarga Guru Jakarta, a cooperative for primary school teachers in Jakarta. This cooperative first began in 1950 by obtaining funds from external borrowing as well as from membership dues. This heavy dependency on external sources of capital spelled its downfall; during the financial crisis of 1983, it went bankrupt when its sources of funding failed.

In 1986 the teachers' co-op came back together, reevaluated its founding philosophy and rebuilt its capital using funds only from its members, approximately $2 US each month in membership fees. Two US dollars a month is not a small amount considering the low wages primary school teachers currently receive. A major function of the cooperative is to provide teachers where needed in the school system. A school principal who needs a qualified teacher or substitute can phone the cooperative and be assured of a highly qualified new staff member. Koperasi, acting as an efficient personnel agency, can assure proper placement of its members in a primary school within the Jakarta area.

Over the years since then, the group has used its retained earnings to purchase and operate a large number of subsidiary businesses ranging from consumer and distribution units to savings and loan units. The accumulation of these resources provided funds for the teachers' current activities as well as handsome retirement benefits for all the members. In 2004, Koperasi reported a budget of 75 billion rupias; in 2005, it anticipates a total budget of nearly 90 billion (about $67 million and $81 million US at 2005 exchange rates).

Overall policy decisions are made by a national council of representatives elected regionally and comprising about 10 percent of the total membership. The council meets twice a year, once to make programming decisions and a second time to transact financial affairs and elect officers. All decisions are made by a vote of a plurality of council members present. Hiring of staff and implementation of other policy decisions are accomplished by a small committee authorized by the council. The working staff numbered 12 persons at the beginning of 2005.

In addition to retirement benefits, the cooperative also offers low interest loans to its members as well as holiday gifts of food and money. Since its reorganization in 1986, the cooperative has been in excellent financial condition. It maintains connections world wide, including regular meetings with similar cooperative groups in Belgium, France and Germany. Each year, it offers free training to its members in cooperation and the philosophy of the cooperative movement.

There have been recent challenges to the cooperative by the arrival of Wal-Mart and other large transnational consumer corporations. A number of the cooperative's subsidiary consumer groups have gone out of business because they cannot compete with the large, modern stores. The savings and loan groups, however, have survived and have even grown a bit. Now these groups may need to make up the losses caused by the failure of other consumer units.

Micro-Banking

A groundbreaking effort to serve persons and small businesses that could not get loans for starting a new enterprise or for maintaining an existing business began with a grant from the Bank of Indonesia in 1992. The grant was aimed specifically at establishing a new organization called Bank Rakyat Indonesia (BRI). The words *Bank Rakyat* mean "People's Bank." At the end of 1992, BRI already reported 700 borrowers and 9,024 savers.

The organization begins with neighborhood units made up of a neighborhood leader as a general manager and other local persons as an account manager, a teller or cashier, and two customer service persons. New employees begin as customer service personnel and work up to the position of general manager. Managers are never hired from outside the system. As soon as the number of borrowers in the unit reaches 400, the company begins training a second account manager, who may come either from the unit or from another unit in the branch area. As soon as there are more than about 800-1000 borrowers in a unit, the unit is split into two units. Fifteen to twenty units form a branch, and 25 to 50 branches then require a supervisory office.

Although BRI was started as a project of the Bank of Indonesia, by 1993 it was entirely self-supporting and became an independent commercial venture. The bank was never organized as a cooperative, yet the leadership has come entirely from the ranks of people who needed an institution to support the formation of their businesses. The idea was a very popular one and each year 100 new units were added until, by the end of 2004, there were over 4 million borrowers and 10 million savers. In March of 2003, for the first time, BRI went public and began selling shares. Before the end of 2003, the share price had more than tripled.

Surpluses in retained earnings are all put back into training, promotion of savings, employee retirement funds, and community education. BRI never invests in any other equities and all employees are included in a voluntary Employee Share Ownership Program (ESOP). The maximum number of shares an employee can purchase is pegged to salary levels. The compensation and share-holding amounts are capped for upper management. The company's financial position is totally transparent and published in an annual report. Internal audits are performed annually, and external audits are performed by an independent accounting firm every two years.

BRI has an extraordinarily small default rate. Collateral is required, but usually it is comprised of very simple household possessions. Foreclosure on such small loans is not really feasible, so the company depends on account managers working with the borrower to help get the loan repaid. Of course, a few loans must be written off but only after two years of trying to work out other repayment methods, and the default rate stands at only 1 to 1.5 percent. Those are mostly student loans.

The company is totally supported now by loan interest, a flat 15 percent, and by outstanding shares. The company has never had to take out loans from other banks or companies and holds no other kinds of debt instruments such as commercial paper or government bonds.

The employees report feeling a sense of ownership in the company and state that retirement and other benefits are quite satisfactory. They receive training every year, and the company encourages all employees to better their education and overall quality of life. Managers take a personal interest in their co-workers' welfare and occasionally use unit reserves to help in case of medical emergencies.

Challenges

When asked about their greatest challenge, managers and employees alike cited increasing competition from transnational corporations. Micro-banking has been so successful that every bank in the region wants to get into the act and establish some kind of micro-lending programs. BRI now has to provide ATM's, increase its level of information technology, and hold raffles on Indonesian built automobiles and motor-cycles to spur savings. All in all, growth in unit formation and deposits has slackened a good deal in the last two years.

Another challenge, brought out by criticism from the Grameen Bank and others in the Southeast Asian microfinance community, is that the commercial model of The People's Bank has not been able to reach the lower 10 percent of the population, especially the urban poor. One of the upper managers of the People's Bank has expressed an interest in developing a project within the poorer urban neighborhoods of Jakarta that would, in fact, reach the lower 10 percent of the population. Following the Grameen model, it would seem that one element of such a project would have to be the relaxation of the requirement for collateral.

In order for such a plan to work, the structures of urban neighborhoods would have to become more stable and self-sustaining—more like villages. Due to the urban ethos of strong individualism and privacy, such a project could prove much more difficult to achieve in the urban setting than in rural villages, where people are much more dependent on each other for survival and social identity. Another component of that project would have to involve creating much more social solidarity than is now present in the city.

Cooperatives in Australia

The historical backgrounds of Australia and New Zealand differ considerably from their Indonesian neighbors. Almost no cooperative experiences of their neighbors have stimulated ideas, promoted progress or influenced the Australian and New Zealand economies. Still it is interesting to note that the cooperative and social experiences of their English ancestry have had some influence.

From the beginning of English settlements in Australia, the six states and two territories were virtually autonomous, each with its own royally appointed governor, legislature, and legal system. It was only in 1900 that the states agreed to become federated, and the lazy, inland town of Canberra was chosen as capital. Canberra was chosen partly because it was sufficiently inland to avoid possible naval bombardment. The federation learned from the experience of the United States, when the British bombarded, sacked and burned Washington, DC, twice in the 1800s. The choice of Canberra was a good one also because it was approximately equidistant between the two largest cities of Australia, Sydney and Melbourne, which had been vying strongly for the capital's location.

At the beginning of the twenty-first century, Australia enjoys a certain prominence in the South Pacific region, with a reasonably stable democratic government and an economy strong enough to hold its own in the Pacific Rim consortium. A country with approximately the same land area as the United States, Australia provides a very comfortable homeland for a little over 20 million people, up almost 3 million since the 1996 census. Well over 50 percent of that population lives in the three states on the east coast, New South Wales, Victoria, and Queensland, plus, of course, the Capital Territory (ACT). Queensland is the fastest growing state and accounts for a large percentage of the population increase since 1996.

Like other areas of the world colonized by Europeans, the continent was previously inhabited by a large number of tribes of aboriginal peoples. Also, like other areas where European settlers encroached on primitive cultures, racism was the norm, and tribal inhabitants suffered heavy decimation by disease, wanton killing by the British settlers, and various forms of economic oppression. In fact, settlers on Tasmania claim to have destroyed virtually all the aboriginal people on the island.

Currently, major economic indicators show a strengthening economy with a steadily, though not rapidly, decreasing trade balance stabilized at approximately

$2 billion. Growth of the GDP remained at about 4.1 percent during 2001 while the rest of the world was experiencing a relatively large drop in total production and consumption. The GDP, expressed in terms of parity dollars (PPP), remains around $400 billion. In 1996, unemployment stood at 8.9 percent. By early 2005 it had dropped to 5.2 percent. It should be remembered that this measure will always be adjusted politically to favor a current administration by eliminating certain classes of unemployed from the rolls or by not counting the under-employed, that is, employable persons working less than half time.

The present work force is composed of approximately 2 percent in agriculture, 14 percent in manufacturing, 4 percent in mining/extraction, and about 80 percent in services. A shrinking manufacturing sector probably accounts for most of the trade deficit. Australia is only recently feeling the effects of consumerism and global lifestyles such as dependence on US entertainment (music, movies, and so on), and dependence on Japan for high-tech equipment and automobiles.

Racism in Australia, especially in relationships with the remaining aboriginal people, is still thoroughly ingrained. Those attitudes, combined with the increasing activities of trans-national corporate globalization, will inevitably place severe limits on economic growth and stability on the "big island."

Overview of Cooperatives in Australia

The first cooperative in Australia was formed according to Rochdale principles (see Chapter 1) in 1859 in Brisbane, Queensland. In those early days, a great deal of conflict followed the formation of cooperatives. Consumer co-ops feuded with production co-ops, and the labor movement was very suspicious of co-ops. A great deal of conflict and suspicion has accompanied the movement since those inauspicious beginnings and continues today. More recently, two large private banks did not succeed in an attempted hostile take-over of several credit unions. Perhaps this take-over trend will eventually prevail and eliminate the credit unions from the banking community.

In a typical interventionist move, the federation government in the 1920s required the formation of compulsory "marketing boards." The government promptly instructed the boards to purchase and market designated products in order to ensure their distribution and, at the same time, to fix farm prices. This government intervention removed the need for cooperatives to help distribute resources equitably and led to the collapse of many of them.

At the same time, medical societies complained strongly that "friendly societies" and "lodges," cooperative-like organizations providing medical aid and financial services to unemployed families during the Depression of the late 20s and early 30s, were forcing down the doctors' fees. Again, the federal government intervened to limit the activities of these co-ops.

Since the mid-1980s the so-called "neo-liberal" philosophy of economics (see Chapter 3) has moved the government and the people first toward indifference toward cooperation and then to outright hostility. The "old-fashioned values" of cooperation have been overshadowed by the post-modern pursuits of individualism, competition, and consumerism.

Still the cooperative movement has flourished. As of 2003 there were approximately 2,400 registered cooperatives in Australia. By Australian corporation legislation, cooperatives are either "general" or "cooperative-like" companies. The "general" cooperatives are those that adhere to the Rochdale principles laid out by the International Cooperative Alliance (ICA—see Chapter 1). In 1992, special legislation actually spelled out these cooperative principles. "Cooperative-like" companies may or may not adhere strongly to these principles and primarily include an Australian version of credit unions.

Legislation also distinguishes between cooperatives that are permitted to distribute profits to members, called "trading co-ops," and nonprofit cooperatives, usually very small and often called "community advancement co-ops." The latter category includes gaming or sport clubs. These "clubs" are an outgrowth of a variety of small social clubs that existed at least a half-century before the federation, during British colonial times. In the late 1970s, legislation was established requiring these clubs to register as non-profit companies. By and large, the designation of cooperatives with respect to these "clubs" remains very loose.

The largest number of cooperatives (81 percent) are found in two states, New South Wales and Victoria. Most of the cooperatives in New South Wales—more than 200—are gambling casinos. Wholesale and retail cooperatives comprise the remaining hundred or so co-ops in the state and are found mostly in the rural areas. Although cooperatives for agricultural production are relatively few in number, they tend to be quite large and account for 66 percent of the total cooperative market, with a turnover of more than $2 billion Australian dollars (Lyons, 2001).

In 1998, 14 cooperatives were among the thousand largest companies in Australia. Three had a turnover of more than $1 billion each, and all 14 grossed over $6.5 billion. Seven of these 14 were farm co-ops and seven were dairy co-ops (Lyons, 2001).

Incorporated cooperatives in New South Wales have almost 1.5 million members. The largest of these, in terms of membership, is the University Cooperative Bookshop with more than 40 stores and over 1 million members. The total cooperative membership in Australia includes "club" memberships, which in New South Wales total 150,000 members. Many persons belong to two or more cooperatives, thus being counted at least twice in the total. Such a huge cooperative membership is certainly significant in a state whose adult population is about 4.5 million.

Summary and Conclusions

The star of the cooperative development in Southeast Asia is certainly the Grameen Bank of Bangladesh, with its model of village women's groups for borrowing, saving, and family improvement. Muhammad Yunus, banker to the poor, led the way to the eventual elimination of poverty in that area of the world. Indeed, the Grameen model has gone global, with 50 Grameen Foundation partners in 20 countries around the world, with a total of over 5 million borrowers. The foundation estimates that Grameen lifts 10,000 families each month out of poverty in Asia, Africa and the Americas. Currently (in 2005), savers can receive a record 8 percent interest on their savings accounts.

Bank Rakyat Indonesia (The People's Bank of Indonesia) adapted the Grameen model to its micro-finance department, and by the end of 2004, had reached over 4 million borrowers and 10 million savers. The People's Bank, because of requiring collateral, fails to reach the lower 10 percent of the population. Growth rates have slackened somewhat recently because of competition with transnational commercial banking enterprises.

Cooperatives in Australia have experienced a much more difficult struggle for survival. The government of the federation of Australia has never been supportive of the cooperative movement; in fact, there have been incidents of deliberate suppression of cooperatives. During the Depression, the government intervened to limit the activities of "friendly societies," organized to give medical and financial aid, because they were "driving down doctors' medical fees." Recently two large private commercial banks made a serious bid for a hostile takeover of several credit unions. That bid failed, but the economic philosophy of the government continues to be hostile toward cooperation.

In spite of the challenges of flood, *tsunami*, competition from transnationals, government interference, and hostility, cooperatives in Southeast Asia and Oceania have survived and have even thrived. This survival has been largely because of the cooperatives' ability to involve people at the lowest levels of society in their own socio-economic growth and increasing quality of life. Millions of people have been lifted above the poverty line by micro-finance, cooperative production, and more equal distribution of resources and goods. No natural catastrophe, greedy economic globalization, or hostile government has yet been able to quash the movement.

References

Alinsky, Saul (1935). *Rules for Radicals.* Random House, N.Y.

Charitoneneko, Stephanie, Anita Campion and Nimal A. Fernando (2004). *Commercialization of Microfinance: Perpectives from South and Southeast Asia.* Asian Development Bank. Manila, Philippines.

Friere, Paulo (1968). *Pedagogy of the Oppressed* (trans. From Portuguese). Seabury Press, N.Y.

Grameen Foundation Website, www.grameenfoundation.org/about_us/.

Korten, David (1980). "Community Organization and Rural Development: A Learning Process Approach." *Public Aministration Review*, 40.

Lyons, Mark (2001). "Cooperatives in Australia—A Background Paper." ACCORD Paper No. 1, Australian Centre for Cooperative Research and Development. www.accord.org.au.

Yunus, Muhammad (1998). *Banker to the Poor: the Autobiography of Muhammad Yunus, founder of the Grameen Bank.* The University Press Limited. Dhaka, Bangladesh.

Chapter 5

The Cooperative Movement in India

Untouchables tap
Source of self-empowerment
Microfinancing   (Haiku by BL & BF)

Civil society in India has gone through a number of phases over the last couple of centuries. Before the British invasion in the late 1700s, civil society did little more than collect food for the poor and distribute old clothing—the almsgiving phase. The British brought with them their own brand of domination, which subjected virtually all civil society to the whim of the crown's governors. Local cultures, particularly in the south and west where Portuguese trading was the dominant activity, survived this British brand of domination in better condition than did the bulk of central India.

When the missionaries came, they made many mistakes in relating to the native cultures of India. On the other hand, the missionary phase of civil society contributed two very significant institutions to the development of modern India. One of those was the building and operating of schools for the children. Much of the middle class in India today has been educated in mission schools. A second major contribution of the missionaries was providing healthcare for the poor. When Christianity is mentioned today, most Indian people think of the local hospital or the school they attended. Another immediate association flashes in their memories, the very abusive use of "evangelism" as practiced around the beginning of the twentieth century. The missionaries often attempted to convert rather than help, denigrating the local customs and religious practices.

Under British rule, little work was available to Indian people except as servants for British upper-class families. Their only alternative was living on the edge by scratching what they could from the earth. This phase lasted for almost 200 years. After independence in 1945, the people of India were free; they could establish a democratic government. They immediately looked to their new government to bring equity and quality of life to all. In this way, civil society simply became the handmaiden of the government.

The great reawakening of civil society toward self-determination came in the 1950s and 1960s. There were many false starts, but with the hopes for equity and justice and with liberation in the air, more people became conscious of their power to do something about their own condition. Gandhian awareness of their political power energized people in the middle and higher castes. Unfortunately, the momentum of liberation was slowed by Gandhi's assassination and also by a failure to include the lowest of the castes in his movement.

The Role of Castes in Indian Culture

There probably are not sufficient archaeological or historical grounds for the much touted Aryan incursions, between 1000 and 500 BCE, from northern Persia or the Caspian area. It is likely that the Vedic portrayal of Arya (means both "white" and "noble"), Krishna's legendary general, had some influence on the formation of the modern caste system. The caste system was probably not brought into India from European invasions or incursions. More likely, it should be attributed to the more influential Harappan civilization of 3000-2500 BCE in the Indus Valley.

In the Rig Veda, the Aryans are not presented as particularly important components of Hinduism. Still, a number of elements could point to an eastern European influence on Indian life before the domination of the British. Vedic Sanskrit forms the basis for several of the 16 official Indian languages and is unmistakably related to European languages, mostly through Avestan (ancient Persian). The strong philological evidence for this relationship does not show much more than a kinship between the European and Indian cultures, and should never be used to prop up any sense of superiority of European over Indian culture—as British colonists tended to do (Leach, 1990).

In any event, the caste system has operated now for over 3,000 years. According to the earlier myths, "Manu the lawgiver" created human beings from the body of Brahma. Out of his head, Brahma created the purest and highest form of human existence, the *Brahmins*. The Brahmins have performed the priestly and religious functions of Hindu society. Out of his arms he created the *Kshatriyas*. These are the warriors and rulers. Out of his thighs he created the *Vysyas*, the traders and merchants. Out of his feet came the *Shudras*, the artisans, laborers, and service providers. The Shudras are also often referred to as the "Other Backward Communities" (OBCs).

Most relevant to this study, a large number of people did not fit into any of this four-fold caste system (Brahmins, Kshatriyas, Vysyas, and Shudras). They are listed in the Indian constitution as the *Scheduled Castes*. People in the lowest part of the largest of these Scheduled Castes call themselves *Dalits*, meaning the oppressed. Combined with another large undesignated Scheduled Caste, they often refer to themselves as *Dalitbahujan*. Bahujan means majority, because they comprise well over 60 percent of the Indian population. These lower groups together were often referred to as "untouchables."

Although illegal according to the modern Indian constitution, the caste system remains at the core of modern Indian society. It demands a strict compartmentalization that is seldom breached. Indian people are born into a caste and have no way of ever changing their caste designations. Everything in life relates to the caste system: where one lives, what one eats, what kind of work one can do, what assets can be held, and what institutions and resources of society can be accessed. Although the caste system originated in the Hindu culture and was institutionalized by the Hindu religion, it permeates all the other cultures and religions of the nation as well.

As a result of this feudal hegemony, the Dalit communities have, by and large, been systematically excluded from all economic, political, social processes, and institutions of the society. The caste mindset has set the stage for all the "higher" communities to practice untouchability, harassment, and even violence on the Dalitbahujan communities with total impunity. Furthermore, caste separates work from interests and natural ability, disconnects intelligence from manual labor, and renders everyone, regardless of their caste, less than complete human beings.

There are always exceptions to the "hard and fast" rules of society, and Dr B.R. Ambedkar was one of them. He was born Bhimrao Ramji Ambavedkar on 14 April 1891 of an "untouchable" family in a small rural district south of Mumbai (Bombay). Even before going to school, he was fond of books. His father somehow scraped together enough money to send him to a local elementary public school. Bhim soon learned that he was not to drink at the drinking fountain used by his classmates. He was not allowed to sit on a bench or at a desk like the other students. He had to sit on the floor. The Brahmin teacher noticed that he had an unusually sharp mind, began encouraging and complimenting his work, and eventually bestowed upon Bhim his own Brahmin family name, Ambedkar.

After his years at elementary school, Bhim decided that the proper place for him would be at Elphinshire High School in Mumbai. With the help of his teacher, he was admitted, and the family moved to the city. The only housing available to the "untouchable" family was a little one room shack on the edge of the city; the one room served as kitchen, bedroom, living room, and bathroom. There was scarcely space for two people to sleep in it.

At night Bhim would go to bed early and his father would stay up late. At about 2 am, his father would go to bed, and Bhim would get up and study the rest of the night, by a chimneyless kerosene lamp. He learned everything the teachers could teach him, except that he was not allowed to learn Sanskrit because of his caste. He did learn it anyway, on his own, later in life.

He married at the age of 17 and graduated later in the year, 1908. Miraculously, his marks and recommendations from his teachers allowed him to matriculate at Elphinshire College where he earned a BA degree in 1912. At his graduation he was presented with a job with the Maharaja of Baroda. He was again restricted by his caste in his associations with other workers. It was a sin according to many Hindus to touch him, hand him materials, or allow him to sit on chairs. Complaints to the Maharaja availed him nothing.

One year later, just as things were looking up a bit, his father died, and the Maharaja sent him to the United States, where he enrolled as a graduate student at Columbia University. In a letter to a friend in India, Ambedkar commented on his very fortunate situation, roughly in the words of Shakespeare, "In the life of man now and then is a swelling wave; if one uses this opportunity, he will be carried to his fortune." He studied Political Science, Ethics, Anthropology, and Economics, and finished with an MA in Political Science and a PhD in Economics.

Back in India, Ambedkar, with his MA and PhD, was again embedded in the caste system. When the Maharaja and the British Viceroy installed him in a high government post in Baroda, no one welcomed him. His assistants would not hand files to him; they threw them at him. No one would bring him water, tea, or anything else edible or drinkable, as they would for each other. He was unable to get a house to live in. He had to live in a shack with another "untouchable" family. Again, protests to the Maharaja got him nowhere.

After a year of little else but abuse, in 1920 he left again to study economics at the University of London. He studied constantly, including an independent study of law. In 1922 he was admitted to the bar with full practicing status. Back in India, where he returned a second time in 1923, he was only to suffer more caste abuse.

A turning point in his public life came when he led a demonstration against the Chowdar Tank, a source of water traditionally denied the "untouchables." He and his associates were attacked by a group of Hindu rowdies, and Ambedkar was injured. This incident attracted a great deal of attention. As a result of the publicity, Ambedkar was invited to attend a series of conferences to discuss the rights of lower caste citizens. In the meanwhile, the Chowdar Tank incident went to court. Ambedkar won, and attracted the attention of a fellow barrister, Mohandas Gandhi.

The next round of conferences was held in London, and both Ambedkar and Gandhi attended. In 1942 Abedkar was appointed to the Viceroy's Executive Council where he served until Indian independence, working for the rights of workers and common laborers.

After India declared independence and the Constitution had been drafted, Ambedkar and Gandhi began to disagree over the idea of separate electorates for the lower castes. Ambedkar was persuaded that only by holding separate elections for "untouchables" could they hope to gain a voice in the policies and plans of their country. Gandhi went on a fast to protest that idea. Ambedkar responded angrily that Gandhi did not fast over the formation of separate electorates for Muslims, Christians, and Sikhs. Why would he fast because the "untouchables" also wanted to be able to elect representatives and run for government office?

In 1947, he was called to join the seven-person Committee to draft a constitution for free India, and he agreed to serve as the committee's chairman. Each giving excuses, the other six members could not (or would not) serve, so Ambedkar was left to draft the Constitution of India single-handedly. With few changes, the constitution, as drafted by Ambedkar, passed the Indian legislature on November 6, 1949.

He was appointed by the Prime Minister of the new legislature to serve as Minister of Law, which he did for two years, his followers pronouncing him a "Modern Manu" (Lawgiver). In 1951 he resigned in order to run for legislature from his old district near Mumbai and was defeated. The entire world was shocked by his defeat. He ran in a different district and won, serving in the legislature and championing a 1953 bill to punish the practice of untouchability. Perpetrators, caught and sentenced, would pay fines, be dismissed from their jobs, lose their professional licenses, or even go to prison.

Dr Babasaheb (beloved) Ambedkar died on 14 October 1956. Thirty-four years later he was awarded the highest national honor, "Barat Ratna."

Born in a caste—lowest of the low—Bimrao Ramji Ambavedkar followed a strong spirit and brilliant mind to the highest honors of his people and became Dr B.R. Ambedkar. People said it was a sin to offer him water, and if he sat on a chair, it would become unclean. His personal life was miserable, he was totally rejected by the unenlightened elites of his country, deprived of his first wife and sons by disease at a very early age, and foiled time and again by the barriers of caste. Yet he was the lion-hearted man who fought for equality and justice for *all* humanity.

Dr Babasaheb Ambedkar, the first Dalit (the lowest of the untouchables) to take political leadership, inspired the lowest levels of civil society to aspire to political activity as well. In his words, "Ours is a battle not for wealth or power. It is a battle for freedom. It is a battle for the reclamation of human personality" (Ambedkar, 2001, Preface).

Following the life, writings, and teachings of Dr Ambedkar, a number of NGOs sprang up in the 1980s and 90s. Among them was the collective for Dalitbahujan (Dalit majority) empowerment and eventually a cooperative in the state of Andhra Pradesh called Ankuram-Sangaman-Poram (ASP). Of this phase of civil society, Dr Vithal Rajan, a retired Professor of Economics from the London School of Economics living now in Hyderabad, commented, "I think with this new group of NGOs, like ASP, we have finally punched a hole in the old system and can now grow very rapidly. Visit us again next year to see what we have been able to do" (personal interview, January, 2005).

The constitution formally banned the caste system. This was the "talk." The "walk," unfortunately, led down the same rutted road the Indo-European culture has walked for millennia, the road of hierarchy and social discrimination. Eventually it has led to violent conflict and a painful gap between the very rich and the abject poor. The caste and class systems live on in the hearts, minds, and behavior of large numbers of people, in India and the United States alike. Racism is outlawed in the US, yet it still continues at every level of society.

To illustrate how caste and class work, a gentleman in Secunderabad, Dr Kurian, tells a story from his days as a school boy.[1] He was not of the *Dalitbahujan* (the lowest "untouchable" castes) but his best friend was. Kurian was always frustrated, because his friend was just a bit better in school work. He was a hard worker. His English was better. His understanding and facility with mathematics was better. His grasp of social studies excelled. In fact his friend ran far out in front of his class, with Kurian running a rather distant second. Try as he might, Kurian was never able to match his friend's achievements. Still they were best friends.

Even though caste distinctions were strictly illegal, the habits of discrimination remained in the culture. When Kurian and his friend both graduated, his friend with top honors, they went separate ways and their paths never crossed until many years later. When they chanced to meet each other, Kurian was the chairman of the board of a large company; his friend, on the other hand, was a common clerk, just managing to stay above the poverty line. Caste made all the difference.

Caste and class make more difference in the common culture of all Indo-Europeans than many in Europe, the United States, Britain and India are willing to admit. So it is remarkable that Dr Ambedkar could rise into a position of respected leadership. It is even more remarkable that a group of Dalits can make any progress at all in such a rigid caste system. The following account of cooperatives in a large network tells that remarkable story. Maybe that "hole in the system" has finally been punched.

A Network of Cooperatives in Andhra Pradesh

A Dalit man and his wife worked together in five villages of a district in the state of Andhra Pradesh in 1994. They signed up two other volunteers and began a retraining

---

1   Permission to use this story granted by Dr Kurian in interview, January 2005.

project with 29 women called "Jogins or Dedasis" (a class of temple prostitutes) and their 22 small girl children. The experience with them was intensive, but the impact of the work began a new life style for a large number of these women. Yet it seemed to the Dalit couple as if such work served merely as a band-aid on a huge wound caused by caste in Indian society. As successful as it was, they could not replicate their project because of a lack of human resources.

The answer came to them when they tried to explain their frustration to workers in other NGOs. Together they formed an NGO network for the district. In 1996 they gathered 11 NGOs together and called the new organization "DOWCALM." Later it became the statewide network called DAPPU, which stands for a Collective for Dalitbahujan Improvement, comprising 85 small and medium sized NGOs. They began repositioning these NGOs into two sets of entities, unions and cooperatives. The unions were organizations of workers focused on worker rights, and the cooperatives were an assorted set of agricultural enterprises, women's credit programs, and artisan guilds.

The Social Context

Indian society had long marginalized the Dalits and continued to do so within the context of a new democratic state. Managers of economic institutions, operating on the "power and might" principle, totally ignored the welfare of their lower caste workers. Mechanization of agriculture threatened the traditional families and community farms with extinction, and farmers began to sell their farms to large agricultural concerns. All this started the Indian people on a downward spiraling road to migration and occasional low-paid work on the larger farms. Custom nearly always barred the Dalits from accessing government institutions and they had no access at all to commercial banks. The "lower castes" were stereotyped by the banking community as chronic loan defaulters without collateral.

The lower castes saw no way open to them except to build their own institutions that would furnish them more respectable identities and enhance their resource base. In the mid 1980s some Dalit NGOs began small programs of women's thrift and credit on the Grameen model. The success of that cooperative model proved that Dalits were indeed "bankable." "It helped them build assets, increase incomes, and reduce their vulnerability to economic stress" (Neelaiah, 2004, 4).

Why Choose the Cooperative Model for the Dalitbahujan?

The coalition of NGOs were familiar with the cooperative model through recently formed global networks of NGOs and deliberately chose that model to form their Dalit-based network. By 1996 they had chartered a new cooperative named Ankuram-Sangaman-Poram (ASP). The cooperative model promised to bring "…freedom from poverty, illiteracy, and accessibility to the markets" (Neelaiah, 2004, 4).

In Telugu the word *ankuram* means "groups"; *sangamam* is a gathering or "coalition"; and *poram* refers to a leather-working tool, a shoe last. The organization works strictly for the Dalitbahujan castes. Dalits are the lowest level of "untouchables," and bahujan (meaning majority) refers to a combination of the dalits, the so-called

Scheduled Castes (SC), the Scheduled Tribes (ST), and the Backward Caste (BC). The Scheduled Castes and Scheduled Tribes are "scheduled" in the sense of being identified specifically by India's constitution. The dalits were totally unrecognized by official documents. Presently the combination of these castes comprises well over 60 percent of India's total population.

It is interesting that, since the organization of ASP, members of these "lower" castes are beginning to be proud of their identity and, inspired by the teaching of Dr Ambedkar, fully intend to assume prominent leadership in government and business. They could do this by providing a base for social action from within the community and a vehicle for building their own institutions and community identity; thus they could ignore the rules of the Standard Economic Model which drove the rest of India's economy.

All of this was accomplished through a cooperative model that would free the "lower" castes from the tyranny of the political and economic power of a small and corrupt elite class. In a very short time, less than ten years, ASP has attracted the attention of prominent members of the nation's secretariat. In a frontispiece of ASP's 2003-2004 Report, Chief Secretary, Dr Mohan Kanda of the state of Anhra Pradesh, writes, "The organization has taken a welcome lead in building a cooperative movement comprised of the poorest of poor families ... and ... this year will see a massive increase in bank-lending to the poor ... I wish them all success in the future" (ASP 2003-2004 Report, facing iv).

Organization and Strategic Plans for the New Cooperative Network

The base of ASP is built on its members organized in small rural villages and a few very small urban groups. These groups of 15-20 members, ages 18 to 45, called Self-Help Groups (SHGs), cluster into independent Mutually Aided Cooperative Societies (MACS). The small groups begin local projects with the help of very small unsecured loans using the Grameen (village) system begun in Bangladesh (see Chapter 4).

Each small group sends two leaders to comprise its regional MACS, meeting every two weeks. Although MACS are totally independent in their decisions, they create many collaborative linkages among each other. Each MACS has its own set of officers and, in some cases, staff. These small groups, clustered into MACS, form the heart and soul of the organization. Each MACS also sends five representatives to a general council that meets periodically to discuss policy issues and logistics (see chart below).

The rest of the organizational chart shows the support network, CEO, Board of Directors, Departments, and Special Projects. The Board of Directors, made up of 12 to 13 delegates elected from the MACS, creates general policy for the organization, and hires the CEO. Four other persons also sit on the board, a representative from the unions (APOVUU), a representative from DAPPU, one permanent invitee, and a representative from the Advisory Committee (*ex officio*). The invitee and The Advisory Committee are all professionals and experts in micro-finance or cooperative organization/policy. Council and Board make all policy decisions by consensus. The most striking aspect of the organizational chart (see Figure 5.1) is that it appears upside-down compared to the usual corporate organization. The village people sit on top and are, in fact, in charge, hiring their own staff, by the representatives, the staff

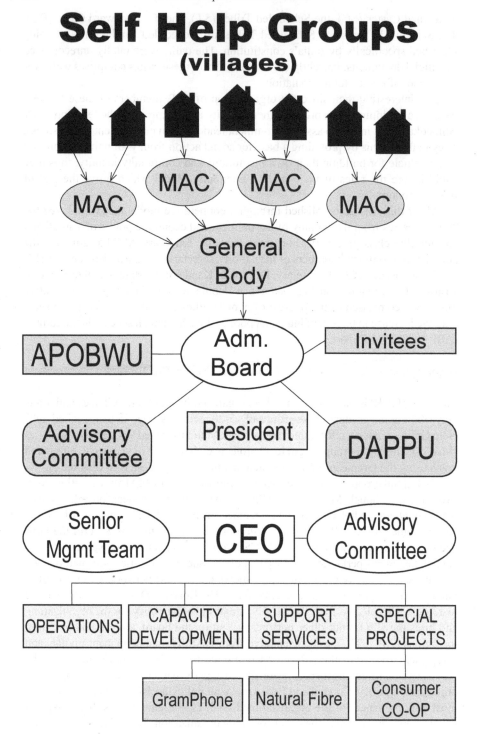

Figure 5.1   ASP Organizational Chart

of MACS and all officers and staff down through the organization. They invite all their "experts" to advise but not vote on decisions.

In addition to the internal loans made by the MACS, the SHGs, and ASP, the Board forms partnerships to help finance these loans. As of March 31 (end of fiscal year), 2004, there were 25 million rupees (Rs) in loans from eight different commercial banks in the state of Andhra Pradesh. The members from the villages also supervise the formation and operation of cooperatives, listed under special projects in the organizational chart. Currently (March, 2005), these new enterprises include GramPhone, a cell phone system especially for members; Natural Fibre, an artisan cooperative that makes attractive containers out of natural fibers; and a Consumer Co-op, a cooperative store selling food, notions, and other merchandise.

The strategic plan also includes (1) interfacing with Dalit mass organizations, (2) engaging in rights struggles, (3) attaining gender equity, (4) recruiting and training Dalit leadership, (5) developing entrepreneurs, (6) providing insurance and more social security to staff and members, (7) maintaining financial viability, and (8) maintaining total transparency and accountability.

Where is ASP Today?

ASP has organized in 12 of the 22 districts in Andhra Pradesh, with MACS in 108 mandals (large subdivisions of the state). These MACS organizations contain 10,000 small groups with a total of 150,000 members. Loans disbursed from ASP now total Rs. 5.21 Crore (US$1 million). The total of internal loans from MACS/SHGs has surpassed Rs. 10 Crore (US$2.2 million).

Currently outstanding loans to ASP from external banks total about 25 million Rs (US$543,000). These loans are payable to four different commercial banks. With total earnings, including a grant from Ford Foundation, totaling 28 million Rs (US$600,000), ASP's Debt/Earnings ratio stands at 0.90, far lower than most commercial banks. Net current assets stand at 53 million with 31 million in cash surpluses. Of the 150,000 members there are currently (Jan, 2005) over 10,000 borrowers. These externally audited figures present a respectably solvent and successful picture for ASP.

Goals for the Future

Immediate Objectives   For the present, plans are to keep the organization within its twelve present districts, made up of 130 mandals, but to expand the number of self-help groups to 27,443 with a total of 400,000 members. The principal objective is to increase the number of borrowers from the present number of just over 10,000 to 125,000. This would mean a total loan disbursement of 60 Crores (about US$13 million). In addition, ASP plans to cover all of its 400,000 members under micro-insurance.

Challenges   The Board of Directors plans to reorganize so that all Board members are either members of the cooperative or direct stake holders in the operation. The

Board then will conduct a thorough review of cooperative principles. The Advisory Committee also has suggested that the Board develop and implement a set of clearly written norms for administrative behavior. There should, for instance, be no discretionary powers available to officers of the groups in making loans. Everyone should follow the same specific rules in order to prevent any patronage in the administration of loans. The available loan fund needs to be raised to 100 Crores (US$22 million) and be allotted for optimal use. As the organization grows larger, it will need to devote more attention to the development of healthy relationships between the rights-based Dalit organizations and the cooperatives. Also there are challenges to maintain good relationships between the management and the governing bodies.

One of the most serious challenges, as in all cooperative organizations, is to maintain a strong commitment to the principles and mission of cooperativism. There is a strong tendency to revert to the surrounding economy, including a relaxation into non-participation of members in serious decision making, as cooperatives grow larger. Focusing attention on the mission and culture of the organization, while training management staff and new members, should be a high priority. Refresher courses for both groups (members and management) also must be available on a regular basis. The Board may need to create a new management division "Staff and Member Capacitation" to achieve these goals. It would be sad if all the work up to now were lost through a deterioration of the cooperative spirit.

In most of these challenges the leaders of ASP see real opportunities. There is now opportunity and adequate scope for replication of this model in other parts of the nation. It is possible at this time to create a non-commercial finance company for greater internal self-sufficiency and for enhanced credit-worthiness. Also, the organization is now well enough established to attract and train more Dalit professionals.

Common to every other part of the world, increasing urbanization is a growing problem for the largely rural based village system. In the streets and public markets of Hyderabad, for instance, are a large number of "professional" beggars. They are principally women who ask for money for their sick babies. ASP sees the urban beggar population as one of its next challenges to organize cooperatively. Whether or not the beggar-women will respond to a microfinance opportunity remains to be seen.

If there is even a modicum of success in meeting these challenges, the government and other financial institutions in India will see ASP as a good business venture and a viable target for investment. ASP is now discussing the possibility of creating public, non-member and non-voting shares up to 49 percent of its outstanding shares. This, of course, would increase the challenge to maintain the mission and participation of the group and would reemphasize the need for firm commitment and control by the members.

Two Groups Still Left Behind

In the early economic development programs of the Indian government and state governments, two rather large populations were left behind, the fisher people and the dairy farmers. These large groups live mostly in southern and western India, in the states of Goa, Karnataka, Kerala, and Tamil Nadu. This southwestern region has become very important to the future economic development of India.

Goa

The state of Goa has a distinctive history, colonized and maintained by Portuguese traders instead of by British government functionaries. During the mercantile era, in the sixteenth and seventeenth centuries, the west coast was a major stop for trade between Europe and the Far East. The Portuguese settled and maintained much of the southwest coast as a strong colony, primarily for trading in spices and timber. The tiny state of Goa became a free and separate country and remained so for four decades after independence, until it became the 23rd state of India in the 1990s. Portuguese is still spoken widely in Goa, and Roman Catholicism is the major religion.

Kerala

About 300 kilometers to the south of Goa lies the northern border of the state of Kerala, a slender strip of very fertile land between the coast and a range of mountains called the Western Ghats. The Ghats, although not particularly high, are rugged and effectively isolate the coastal regions from the broad inland areas of India.

Even before independence in 1945, the Communist Party was gaining strength among the population of Kerala. The British paid less attention to this somewhat isolated region, marked off by the mountain range and dominated by Portuguese traders. As a result of such isolation and the socialist doctrines of the Communist Party, Kerala's people are much more assertive, socially and politically, and on average more highly educated than the people of any other state of the Republic.

Kerala has achieved an impressively high life expectancy, low fertility rate, high literacy rate, and other favorable indicators of quality of life despite its low per capita income (World Bank, 1996). Such an achievement doubtless is a result of a high degree of income support and social services for the lower two deciles of the population. That, along with the absence of a very rich class, tends to lower a mean income statistic and still produce a relatively high quality of life. This supports the argument that a developing country need not wait for a high GDP in order to begin spending on health and education. Certainly a high per capita GDP, without an attendant high level of income and wealth equity, is a poor indicator of economic development (Sen, 46ff.).

Following independence, the Communist Party gained control of Kerala's government. This version of communism was much more democratic than the national socialist models of Leninism and Maoism. Statewide elections were held every five years, however, and a more conservative "neo-liberal" party defeated the Communist Party by a small margin in 1990. Since 1990, the pattern of state control has been first the communists and then the neo-liberals, with a change in administration and legislature every five years. This political situation provides a curious contradiction between a neo-liberal emphasis on transnational corporations with their version of "free trade" and the traditional communist hostility toward the capitalist model.

It is also curious that, with the traditional distrust of cooperatives by both capitalists and communists, the Kerala government has been so friendly toward the cooperative movement and has intentionally fostered its growth. One striking aspect of the Kerala government has been its strong fiscal and legal support of cooperativism. This support may be both a result and a cause of the singular successes of the cooperative model within the two "forgotten" populations, fishers and dairy producers.

Fishing   Southern Indian Federation of Fisherman Societies (SIFFS) follows the broad outlines of a cooperative association but differs in many significant ways from the usual model. So far all members and workers in the fishing industry have been men, but not every fisherman can be a member of a local society. Only an owner of a certain class of fishing boat, an "artisanal" boat, a small craft (14 to 20 feet long with a single sail or outboard motor), is qualified to become a full member. To join, the owner must be between the ages of 18 and 40 and cannot remain a member after the age of 60. Each boat requires a crew of four to five non-owner fishermen for the smaller boats and up to eleven or twelve for the somewhat larger artisanal boats. The owner/captain of a boat may be a member of SIFFS, but not the hired crew, who are engaged by the captain for specific expeditions. The captain member also owns the fishing equipment, sails, and outboard motors (OBMs).

The original impetus for SIFFS came from the church, and the cooperative model was inspired by the Dalit model in Andhra Pradesh. Because ASP's cooperative project in Andhra Pradesh had successfully reached the very poorest of the poor, it seemed like the model to use with the very poor fishermen. The cooperative would also be based in the villages and involve the women very strongly in micro-finance projects, even though they could not be members of the fishing society.

A local society is formed in a specific fishing village and, depending on the size of the village, may have up to 100 members. Each society then selects two of its members to serve on a federation board of directors, which hires the CEO, who, in turn, hires the federation's staff. The staff and CEO cannot be members of the cooperative since they cannot both serve as professional staff and own and operate fishing boats.

The legal status of the federation is as a "society" under the Society Registration Act in both the states of Kerala and Tamil Nadu. This arrangement is necessary because the federation does business in both states, and Kerala will not allow the organization to register as a cooperative; only a government enterprise can be called a cooperative. Still the basic nature of the federation is cooperative, because the boat owners are definitely the legal owners of SIFFS. A conversation with an older fisherman in the village of Mottum affirmed, "I am a member of the fisherman society and I certainly consider myself an owner of the society."

SIFFS hires auctioneers who arrive daily as the fishing boats come in from their expeditions and auction off the fish to the highest bidder. Thus the fishermen are not captive to a single buyer's fixed, low pricing. Of a society's daily take, members of the federation must contribute three percent to the district federation, two percent for savings to be deposited in their own local bank account for society contingencies and emergencies, and another five percent to any loan payments that may have been incurred. The rest, 90-95 percent goes to the fishermen. Any surpluses at the district level return to the fishermen each year as bonuses.

The federation requires that at least a minimum living wage be paid to non-member workers, and it provides repair services both for boats and equipment. The prices for these services are usually much lower than they would be for individual fishermen in the "open" market. There are plans now to provide federation-built boats and specially ordered motors for members. In addition, a high-tech group is researching low-cost communication equipment for the members. One of the challenges of the artisanal class boat is to maintain effective and dependable ship-to-shore communication.

Because of the superior marketing provided by the association of cooperative societies, membership is very popular. As of January, 2005, 120 societies served over 6,000 members in villages in three states: Kerala, Tamil Nadu, and Karnataka. The larger fishing industries present little competition, because they catch a larger species of fish, and the smaller fish that the artisanal boats bring in are in high demand everywhere. The auction system prevents buyers from fixing their own prices and allows the free market forces to operate; large commercial groups have no more status and power than individual families in bidding for the fish.

SIFFS's credit department issued more than 2,000 loans in the year 2004 with fish sales of over 30 Crores (US$ 6 million), a 21 percent increase over the previous year. But near the end of the year, on the day after Christmas, came the *tsunami* with waves 400 to 500 feet high, destroying entire villages even as far from the epicenter as the southern and western coasts of India.

The *tsunami* of 26 December 2004 destroyed entire villages where SIFFS members and their families lived. The cooperative structure, from its member savings, were able to replace boats, engines, and nets for surviving SIFFS members by mid-March of 2005. Private and commercial fishermen do not have the resources to accomplish this feat. Volunteer psychologists with training in trauma recovery, social workers, and SIFFS staff are working to reduce the remaining fisher communities' fear of returning to the sea for their livelihood. Thankfully the *tsunami* occurred on a Sunday, so there were no fishing boats on the open sea. On the other hand, entire families perished as their homes were destroyed, with them in it; the huge tidal wave inundated them within minutes and without warning.

The SIFFS cooperative structure has allowed fishermen and their families to catch up with the rest of the Indian economy. Those who were once forgotten by the new government have found their way, through the cooperative, into a stable and viable economy.

The Dairy Producers The geography of Kerala is unfriendly to all forms of agricultural activity. It is densely populated, and urban development has encroached on what little arable land is available. Family farm plots are much too small for grazing or for raising grasses and grains for feed. Therefore all feed must be imported from other states. A small farmer, as one individual, cannot afford the high cost of such an operation.

Economic development has proceeded much farther in Kerala than in any other state of the federation of Indian states. That makes the necessary daily wage for farm workers as high as Rs 180-200 per day, in contrast to the average farm wages of Rs 18-19 per day elsewhere in India. Also, family size has diminished in Kerala to an average of fewer than two children, further reducing the number of people to work on the farms. Finally, division of land to support offspring who want to remain in farming has reduced all family farm plots below a sustainable size.

Today, if a family owns animals at all, they cannot support more than two diary cows. In fact the average number of cows owned by individual farmers is 1.8. Some years ago, dairy farming in Kerala reached a crisis. No dairy farmer was able to sustain a family on the income from 1 or 2 cows. The idea of a cooperative was introduced on the west coast of India.

In the 1950s and 60s, a cooperative dairy system was developed in the nearby state of Gujarat, in a little town named Anand. The cooperative, named Amul, spread all over the state and throughout the area including Mumbai (Bombay) and has become one of the largest dairy producing enterprises in the world. The organizational pattern that made it such a success is now called the "Anand Pattern."

The Anand Pattern, developed by Dr Kurian, eliminates the middleman by bringing the organization of producers directly in contact with their consumers. Working together in cooperative mode, the producers make their own policy, shape their own development, and achieve an economy of scale to maximize the producers' incomes. A cooperative society of about 100-200 farmer members establish a dairy to which they bring their milk and receive payment daily. The producers set their price to provide the cost of dairy processing, incomes for themselves, and individual savings accounts.

In 1965, the capital city of Kerala, Thiruvananthapuram (Trivandrum for short), developed the City Milk Supply Scheme along the same lines as the Anand Pattern used by Amul. Dairy farmers were organized into "societies" in order to pool their resources. The first project of City Milk was to develop a higher yielding breed of cattle. After some research, a cross between the local breed and the Swiss Brown, called Sunandini, was created. A "Bull Station" was established by the state and funded by a grant from a Swiss NGO. Today, about 68 percent of all dairy cattle in Kerala are high-yielding Sunandini.

Operation Flood, a government sponsored program, has helped the dairy farmers in India to direct their own development, placing control of the resource in their own hands. A national milk grid now links milk producers in over 700 towns and cities, reducing seasonal and regional price variations while insuring that the producer receives a major share of the consumer's rupee. Operation Flood's main objectives include (1) increased milk production ("a flood of milk"), (2) augmented rural incomes, and (3) fair prices for consumers.

Operation Flood operated in three phases. Phase I (1970-1980) was financed by the sale of skimmed milk powder and clarified butter contributed by the European Union through the World Food Program. During this phase Operation Flood linked 18 of India's "milksheds" with four major metropolitan areas, Delhi, Mumbai (Bombay), Kolkata (Calcutta), and Chennai (Madras). Phase II (1981-1985) increased the number of milksheds to 136 and urban markets to 290. By the end of this phase, the operation comprised a self-sustaining system of 43,000 village cooperatives linking 4.25 million milk producers. Phase III (1986-1990) enabled dairy cooperatives to expand and strengthen an extended infrastructure of veterinary first-aid, feed supplies, artificial insemination services, and intensified member education.

In 1976, during Phase I of Operation Flood, Kerala's legislature created the Land Development and Marketing Board, which set up markets for selling dairy products from the City Milk project both inside and outside Kerala. The Anand model succeeded as well for City Milk as it did for Amul, and dairy cooperative societies began to replicate rapidly throughout the coastal area.

In 1980, as a part of Operation Flood, Phase II, the dairy cooperatives began to spread over India under the encouragement of a newly formed National Development Board (NDB). In Kerala, Operation Flood II helped to reorganize the project, and Kerala formed Cooperative Milk Marketing Federation, Ltd. (MILMA)—again according to the Anand Pattern. Grants from the state government's Operation Flood II provided about 30 percent of the capital necessary. Loans from donors and banks made up the remaining 70 percent.

The individual dairy farmers in each district, each producing a certain number of liters a day for 90 days, have formed a society called Anand Pattern Cooperative Society (APCOS). Some APCOS now have up to 200 members. A member family brings milk to the dairy each day and receives payment. A small percentage of the price goes to the APCOS and another percentage goes into a personal savings account for the family. With its percentage, the APCOS provides a low-priced feed supply, a veterinary service, and a business consultation.

The first APCOS were registered on 30 September 1981 and new units have been forming continuously since. The entire cooperative enterprise is divided into districts that are clustered into three regional "unions" made up of representatives from all the APCOS. In March, 2004, there were 880 APCOS in the Trivandrum regional union (4 districts), 861 in the Middle regional union of Kerala (4 districts), and 819 in the North (6 districts).

A general governing board of 14 members is composed of 9 farmer representatives (three from each of the three regional unions) elected by the APCOS and 5 government appointees, 3 from the state of Kerala and 2 from the national government. The board meets regularly once a month with the CEO in attendance *ex officio.* On paper, the board is to decide by majority rule, but in practice virtually all decisions are by consensus.

Each year APCOS continue to form, and at the end of March, 2004 (the fiscal year), 2,560 primary cooperatives encompassed 706,000 members, 10 dairies capable of handling 850,000 liters of milk per day, 14 milk chilling plants, two cattle feed plants, a milk powder plant, a well established training center, and 8,000 distribution outlets. Each day, the APCOS delivered milk and milk products to the 8,000 outlets run by private owners, trained and approved by MILMA.

The farmers characterize their organization as "…very democratic…truly an organization of producers, run by the producers, and functioning for the producers." The members genuinely feel a strong sense of ownership and pride in the cooperative. The private owners of the outlets also feel a close relationship to the cooperative, akin to membership. Everywhere in Kerala, in every city square and every town center there is a MILMA milk product outlet.

The financial state of MILMA is very strong and growing at the rate of about 10 percent each year since its inception, even during the years of economic slowdown experienced by other sectors of the economy. Gross income in 2003-2004 was Rs 1.138 billions. Sale of products alone yielded Rs 1 billion, broken down as nearly Rs 300 million in milk products and Rs 700 million in cattle feed.

The original capitalization loans taken out in the early 1980s have been repaid and new loans approved for expansion purposes. Current debt (March 2004) rests at Rs 79 million.

These figures indicate about a half of one percent debt/earnings ratio. Such figures reveal a particularly solvent and expanding enterprise.

Challenges for the future include continually diminishing land holdings by the member farmers, shrinking family size, and high costs of hired labor. Farmers still must deal with increasing costs of inputs such as feed and concentrates. Due to the demand for milk increasing more rapidly than the local supply can satisfy it, there is continuing need for procurement of outside milk. The farmers also worry about the impending crossfire between globalization, with its neo-liberal trade policies, and the cooperative mission.

Economic challenges include recent shifts in demand for exports from India toward products like rubber, cocoa, and cardamom. Filling these demands tends to pull workers and capital away from the dairy industry. In addition, hired hands are becoming difficult to find even at increased wages, because more and more day laborers work in other markets and outside India, primarily in countries of the Middle-East. For example, salaries in the Persian Gulf area are considerably higher than they are in India—even in Kerala. As a result, the economy of India is becoming increasingly dependent upon workers abroad sending their wages home. Add to this the fact that the costs of feed, concentrates, and other dairy sector inputs have risen more rapidly than the income from milk products in the last couple of years.

Although the pressures of large transnational dairy concerns have not yet been felt in Kerala, MILMA is aware that most of their economic challenges arise from the increasing pressure of globalization from above on the general economy. It remains to be seen what kind of challenges will arise in the next few years, especially if the present neo-liberal government continues after the 2005 elections.

Conclusions

Three examples of cooperative enterprise in India have a number of factors in common: (1) Small village groups learn to direct their own development. (2) The cooperative groups use principals of micro-finance to capitalize their enterprises. (3) All kinds of cooperatives are finding ways to replicate themselves, and see themselves spreading over increasingly large areas of India.

The most distinctive element in the Indian cooperative experience involves the caste system. The Dalits (the lowest level of the "untouchable" castes), long barred from the main stream of economy in India, can now find ways to build a satisfactory life through microfinance and cooperative projects of their own. Ankuram Sangamam Poram (ASP) cooperatives offer a full economic system for the poorest of the poor.

These village cooperative "self-help groups" are organized and directed by the people. They have side-stepped the Standard Economic Model and have provided their own living.

In all three types of cooperatives described, the ASP agricultural cooperatives, the fishing cooperatives, and the dairy cooperatives, members use the principals of micro-finance to capitalize their economic projects. These projects were all small enough that they needed very little capital, and what was needed was available in the form of small loans. All three cooperative groups have grown considerably and are able to support large numbers of members and their families. The fishing cooperatives found that they could survive a serious catastrophe, the *tsunami* of December, 2004. Because of their practice of regular saving, the fishermen had enough set aside so that they could replace destroyed boats, motors, and nets within a few months after the total destruction of their fleets.

All three of these models in India have been able to grow and replicate themselves over large geographical areas, and at the same time they were able to maintain their commitment to the mission of cooperativism. So far ASP and MILMA have been able to operate to some extent in the urban as well as rural areas, and they have all survived the process of corporate globalization by keeping in communication with other grassroots organizations in India and around the world. For the poorest of the poor in India, cooperativism is their best hope for ensuring a reasonable lifestyle in the future.

References

Ambedkar, B. (2000). *Writings and Speeches, Vol. 6.* Education Department of Maharashtra, India.

Keer, Dhananjay (2003) *Dr Ambedkar: Life and Mission.* Pradash Private Publishers, Delhi, India.

Leach, Edmund (1990). Aryan invasions over four millennia, in Ohnbuki-Tierney (Ed.), *Culture through time: Anthropological approaches.* Stanford University Press, Stanford, CA, 227-245.

Neelaiah, J. (2004), "Making the Difference ... Where It Matters Most" Power-Point presentation. Ankuram-Sangamam-Poram, Secunderabad, India.

Sen, Amartya (1999), *Development As Freedom*, Oxford University Press.

Ward, Geoffrey C. (1997), India: Fifty Years of Independence. *National Geographic*, Vol 191, No. 5, 2-57.

Chapter 6

Mondragón: The Basque Cooperative Experience

If we don't sing out
Then who? The Sphinx? The shaggy
Arrasate sheep?   (Haiku by BL & BF)

Nestled among the high mountains of the western Pyranees in north-central Spain and spilling down into the rocky coast of the Bay of Bizcaia, rests a land known as Basque Country. The Spanish still refer to this area as "País Vasco," although to most natives of the area, it will always be Euskal Herria. A more common term, Euskadi, was coined by nationalists near the end of the 1800s. The Basque people enjoy a measure of freedom from the Spanish government and have their own participatory form of democracy similar to that found among other relatively isolated peoples of the world.

The Basque language, Euskara, differs so greatly from other Indo-European tongues that its origins still baffle linguists. The culture, as well, has a distinctive flavor, radiating an energy and self-confidence doubtless born of the area's mountainous isolation and the self-sufficient life of centuries of herding sheep and building fishing ships.

Throughout much of the medieval era (1000-1450 AD) the Basque people were constantly torn between the ambitions of rival warlords. País Vasco (Basque Country) occupies a region at the western end of the Pyranees mountains and along the Bay of Bizcaia in Spain, but a small population of Basque people still live on the northern side of the Pyranees in France. Today the major Basque population is contained in five northern Spanish states: Navarra, Rioja, Gipuskoa, Araba, and Bizcaia. In the late fifteenth century, the Castillian royalty gained a modicum of control over the territory, but prevailed only with great difficulty. The state of Navarra operated as a separate kingdom until 1512. Even now, Navarra, Rioja, and the three original provinces of País Vasco—Gipuskoa, Araba, and Bizcaia—express their independence by forming the Comunidad Autónoma Vasca (CAV). These autonomous communities reached agreement for a broad autonomy (*fuero*) three centuries ago at a conference in Cádiz.

The first monarch to repeal the *fuero* agreement, Napoleon in the early nineteenth century, was also the first to propose the idea of a central Spanish state. The more conservative Basques considered such an idea anathema and tended to support the reactionary Don Carlos, brother of king Fernando VII. When Fernando again (later in the nineteenth century) scuttled the democratic Constitution of Cádiz, Don Carlos laid claim to the throne and began a full-scale war against the supporters of Fernando's daughter, Isabel. During this First Carlist War a violent anticlericalism broke out, religious orders were closed, and church lands were seized and auctioned off. As usual, the rich emerged the only beneficiaries of these confiscations and auctions.

After the Second Carlist War (1872-1876) the new constitution, created by a coalition of the Church and large landowners, stripped all of the provinces except Navarra of their autonomy. This proved to be a huge mistake, because, in 1894, the Basque Nationalist Party (PNV) formed and proposed a new plan for independence that began a long and violent struggle. Support for the plan was never uniform, however, as Navarra and the Basque province of Araba contained large contingents of Castillians; the strife continued and lasts even until today. Navarra in particular, with its *fuero* rights still intact, had little to gain by supporting the Nationalist Party's plan.

When the Spanish civil war erupted in 1936, most of the Basque provinces tended to support the Republicans, but the conservatives in Navarra and Araba backed the fascist contender, Francisco Franco. During the war and after Franco's victory in 1939, the provinces of Bizcaia and Gipuskoa paid a heavy price for their support of the Republic. The historic event that still sticks in the Basque people's minds was when, on April 26, 1937, at the behest of Adolph Hitler, Franco bombed the community of Gernika. Gernika was the ancient political and spiritual capital of Basque Country, where the original idea of *fueros* was first conceived. The bombing happened on a Monday, a market day. Thousands of people died. The event is memorialized by one of the most famous of Pablo Picasso's paintings, "Guernica." The idea of the bombing was to break the backs of the Republican supporters, but time, as usual, proved otherwise. After Franco's death in 1975, the Republicans assumed office quietly and restored some of the Basque autonomy.

The Mondragón Cooperatives

In early 1941, only two years after the fascist victory and while the National Socialists were gathering "power" in Germany and claiming *Lebensraum* in central Europe, a twenty-six year old priest, freshly ordained, assumed his post in Mondragón. Mondragón is in the province of Gipuskoa, in the upper Deba River valley near the center of Basque country. Fr José María Arizmendiarrietta, or Arizmendi, as he was affectionately (and more easily) called, was a socially committed but hardly charismatic priest. His appointment was as a youth pastor in the parish. At that time fewer than 5,000 people lived in what is now called the "old town."

Although the war economy had already enriched the elite classes of central Europe, it was mostly at the expense of the ordinary folk of more modest circumstances. In fact, the primary social problem affecting the youth of Mondragón, Arizmendi noticed, was a severe rate of unemployment. He and five local engineers decided to start a school of technology to help fit upcoming youth for jobs in the local steel mill.

Arizmendi was aware of the progressive, early cooperatives in Catalunya (the province in eastern Spain where the prosperous modern city of Barcelona now is) and the experience of Rochdale, England, in the middle 1800s. They founded the school on what he and the engineers called the "third way," a model built on the best principles of cooperation and democratic participation. All of this activity took place during the most reactionary, violent, and autocratic period of European history, World War II.

Soon a large manufacturing corporation, the Mondragón Steel Works, announced the closing of the large mill near the center of the town, and the community realized that hundreds of jobs would be lost. Although not a commanding public speaker, Arizmendi, by personal contact and persuasion, convinced the workers to purchase the steel mill and run it themselves as a cooperative. Eventually, capitalization became a problem, so in order to prevent the cooperative from selling its soul and issuing public stock, the road to failure of many earlier cooperative attempts, Arizmendi single-handedly obtained a charter for a cooperative bank. Thus, in 1959, the Caja Laboral Popular (Working People's Bank) was born, providing, through a growing fund of local deposits, sufficient capital for all the cooperative projects.

These first three stages of development were crucial: first the capacitation of workers through a technical training cooperative (Mondragón School of Technology), then the start of a cooperative steel manufacturing company (ULGOR, the forerunner of today's FAGOR) manufacturing paraffin based stoves, and third, the establishment of cooperative institution of financial credit (Caja Laboral). "Cooperation is an authentic integration of the person in the economic and social process, and it is central to a new social order; employees working cooperatively ought to unite around this ultimate objective, along with all who hunger and thirst for justice in the world of work" (Arizmendi, 1983, 175, trans. Cheney, 1999, 39).

In 1966, the cooperative group sent its first exports beyond the borders of Franco's Spain. Machine tools were in great demand, and FAGOR was uniquely fitted to supply that demand with some of the finest. The manufacture and distribution of machine tools, incidentally, provided an important economic impetus for advanced industrial development. Until the formation of the European Union (EU) in 1992, the Mondragón cooperatives enjoyed a unique and unchallenged place in the European economy.

In 1969 consumers and distributors formed a new cooperative, EROSKI (meaning "group buying"). EROSKI grew rapidly, and by the end of 1997 became the largest supermarket chain in Spain with over 200,000 consumer members. Currently, February 2005, all but 12 percent of its nearly 15,000 employees work full-time and, by the company rules, are also owner members. This represents a significant change from 1997, when the large number of temporary, part-time workers hovered around 50 percent.

In 1974, the cooperatives initiated a research and development group, Ikerlan, providing a fourth support leg for the enterprise. The consulting wing of Ikerlan now counts many significant EU corporations among its clients. That year, the cooperatives also saw their first and only strike. This strike was a very important event in Mondragón's history as it called attention to problematic power relations within the cooperatives. The strike was largely precipitated by the Management Council's downgrading a large number of jobs in an effort to achieve more "efficiency."

Company spokespersons claim that there is no such thing as management vis-à-vis labor within the co-ops and that a strike within the cooperatives makes no sense, because it is actually a strike of workers against themselves. Yet honesty would demand that problems be identified and corrected. Even the Catholic Church aligned itself with the strikers and criticized the company for a certain managerial elitism that distanced itself from the workers. The diocese of Vitoria stated openly that, "The virulence and crudeness of the cooperative leaders greatly surpasses that of the firms that they disrespectfully call capitalist" (Cheney, 44).

At that time, ULMA and two other cooperatives left the association, criticized the treatment of striking workers (a number of them were "fired," that is, relieved of their memberships and full-time jobs), and objected to the new name for the association, Mondragón Cooperative Corporation. In less than a year, however, the General Assembly—made up mostly of workers themselves—recanted and restored these "fired" workers to their original positions. These workers were all women, and that fact apparently embarrassed the assembly into reconsidering their earlier precipitous actions. Also, since 1997, ULMA and one other defecting group have returned to the fold; a third one is seriously considering returning.

A consensus, in discussions following the strike, concluded that the functions of the councils needed to be reevaluated. Also, some member owners remarked that the personnel/human-resource policies of the cooperatives, "…need to recognize the dignity and potential of the individual person in attempting to maximize production" (Cheney, 46). As a result of these discussions, the cooperatives were completely restructured.

The New Organizational Structure

Currently (2005) the Mondragón complex of cooperatives consists of 218 companies with a total of over 70,000 full worker members distributed among 50 cities of the three Basque provinces and 21 countries around the world. The new structure divides the cooperatives into three broad categories: (1) Industrial Sector, composed of 87 production cooperatives; (2) Financial Sector with a cooperative bank, Caja Laboral, an insurance company, Seguros Lagun Aro, and a holding company for retirement funds, Lagun Aro, E.P.S.V.; and (3) Distribution Sector with seven consumer cooperatives, EROSKI for general product distribution (including the largest supermarket chain in Spain) and seven agricultural groups. The Technical University and Ikerlan, the research cooperative, still support the cooperative enterprises.

With such a large number of independent cooperatives, the Assembly found it necessary to link them all within a single cooperative corporation called Mondragón Corporación Cooperativa (MCC). A new General Assembly, governing the entire cooperative corporation, consists of 650 worker members meeting annually to determine policy and to review the work of the various councils and commissions; the Permanent Commission; the General Council; Commission on Vigilance (fiscal responsibilities); Governing Council (Consejo Rector, the general on-going governing body made up of 100 worker members); the new Social Council (established to review management-worker relations and worker concerns); and finally, the Directorship (composed of the CEO and an advisory council, both appointed and closely supervised by the Governing Council). See organizational chart, Figure 6.1.

In addition to the above overall structure, there are numerous *consejos* (councils) within each individual cooperative. The *Consejo Rector* is the principle governing

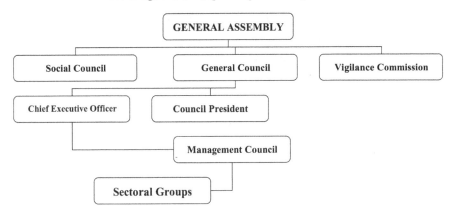

Figure 6.1   Basic Mondragón Cooperative Organizational Chart

- *The General Assembly, Social Council, and General Council all consist of worker/owner delegates from the cooperatives.*
- *The Vigilance Commission is the financial organ of the entire cooperative structure and consists of treasurer, accountants, and internal auditors. NOTE: the Basque government also requires biennial outside audits.*
- *The Sectoral Groups (total=120) consist of (1) 87 Industrial Cooperatives; (2) 1 consumer co-op (EROSKI); (3) 4 Agricultural Cooperatives; (4) 1 large credit cooperative (Caja Laboral); (5) 13 Research Cooperatives; (6) 8 Educational Cooperatives, including 3 universities and 4 Basque Language Schools (consisting of 36 different individual schools); and (7) 6 Service Cooperatives, including holding companies and insurance carriers. In additional, the Mondragón Cooperative Corporation (MCC) is in the process of incorporating 17 new housing cooperatives.*
Sources: MCC (2003), MCC(2005), Catalá (1996).

body of each cooperative on a day-to-day basis. The general membership of the cooperative elects director-members of this council for four-year terms, overlapping, in order both to provide continuity of council membership and to ensure a regular rotation of directors. The *Consejo de Dirección* is the management council and is chaired by the General Manager. It is composed of managers of various divisions of the cooperative. All of these managers, including the General Manager, are hired by the *Consejo Rector.* Probably the most important council from the point of view of the "shop floor" is the *Consejo Social.* The presence of this social council recognizes that the management council (*Consejo de Dirección*) is not the proper group to deal with concerns of the shop floor and that participation of the workers should not end with membership in the General Assembly, or even with the *Consejo Rector.*

The three broad categories of cooperatives also have councils that provide pillars for three of the four corners of the structure (see Figure 6.2). Several institutions for research and development now provide a very important fourth pillar. When the research groups were first formed, there were only three small groups, but as economic pressures from globalization and the new United Europe increased, the Assembly formed nine more, because MCC needed to find new ways of "competing" in the world market.

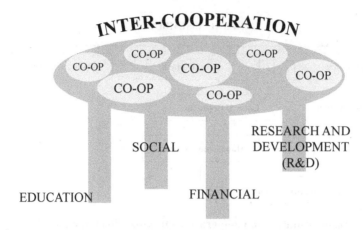

Figure 6.2   Four Legs of the Inter-cooperative Structure

The best way to ensure MCC's leadership in the world market seemed to be to increase the amount of innovative research. For example, in the early days, the paraffin-based heater and stove became FAGOR's leading product. Soon technology of stoves had outpaced these products and FAGOR began to lose money. Through high-tech research, FAGOR now produces a cooking stove based on electrical induction technology. The research division of MCC supports 13 highly innovative groups, and each cooperative in the Industrial Sector is encouraged to establish its own research group.

After 1997, the General Assembly perceived that communications within the rapidly growing organization were becoming problematic. Communications improved dramatically when in 2002 the General Assembly, on the advice of the Governing Council, established "interest groups" among worker members with similar professional interests. Attendance at General Assembly concurrently improved noticeably from around 60 percent in 1997 to over 80 percent in 2004. The interest groups now discuss all kinds of problems from worker relationships to future challenges.

Worker members now almost unanimously report that conditions are vastly improved and that they would work for MCC even if the pay scale were significantly lower than the general labor market. Pay rates plus profit sharing for most members at this time keep up with or exceed the going labor market. The only exception involves compensation for upper managers and the CEO. According to a current company rule, a division manager's salary and a CEO's total compensation can be no higher than 70 percent of the general market rate for large companies. The Management Council began discussions in the early 1990s to increase to CEO's income by the addition of something like stock options, but the Social councils and Interest Groups strongly objected, and management dropped the issue.

In practice, the actual salaries of upper level management are much lower than the "70 percent of market rate." FAGOR's manager, for example, receives only about 7 times, the bank manager (Caja Laboral) receives 8 times, and the rest receive only about 4.5 times the lowest pay of their groups. The CEO, at his own request, makes only 9 times the lowest full-time wage in the entire corporation. For a little perspective, the typical CEO in the United States draws nearly 600 times the lowest full-time wage in the company.

As an adjunct to the new structure, MCC introduced a number of new provisions for the functioning of the organization:

- Reallocate staff among the cooperative to obtain better staff-worker relations.
- Restructure results to ensure an optimum workload, especially
    1. within sectoral groups (from 15 percent to 40 percent) and
    2. within corporation funds in MCC (from 10 percent to 12 percent).
- Maintain solidarity in profit distribution, using more for worker and staff compensation.
- Retain a portion of profit for capitalization.
- Increase funds for continued worker compensation in cases of loss (up to 2 percent).
- Realign the price of initial share purchase for more equitable load on new workers and staff.
- Maintain solidarity in remunerating managers.
- Increase transparency in reporting all data to MCC Headquarters.
- Eliminate internal competition between co-ops within MCC.

(MCC, 2005)

MCC appears to be very diligent in maintaining the original principles of its cooperative mission and has succeeded in answering one of the most severe criticisms of the corporation: that the Management Council was seriously considering increasing top managers' salaries and share/option ownerships in order to compete with other large companies. The company has apparently concluded that there is no empirical evidence that a CEO's performance is correlated with the size of compensation. Rather, MCC seems to have discovered that high management performance is actually much more related to the manager's commitment to the cooperative's values rather than to any compensation that can be offered.

At this time a couple of anomalies have emerged in the corporate structure, new developments that diverge noticeably from the cooperative model. The Directorate has recently created or become associated with a small number of standard corporations as subsidiaries of MCC. Most of them are nothing but holding companies created to provide capital for their sectors. MCC, through the Basque government, chartered the insurance sector as an SA (Sociedad Autónomo), a standard private corporation, because of certain restrictions of Basque law. Also MCC has partnered with ONCE (a public finance corporation) and BBKA (a public bank) to create GESPA.

GESPA originally emerged in order to provide a distribution center for partnering public corporations. Plans are in process for changing the structure of GESPA to resemble a cooperative more closely, with democratic worker participation and more equitable pay scales in the subsidiaries. At present (February, 2005), 66 percent of GESPA is owned by MCC, 24 percent by ONCE, and 10 percent by BBKA, so substantial control is in the hands of MCC. They are now negotiating partnering relationships with corporations in EU, Brazil, Mexico, USA, and 17 other foreign countries. Production centers have already been established in all of these countries. It should be understood that these foreign production centers have not caused a reduction in worker memberships within the Basque provinces. In fact, local memberships are still growing but, because of global economic conditions, at a somewhat slower rate than in the 1990s.

Reasons for Mondragón's Success

Certainly there is no question that the Mondragón cooperatives have been remarkably successful. Between Cheney's 1997 study and the end of 2004, the number of member owners nearly doubled (from 38,000 to over 70,000). During that time, total sales increased from just over 6 billion to a little over 10 billion euros (nearly US$ 14 billion). The company advanced from the fifteenth to the seventh largest corporation in Spain and is now one of the largest multi-national corporations in the world.

Cultural Setting

Theorists have advanced several sets of reasons for this unparalleled success. Some have emphasized the system's uniqueness from a *cultural* standpoint. Whyte and Whyte (1991) provides the most complete literature on this subject. They point out the strong Basque cultural emphasis on self-reliance and, at the same time, a collective solidarity based on a staunch sense of national pride. They contend that these two cultural traits have produced a combination of individual enterprise and social collaboration.

The actual Euskadera wording of the Ten Principles in the constitution of the Mondragón cooperatives, approved in 1987, contains the word *elkartason* (or *solidaridad* in Spanish). This concept is certainly consistent with the principles of the International Cooperative Alliance (ICA, 1996). Although the word is explicitly used only to describe a commitment to wage equity, the last five principles as listed in the MCC constitution, Pay Solidarity, Group Cooperation, Social Transformation, Universality, and Public Education, all include the idea of "solidarity."

Other historic components of Mondragón's distinctive social and economic orientation include the strong opposition of the Basque people to the Franco regime. On the other hand, the communities warmly welcomed the extremely positive role of the Roman Catholic Church. While the Church itself provided no direct influence on the formation of the cooperatives, it contributed a strong impetus through Fr Arizmendi's tireless work. Also one should never underestimate the power, throughout the twentieth-century, of its stress on workers' rights and the ethics of social justice for workers to organize (*Rerum Novarum*, 1891).

Organizational Structure

Probably more important than cultural considerations is the organizational structure of the cooperatives with its strong network for cooperative and participatory governance. It was fortunate, if not by conscious design, that the cooperatives began with a technical school, now three universities, to ensure that member workers would be trained to operate an entrepreneurial effort without recourse to the hierarchical forms of a standard corporation. The so-called "secondary cooperatives" featuring the Caja Laboral and other financial organizations ensured that capital would be available when necessary. This method of capital formation was and is an essential part of the support system. It is important to recognize that during the years 1959 to 1986, Caja Laboral's entrepreneurial division, LKS, has presided over 100 new cooperative starts with only one failure (Cheney, 57).

The General Assembly, composed of representatives from members of all the working cooperatives, forms the key governing body of the Mondragón cooperatives. This assembly must study and approve all policies affecting the entire membership. The fact that attendance at its annual meeting has improved over that last few years should indicate that commitment to cooperativism has increased along with the company's growth and continued success.

More direct support groups reporting to the General Assembly, the *consejos*, provide a complex but sturdy system of participatory democracy. Attendance at monthly meetings of the *consejos* now averages nearly 100 percent. These councils are set up and operate both for the corporation as a whole and for each cooperative, and they are a direct way for worker-member-owners to supervise the management of their own corporate and cooperative enterprise.

George Cheney makes a very important point when he states, "I offer internal dynamism as one of the key factors in Mondragón's success" (Cheney, 62). The point is that one should not look only to the *structure* of the organization but to its *operation* for the ultimate answer to the "success" question. The entire complex system must be woven together for ongoing adaptation to external and internal conditions by a vital means of continual *communication*. The *consejos*, now bolstered by the new series of research cooperatives installed since Cheney's evaluation in 1997, provide such a direct, though complex, system of communication.

Communication

From the perspective of a communication specialist, eight qualities of an organizational structure—if maintained faithfully—are bound to make an enterprise a success. They are:

- Open meetings;
- Deep collaboration;
- Access to power;
- Free expression of minority opinions;
- Shared commitment to the culture or the organization;
- Fair treatment of one another;
- Consideration of the individual;
- Ongoing discussion and reevaluation (remaining open to change).

All of these components seem to be top priority for member workers in the Mondragón cooperatives. The Social Councils of some cooperatives were evaluated as relatively ineffective in the early 1990s. ULMA, which separated from the rest of

MCC in 1991, has significantly improved its Social Council since its return to the fold—principally by instituting worker "interest groups." Recent interviews with workers reveal a high degree of satisfaction with the openness of the organization as well as fairness of management in dealing with both workers who are members and the decreasing number of non-member and part-time workers.

The "interest groups," resembling the Japanese model of quality groups but focused on worker-management relationships as well as entrepreneurial future concerns, is a form now recommended for all of the cooperatives. Their implementation and ongoing impetus appears to be preventing the weaknesses found within the social councils of some of the cooperatives in the 1990s. Much improved worker attendance at the *consejos* and remarks made in interviews of workers for this current study would affirm that observation.

Finances

From a strictly economic point of view, the expansion and profitability of MCC has been exemplary over the last couple of decades. This success stems chiefly from two important factors, (1) the effectiveness of the cooperative bank, *Caja Laboral*, in providing a way to adjust available capital to satisfy emergent needs on a virtually immediate basis and (2) the initiation of the several research groups with their focus on the future markets and need for constant innovation.

Continued Dedication to Mission

The factors of good communication and the financial health of the organization would mean little if the original mission for justice in the work place had been abandoned. Probably more important than any other factor contributing to Mondragón's success are the early successes spawned by the organization's high level of commitment to success through the constant application of their basic principles. Conversations with worker members give a strong impression that their interest and sense of ownership is stimulated most by the successes of their company. Indeed, it may be in the last analysis that the most important principle the Mondragón experience teaches is simply that "Nothing succeeds quite like success."

Challenges for the Future

The main challenge for the future of the Mondragón cooperatives is to maintain the pace of its technological development and continue to show the superiority of cooperation in providing a reasonable living for its members and satisfying the demands of its market. A continual and related challenge is to maintain the high level of commitment and participation of its members. At present, excitement seems to remain high as FAGOR, ULMA, EROSKI, and all the other flagships of cooperativism continue to lead the way in the world.

If MCC remains solidly committed to its primary mission to serve its members as well as to provide a model of justice in the workplace and fairness in the marketplace, there would seem to be no reason why it could not continue to outstrip every other socioeconomic model in the global economy. There also would be no reason why democracy in the workplace could not survive the rigors of the world market and overtake the trend of globalization from above by a strong and engaging globalization from below.

Summary and Conclusions

Even under Generalísimo Franco's violent and oppressive rule, especially in Basque Country, the idea of cooperation and worker owned enterprises flourished. Cooperation continued to grow in Catalunya and Basque Country even in the midst of bitter conflicts between advocates of independence and the Spanish government. The Mondragón cooperative technological school was established under the dedicated leadership of Fr Arizmendi and a small group of engineers in the early 1940s and the Mondragón Cooperatives geared up for production with the forming of FAGOR steel production cooperative in 1956. The establishment of Caja Laboral Popular (Working People's Bank) assured financial solvency.

The effective functioning of its wisely constructed organization provides the strongest testimony for the remarkable success of the cooperatives. The combination of establishing a training school and a bank forestalled two of the greatest problems inevitably encountered by new cooperatives. The school solved the worker-member capacity problem, and the bank solved the capitalization problem. More recently, faced with the need to understand its market, Mondragón Cooperative Corporation (MCC) completely restructured its organization to optimize benefit to the workers and to the consumers alike and, at the same time, formed a new battery of 13 research cooperatives to ensure a prosperous future.

The one and only workers' strike occurred in 1974. This strike focused the worker-owners of the already huge cooperative network on the need of better worker advocacy within the structure of cooperation. The move toward unionizing the workers provided a continual discussion about whether workers striking against their own company really made sense. These discussions highlighted the need for a sharper sense of ownership among the workers and better communication between the staff and the owners. This was achieved partially, at least, by the strengthening of the workers' voices in the General Assembly, in the Social Councils, in the formation of new worker Interest Groups, and in a new focus on the cooperative principle of solidarity with all of the workers in the Basque provinces and the nation.

The Mondragón Corporation (MCC) now considers its main challenge for the future the maintenance of excellence in high-tech manufactured goods and the excellence of its distribution system. With such a well designed distribution system there is no need for the conventional wholesaler. Keeping abreast of market changes requires a high priority on research. That is where the priority rests now in Mondragón.

Recent expansion of the cooperatives outside of Spain brings with it an entirely new set of challenges. MCC now needs to demonstrate its ability to keep its cooperative and democratic principles, its sense of worker ownership, and its mission of "globalization from below." If it can do this successfully, then cooperation will become a truly viable alternative to "globalization from above," an imposed globalization created, not for the worker or the consumer, but for the rich and elite populations of the world. Mondragón has already shown, within the bounds of Spain, that it is possible for a cooperative corporation to keep democracy in the workplace and marketplace no matter how large it grows. The real challenge now lies in whether it can continue to accomplish its mission on a global scale.

References

Catalá, F. (1996). *Democraci Obrera: ¿Autogestión o Privatización?* Centro de Investigaciones Sociales. Universidad de Puerto Rico.

Cheney, G. (1999). *Values at Work: Employee Participation Meets Market Pressure at Mondragón.* (Updated Edition) ILR Press, and Imprint of Cornell University Press. Ithaca, NY. (Contains an excellent and complete bibliography.)

Kasmir, S. (1996). *The Myth of Mondragón: Cooperatives, Politics, and Working-Class Life in a Basque Town.* State University of New York Press, Albany, NY.

MCC (2003). *Memoria de Sostenibilidad.* Annual Report, Mondragón, Spain.

MCC (2005). Cooperatives Within MCC [Power-Point Presentation—English and Spanish versions available]. Mondragón, Spain.

Morrison, R. (1991). *We Build the Road As We Travel.* New Society Publishers, Santa Cruz, CA.

Whyte, W.F. and K.K. Whyte (1991). *Making Mondragón: The Growth and Dynamics of the Worker Cooperative Complex*, Second Edition Revised. ILR Press and Imprint of Cornell University Press. Ithaca, NY.

Chapter 7

Cooperatives in Latin America

Trade might shrink the world
But who dares to extract the
Essence of the thing?   (Haiku by BF & BL)

Latin Americans are, for the most part, poor. As in every part of the world, the elite dominate the economy and are phenomenally rich. In 1994 before its economic meltdown, 24 billionaires lived in Mexico—more than in Britain, France, and Italy combined. Persons born in Western Europe or the United States would most likely not go hungry or lack a solid roof over their heads. Born in Latin America, odds are about 50-50 that a person would suffer malnutrition and poor health due to unsanitary living conditions. Economists tend to use the GDP (Gross Domestic Product) and per capita GDP to measure progress, a practice that totally obscures the fact that wealth and income distribute so inequitably within the population. The IMF and World Bank have also exacerbated this problem by their application of the "standard model" so rigidly across the region (see Chapter 3).

Commentators on the world economy since World War II, well aware of the vast disparities in living conditions, have labeled regions of the world according to the prevailing economic strength of the majority of people there. The industrial and wealthy countries of the West and North they labeled *First World*, The Soviet Union and its satellites they called the *Second World*, and everyone else they designated as the *Third World*. These terms stuck, as inept as they were, for nearly a half-century. "*Fat world* and *Thin World* would be far more creative—and more meaningful— descriptions of these highly unequal regions" (Sherman, 2000, 1).

History can offer some explanations and theories about why such a disparity exists between the rich and poor in the Americas, the New World, land of hope for so many for so long. First of all, America is a land of *conquest*. North Americans who are aware and awake realize that "their" land was not always unquestionably "theirs." A philosophically minded Lakota, in a conversation about the "white man" violently wresting the sacred Black Hills from his people, once remarked, "Well, we took them from the Arapahoe, and they stole them from someone else." The fact is, however, that the conquest by the Europeans remains far more devastating in its historical impact than any other land grab in the Americas since the Mongolian tribes migrated from Siberia.

Recent economic domination of the Americas by transnational corporations, IMF restructuring, monetary devaluation, and resource depletion may be seen as no more than a new era of conquest, a type of *neocolonialism*. The new, just as the old colonialism, is intent on enriching its three-piece suited, pale-skinned *conquistadores* at the expense of the darker, already starving, natives.

In spite of the oppression of the new colonialism, or perhaps because of it, the cooperative movement thrives in various places in Latin America. Alan Weisman has recently reviewed one of the most famous Latin American cooperative communities, Gaviotas in Eastern Colombia (1998). Two types of cooperatives in Mexico tell their story of making cooperativism work there. Also in Mexico, the struggle of the Mayan coffee growers provides an exciting and instructive exercise in fitting cooperatives into the so-called "free trade" ethos of modern Latin America.

Gaviotas: Utopia in Eastern Colombia

Colombia, torn by civil strife since any citizen can remember, offers beautiful landscapes from steaming *selvas* (jungles) of the Chocó and high Andean *cordilleras* to *llanos* (desertlike prairie grasslands) east of the Andes. Its abundant and varied resources could provide an idyllic lifestyle—if peace and a just economy could prevail. Its capital, Bogotá, in the mid-twentieth century had not yet become the cauldron of destitute landless folk that Lima, São Paulo, Mexico City, Manila, Lagos *et al.* had become. At that time the population distributed at 60 percent rural and 30 percent urban; by 1990 that distribution had reversed. People flocking from the country-side to the capital had massed toward the southeast of the city into a community bravely called Ciudad Bolívar, numbering over two million—as nearly as anyone could count.

Paulo Lugari grew up in Popayán, a serene colonial city to the west of Ciudad Bolívar. His father Mariano, an Italian-trained attorney, engineer, and geographer, frequently invited prominent persons to dinner for the stimulating conversation they provided. When Paulo was in his mid-teens, the guests included Fr Louis Lebret, a Dominican who taught in Paris at the Institute of Economics and Humanism. Paulo was captivated when Lebret posed the question, "How can we define development?"

After many false starts at the definition—Lebret's comment was always, "No," not by how many kilometers are paved with asphalt…not by the number of hospital beds per capita…not by the gross domestic product divided by the population…not by the total wealth invested in the infrastructure… but, "Development means making people happy…before you spend your money on roads and factories, you should first be sure that those are what your citizens really need" (Weisman, 1998, 24).

Paulo graduated from Universidad Nacional, with honors, as development economist and engineer. After several assignments in the Philippines and the far east studying public health projects, sewage treatment centers, and the International Rice Research Institute, he returned to Colombia. In 1965 he was hired by a commission planning the future of the Chocó, one of the largest remaining intact virgin rain forests. Someday, he was told, a new canal linking the Atlantic and Pacific would slice across the upper Chocó. His final report asked, "What will be more important to Colombia one day, connecting the oceans or maintaining our biology?" (Weisman, 25).

After a few months, his Uncle Tomás, Minister of Public Works, took Paulo on an inspection flight of the Orinocan *llanos* on the other side of the country. The *llanos* were at that time a haven for people who, decades earlier, had fled the civil violence and slaughter between the two Colombian political parties, the Conservatives and the

Liberals. Fugitives from *The Violence* wandered across the mountains and through the roadless prairies. The only government project in that area was a road scraped across the *llanos* by the military engineers in the 1950s making it possible to access the upper Orinoco drainage.

At that time nothing much grew on the sun-baked plains except a few grasses and the *chaparro*, a squat tree with multilayered bark evolved to withstand the chronic prairie fires. Still Paulo remembered the area and one or two grassy and wooded oases where a few western people still lived among the native Guahibo. From 1967 to 1970 he slipped off to the *llanos* whenever his Chocó duties permitted. When he could, he gobbled up the utopian works of Sir Thomas More, Francis Bacon, Thoreau, Emerson, Karl Popper, Edward Belamy, B.F. Skinner, Bertrand Russell, and even Plato's *Republic*.

Lugari eventually gathered a group of interested people, a physician from Bogotá, civil engineers who had worked for his uncle, a soil chemist, and even an astronomer. Together they created a foundation, *El Centro Las Gaviotas* (The Seagull Center). The purpose of the center was to build a new, peaceful, self-sustaining community in the *llanos*.

Through the efforts and imagination of the engineers and soil chemist, they were able to reclaim a significant portion of the infertile prairie for forest and agricultural land. The engineers built a pump, powered by a teeter-totter device, to raise ground water for irrigation, cooking and cleaning. Gaviotas, a small town of dedicated *llaneros*, now graces the prairies and merges harmoniously with the ecology.

The land provides sufficient food, and a steam generator provides power, retiring an ancient 10-kilowatt diesel plant. Colombia's political pains have never eased, but Gaviotas continues to advance. Recently Gaviotas sold its cattle herd and applied new modular techniques for raising rabbits, chicken, and fish. As Paulo Lugari remarked, "… too much red meat is bad for us, … too many cow pastures are bad for the environment, and … too much *hamburgerización* is bad for the world" (Weisman, 226). None of its industry creates any smoke. As a result, the United Nations' Zero Emissions Research Initiative awarded Gaviotas the 1997 World Prize.

Gaviotas is not strictly a cooperative, though they follow many of the usual cooperative principles. Industry, agriculture, and trading are carried on primarily by individual enterprise. The town does meet frequently to plan policy, to make decisions, and to set strict criteria for membership in the community. Ownership, however, has never been communal or owned in equal shares, but so far the community has not sold shares publicly or allowed anyone but confirmed members to participate in decision making. The greatest challenge for the community now is the steady infiltration of the area by guerilla and right wing militias. Consequently visitation by the public is discouraged, and for several years it has been impossible to obtain direct observational data.

Persistence Wins: Two Mexican Cooperatives

Mexico, like much of the rest of the world, is a contradiction. The population is, on the one hand, a remarkably consistent mix of Spanish and Native American.

On the other hand, the social structure rests firmly on assumptions of natural and genetic stratification. The Mexican people understand the three strata as *criollos*, *mestizos*, and *indigenas*. *Criollos* denotes the direct European descent from the Spanish Conquistadores. The *mestizos*, as the term would suggest, indicates people whose ancestry is a mixture of Spanish and Native American. *Indigenas* refers to descendents of one or more of various indigenous cultural groups, Olmec, Toltec, Aztec, Maya, and numerous other pre-Colombian peoples. To the average Mexican, the three "racial" groups sort themselves out by a tacit social contract and assume social, economic, and political roles appropriate to their status.

By far the largest of the three groups are the *mestizos*. Still political leaders, policy makers, and captains of industry come almost exclusively from the *criollo* class. Only one president of the republic, Benito Juarez, declared himself openly as *indigena*. Light skin universally signals a member of the *criollo* caste; a healthy brown color, the *mestizo;* and very dark, *indigenas*. Names and ancestry are instinctively known to the general citizenry, especially those of the *criollo* caste. Two famous leaders of the revolution in the early twentieth century, Emilio Zapata and Francisco (Pancho) Villa, were *indigenas*. Yet, after their heroic contributions to the struggle for independence, and in spite of their popularity, both were isolated from any kind of political leadership and eventually assassinated by *criollo* leaders.

Both Zapata and Villa derived their power from the lower classes of Mexicans who were ready to overthrow the cruel Porfirio Díaz regime. Mexico was, at the same time, seeing a generalized domination (mostly foreign) of its resources and means of production, consequently relegating the lower classes to poverty-level wages or below and a high rate of unemployment (Cockroft, 1998, 87-88).

The attempt at revolution succeeded, but neither Zapata nor Villa were ever able to assume leadership or even to acquire a modicum of influence over Mexico's new government. Zapata was assassinated on his way to represent his state of Morelos at a 1919 "peace conference" with Carranza, a former Díaz supporter. In turn, a rich *criollo*, Álvaro Obregón, probably of Irish ancestry (O'Brian), gained the presidency in 1920, after subduing the opposition headed by Zapata and Villa. Obregón's people assassinated Carranza in 1920 to make way for Obregón to assume the presidency. The Obregón government immediately placed Villa under house arrest in an *hacienda* given to him by the Obregón government. Someone in the government murdered him in 1923. His murder satisfied the first of two criteria laid down by the United States for official recognition of the Obregón "revolutionary" government (Katz, 1998). Needless to say, Obregón was a well-dressed, very European, light-skinned *criollo*. No surprise either that the second of the US criteria required free access to oil extraction and refining in Mexico; not surprising either, it was the Harding and Coolidge administrations that dictated both of these criteria.

Mexico's economic system, of course, is also hierarchical and caste oriented. To understand how the Mexican economy works and to appreciate the successes of cooperatives in modern Mexico, it is necessary to review the historic church, the *hacienda*, and the *ejido* systems. These three forms of land ownership and associated production systems became prominent issues in both of the Mexican revolutions, the fight for independence from Spain in the early 1800s and the democratic revolution of the early 1900s.

The *Hacienda* system, the Religious Institutions, and the *Ejidos*

The structure of the *hacienda* was very much like the plantation of southern United States except that the owner seldom lived on the estate. A few imported slaves and indentured workers bound to the estate by debt peonage operated the entire enterprise. The owners, or *hacendados*, collected and sold the products of the *haciendas*, and in the early days, amassed wealth, keeping the slaves and indentured workers in abject poverty. After the middle of the 1800s, with continued absentee landlordism, increasingly inefficient management, rising rates of alcoholism, high costs of construction and maintenance, and continual strife among the workers, *haciendas* gradually became more trouble and expense than they were worth. Still many *hacendados* hung onto the estates for status reasons and to preserve their family history.

The *haciendas* had enjoyed the status of fixed institution, a heritage of the Spanish conquest, since the time of Hernán Cortez. One of the largest *haciendas*, one of two extensive landholdings in Mexico, lies about 200 kilometers east of Mexico City, near Puebla. The main buildings are now a museum, restaurant, and high class bed and breakfast. These very large *haciendas* were owned by Cortez, and until recently they produced most of Mexico's sugar.

The Roman Catholic Church of Mexico, by the middle of the 1800s, had grown into the largest single landowner in the country. A large movement to curtail the power of the church led to the Lerdo Law of 1856. Under that law, the government confiscated most of the church's landholdings and put them up for public bid, hoping to stimulate growth of a middle class of private landholders and farmers. Only the rich elites could afford to bid on entire *haciendas*, so instead, the large *haciendas* combined with each other and grew into huge *latifundios* or multi-corporate farms, operated largely by *criollos*.

The Porfirio Díaz administration (early 1900s) encouraged the growth of *latifundios* at the expense of native lands. Land reform then became a central issue leading up to the Mexican revolution of 1917-1921. While United States revolutionaries cried, "Life, Liberty, and the Pursuit of Happiness," Mexican revolutionaries 150 years later shouted, "Life, Liberty, and Land." Nevertheless, the *latifundios* survived the revolution and lasted until they were broken up during the land reforms of Lázaro Cárdenas in the late 1930s.

The idea of *ejido* also came from Spain, brought by the Conquistadores. Since then *ejidos* have undergone many legal and economic changes. Most recently, *ejidos* have been owned by the government and turned over to the local peasants to work and live largely in subsistence mode. Ordinarily an *ejido* was divided into two sections, a common plot to be shared by the entire community and a variety of small private parcels held and worked by individual members. The members could not own the plots, either individually or communally, and could not sublet their land to be worked by anyone other than a qualified *ejiditario* (a member of the *ejido*).

Thus an *ejido* could never qualify as a cooperative, because of government ownership and lack of control by the membership, even though they occasionally operated much like a cooperative. During the Cárdenas administration, remaining *haciendas* and large *latifundios* were broken up into smaller *ejidos*, and the *ejiditarios* collected state credit to increase production under a growing demand of the Mexican population for food. Complex laws respecting land ownership, *ejidos*, true cooperatives, and increasing numbers of "civil societies" changed almost annually.

Silver Artisans of Old Taxco

Taxco, a community of shining-white homes and businesses, lies about an hour southwest of Cuernavaca in the State of Guerrero. Its earliest registry dates back to 1529 with a description of the community of Old Taxco (*Taxco Viejo*) about 30 kilometers down the valley from the present city of Taxco. Hernán Cortés "discovered" the community in the early 1500s as he, his courtesans, and soldiers combed Mexico in search of silver.

Despite the wealth of its silver, residents did not fully exploit it until the arrival of Don José de la Borda. Borda, a Frenchman of Spanish descent, crisscrossed Guerrero many times. One day his horse, according to legend, kicked up some earth to reveal a rich vein of silver. Several mines, using local Mexicans as virtually slave labor, made Borda a rich man.

At this time, the new city of Taxco, with white-walled and red-tiled buildings, still clings to a steep hillside just north and a little east of the original community of Old Taxco. Borda contributed some of his wealth to the community in the form of a large baroque church, Santa Prisca. He required that the church be built strictly according to his specific designs and instructions. Also the citizens had to agree that no one could ever change the appearance of the church in any way. Consequently the ornate intricately carved brown walls are no longer a good match for the rest of the simple, sparkling white town. Don José eventually left the area when he became over-extended financially. He merely dismissed his workers and abandoned the mines.

During the war for independence, Spanish barons, who had meanwhile taken over the mines, preferred to destroy them rather than to lose them to the revolutionaries. Silver production in Taxco thus suffered a long hiatus, until the arrival in the late 1920s of a Tulane University professor of architecture. William Spratling came to Mexico from the United States to write a book about Taxco's architecture, but he set aside his manuscript when he learned about the recently opened silver mines. Local silver artisans, though highly skilled, experienced difficulty in marketing their wares. Spratling, a talented artist, gathered several artisans into a workshop for jewelry and tableware, contributing his designs based on local pre-Hispanic art. Through his contacts in the United States, these designs soon became enormously popular. Before his tragic death in an auto accident near Taxco in 1967, Spratling had trained numerous apprentices and had become known for setting the course for Taxco's artistic and economic history (FloraMex, 2003).

In 1987, five families in Taxco Viejo, assisted by a Dutch non-governmental organization, formed a company with two objectives: (1) to sell silver products that they were already manufacturing and (2) to improve the lives of artisans and their families. Up to that time they had been purchasing materials individually and working the silver in their own homes. After two years they reorganized themselves as a cooperative, using the usual definition of one member-one vote-one share. Decision making by consensus was easy with only five members. The cooperative grew rapidly until in 1994 it had 27 members. They called themselves *Unión Progresista Artisanal*.

During 1994 they were forced by changes in the federal law to dissolve their cooperative. Under the NAFTA agreement, incorporating as a cooperative became virtually impossible. The Mexican government charged cooperatives twice the tariffs that they charged standard corporations, plus the government required the cooperative to carry expensive whole life insurance on each of their members. Total federal taxes on cooperatives almost tripled. The only other kind of corporation allowed by law that remotely fit their group was called a "Micro-Enterprise."

For a couple of years the *Unión*, as a micro-enterprise, marketed their silver products wholesale to a number of local distributors and were just able to make expenses. In 1996, a new federal law was passed that forced the *Unión* to reorganize once again under a designation called an SSS corporation (*Sociedad de Solidaridad Social*). The group continued operating as a cooperative but did business publicly under the new legal designation.

The years 1997 and 1998 were very difficult for the *Unión*. Large debts accumulated and the number of members dropped from 27 to 12. Marlin Yoder, a country representative of the Mennonite Central Committee (MCC), took notice of the struggles of the artisan group and provided organizational and business consultation to help them get back on their feet. They began listing products on a catalog of SERRV, an international marketing cooperative.

In 1999, another Dutch non-governmental organization, Fair Trade Assistance (FTA), contributed business training and helped the *Unión* design a quality control system. In 2001, by a refinancing arrangement with FTA, they cleared all past debts, and the cooperative began to prosper. In 2001, they grossed well over $20,000 US, and in 2002 they grossed over $40,000 US, double the previous year's income.

With a more healthy income, *Unión* could now use some of its retained earnings to provide capital for the purchase of materials for new orders, to cover increasing accounts payable, and to pay large dividends to members. As a result, the membership began to increase again. By 2005 about 40 percent of gross income went back to the producers, 20 percent went to purchase materials, 20 percent was set aside for administrative costs, 5 percent went to community social projects, and about 15 percent was allocated to undesignated retained earnings. From these retained earnings, the cooperative provided loans to producers and their families for emergency medical care. Community social projects included improved sanitary conditions, principally a new garbage collection system for the entire town of Old Taxco.

Persistence paid off for this silver artisan cooperative, even during bad economic times for Mexico and the United States. Through all their hard times, they never abandoned the goal of improving the lives of their artisans and their families. Now, they not only improve the lives of their own artisan producers, they improve the life of the entire community.

Unión still faces some stiff challenges. Training artisans for their cooperative remains an important part of the cooperative's work, but it turns out to be one of its most troubling aspects. The current president of the co-op, Manuel Díaz, is the son of one of William Spratling's early trainees. Manuel himself, has trained many silver workers, but as soon as they are trained, they tend to leave the community. There are no schools to train artisans and there is very little quality control in the local trade, either in the quality of designs on in the quality of teaching. Maintaining the quality of their designs and keeping their in-house trained workers are the biggest challenges for the cooperative.

Vicente Guerrero, Tlaxcala

Human beings have inhabited the state of Tlaxcala, Mexico, just north of Puebla for at least 12,000 years. Archaeologists have recently discovered clovis arrow points in the area, similar to those found in the high plains of southwestern United States. Among those discoveries were also remains of a Neolithic tribe demonstrating the beginnings of agriculture in the valley and in the volcanic hills of the northwest part of the state.

As early as 200 CE, in southwestern Tlaxcala, Cacaxtla served as the religious center for an advanced society of Olmec/Maya people. Cacaxtla, therefore, must have been one of the earliest examples of cultural integration in Central America. Rare murals on the walls of temples depicted Figures of Olmec, Toltec, and Mayan faces arranged up and down the cornstalks where the ears of maize should be, demonstrating the mix of cultures already present in the valley. The corn people also symbolized the centrality of the plant for sustaining human life.

By the thirteenth century CE four groups of pre-hispanic peoples inhabited the area, the Tepeticpac, the Ocoteltuco, the Tizatlán, and the Quiahixtlán. Old records testify that these peoples were a sixth of seven lineages descended from the Chicomostoc (peoples of the seven caves). These four groups settled the plain of Poyoauhatlan in 1208 CE. They were soon joined by tribes fleeing from the powerful Aztecs who imposed unendurable conflict and oppression on them in their original homes at Texcoco and Chimalhuacán, in the high plains near present day Mexico City. They wrote in Nahuatl that their god Camaxtli had told them, "Go further east toward where the sun first sends its resplendent rays" (Banderas, 2003).

These people fleeing from the west settled in the volcanic hills of northwestern Tlaxcala. Perhaps some of them joined the thousands who marched with Cortez in 1517 against Moctezuma, remembering their oppression 300 years earlier under the Aztecs.

In the hills of northwest Tlaxcala, in plain view of two volcanoes, Popocatepetl and Ixtacxihuatl, is a small village inhabited by descendents of these eastern Nahuatl peoples. They named their village after Vicente Guerrero, hero of the revolution of 1810-1821. A *mestizo*, Guerrero could speak both Nahuatl and Spanish and dreamed of a Mexico free of caste. His origin and his mission enabled him to assemble a *Moreno* (dark-skinned) majority to support his dream and he was elected president in 1829. His philosophy is best expressed in his own words:

> We have defeated the colossus and we bathe in the glow of a new-found happiness ... [We now know] the way to genuine freedom ... which is to live with a knowledge that no one is above anyone else, that there is no title more honored than "citizen." Such a title applies

to a person in the military, a private worker, a government official, a cleric, a land owner, a laborer, a craftsman, or a writer ... because the sacred belief in equality has leveled us all before the law.
(Speech to the 3-person democratic junta, 1823, Banderas 2003, translated by the author)

Guerrero's dream, as well as his short-lived democratic government, was ended when he was brutally murdered in 1831. Still his dream lives on in the rural areas of Mexico and is carried on by cooperative groups like the village of Vicente Guerrero in Tlazcala. The Vicente Guerrero *campesinos* work the land of an old *ejido* formerly abandoned because of the withdrawal of government support under pressure from the "free" trade agreements.

Early in the 1990s, a group of expatriate farmers arrived from Guatemala. They knew about natural agricultural methods and terracing of the steep slopes. Because of violent conflict caused by right-wing paramilitaries, they were forced to leave their own country. They had received numerous death threats from these paramilitaries. The farmers had heard of the Vicente Guerrero community through common friends, Paul and Mary McKay, who had worked with the Guatemalans on behalf of a Quaker group and had later become the representatives in Mexico for the Mennonite Central Committee (MCC). The Guatemalans shared their knowledge of no-till farming with the Vicente Guerrero farmers, along with a simple but effective method of terracing.

Using these ancient but newfound methods, the farmers at Vicente Guerrero have been able to triple their yield of maize, beans, and squash (all grown together on the same terraced hillsides). Of the approximately 200 families in the village, all but three are members of the new cooperative. Now the Vicente Guerrero Cooperative has set up a staff of administrators and a training group that travels all over the countryside sharing their knowledge with surrounding communities.

What they know is a combination of centuries-old wisdom of the land and new low-tech methods of natural farming without the use of chemical fertilizers, herbicides, and insecticides. The simple method of terracing is accomplished by the use of a heavy metal weight (plumb) and two tent-like supporting sticks that can be easily moved along the slopes to mark the contours. Then they dig wide ditches along the marked contours and face the ditches with sod or stones to prevent erosion. Otherwise, the newly disturbed soft volcanic soil will wash down the hillside with the next rain. Planting trees in the ditches both reinforces the terraces and encourages more birds.

Maize, beans, and squash are all grown together, and the unused parts of the plants become mulch and compost between growing seasons. This practice retains the organic materials and retains more moisture during the long dry seasons. The farmers allow weeds to grow among the crops to provide food for the *chapulines* (grasshoppers) and other insects. Otherwise, the insects would eat and destroy the maize and beans; most of them actually prefer the weeds. This practice avoids the need for both herbicides and insecticides.

The insects, in turn, provide good protein for the birds, free-ranging chickens, and turkeys. Insects are also helpful in the open pollination of the food crops. All these methods take into account the alternate rainy and dry seasons, the loose but fertile volcanic soil, the necessary organic buildup of the soil, the steeply sloped fields now beautifully terraced, and the ecology of insects/weeds/birds/poultry/pollination.

Ecological balance is also esthetically pleasing as one stands in the life-giving and spirit-raising atmosphere of the fields. The untilled field gives off a totally different essence than the plowed, fertilized, herbicide and insecticide-filled earth of the corporate farm.

Vicente Guerrero is not registered specifically and legally as a cooperative. As mentioned above, the legal status of cooperatives and other forms of land and corporate registry in Mexico is tentative and ever-changing. Even so, equipment, materials, seed storage, and work are all shared cooperatively in the community. Their budget is similar to that of the silver artisan cooperative in Old Taxco. The Vicente Guerrero group has used their retained earnings to establish a library for the school children of the community. They also believe that training and the sharing of information with other communities is part of their cooperative work. The training program has promoted a cooperative spirit and a pride of accomplishment in Tlaxcala that is rare elsewhere in North America.

The Mayan Coffee Cooperatives

Gloria spoke in Spanish, although she is a Mayan woman, about thirty years old, and Tsotsil (one of 31 derivatives of ancient Mayan) is her native tongue:

> We had to leave our community, at 3 am on 16 July 1996 with only what we could carry. The problems began when we started to organize as a Civil Society. The people of our municipality are poor, and I go to the meetings of the bases of support for the Zapatistas in order to bring peace and justice to our community. A right wing paramilitary group, responsible for the massacre, killed 43 persons, mostly women and children, at Sunday morning prayer at Acteal. The large paramilitary group calls itself *Paz y Justicia* [peace and justice] and brings to us only war and killing. One of the leaders of *Paz y Justicia* is Marcos, my cousin. He ordered that I be killed because I helped to organize the people and because we do not support the PRI party [Institutional Revolutionary Party, the only party in power in Mexico for 75 years]. It is risky for me to speak to you about all this, but I want the world to know! Because the paramilitary groups are all around us and neither the PRI nor the Mexican military do anything about it, we cannot go anywhere to work. We are suffering, but thank God, we are organized.
>
> (direct interview, translated by the author)

Gloria lives in an "Autonomous Community," a legal designation specifically reserved for the indigenous peoples (similar to the US reservation). Her community is deep in the highlands of Chiapas, the southern-most state of Mexico, close to the border with Guatemala. Since the passage of NAFTA (North American Free Trade Agreement) on 1 January 1994, the right wing paramilitaries and the Mexican and Guatemalan military, using United States dollars, have been steadily displacing the indigenous people from their autonomous communities in Chiapas.

Descendents of the ancient and proud Maya, over 50,000 people, displaced from their community lands, live in makeshift houses in the highlands of Chiapas, the lowland *selvas*, and the rolling hills of Guatemala. These Mayan corn, bean, and coffee farmers traditionally organize their work cooperatively. They pool their resources to maintain a rough wooden barn as a preliminary processing plant, where coffee beans are hulled, dried, fermented and bagged for shipping.

The ultimate insult to the Mayan community occurred when, at the end of the season, the farmers went to the co-op storage barn to gather their hundreds of bags of semi-processed beans for shipping, they found the barn empty. Apparently an army unit posted there to guard the barn had either stolen the coffee or allowed it to be stolen.

Because their organizations are cooperatives, the Maya must pay almost double the tariff that a private farmer or corporate farm pays. The tariff gets higher for every step of processing that they do themselves before selling the coffee bags to companies like Nestle. If they were to roast and/or grind the beans, the combined cost of production and shipping by "free" trade (under NAFTA regulations) would far exceed the price they can get for a kilo of coffee. Under NAFTA, the government cannot subsidize local coffee or corn production, although the US subsidizes its corn farmers, as well as the coffee farmers in South Vietnam.

Two other problems beleaguer the Maya. First, the US and Mexican governments and the transnational corporations continue to apply pressure on them to sell their lands. Since the early years of the PRI, the Mexican constitution protected (Section 22) autonomous lands for the indigenous. However, president Salinas, the leader of the ruling PRI party, without consent from the legislature or the people, recently modified the constitution to allow autonomous lands to be bought and sold. Some local PRI leaders then presented a few indigenous and non-indigenous families with bogus deeds of ownership for land on the autonomous reservations in order to claim private ownership of desirable agricultural and medicinal products for trade through NAFTA.

The second problem is the difficulty in obtaining education for their communities. Most teachers in these autonomous communities are volunteers from among a number of non-governmental organizations in civil society who tend to stay for very short times. Usually they leave after a few weeks because of threats by right-wing paramilitaries. The primary mission of the paramilitaries is to give the Mayan people every problem they possibly can so that the Maya will abandon their lands to "more efficient" corporate farms run by the transnationals.

Still, most of the Maya remain on their autonomous lands. They have organized and call themselves *Las Abejas* (Worker Bees) and span over a large geographical area of southeastern Mexico and Guatemala, bridging many individual communities. Since 2000, several groups in the United States, Canada, and Europe have been organizing to provide a direct market for the cooperatives in the Chiapas Highlands. For example, now shoppers can buy *Zapatista Coffee* directly from a cooperative distributor, *the Human Bean*, in Denver or from several natural food stores and chains like Whole Foods. Similar arrangements make "fair" trade coffee available in other parts of North America and Europe.

Summary and Conclusions

The gap between the rich and the poor is larger in Latin America than anywhere else in the world. The current practices of economists and policy makers is to gauge the economic health of nations of the world by the Gross Domestic Product (GDP) or, worse yet, to assess the common people's welfare by the per capita (average) GDP. This practice totally masks any awareness of the unequal distribution of wealth. The existence of only a few very rich individuals can skew these figures grossly in an upward direction, and there are more than just a few very rich people in Mexico's power elite. To say that the per capita GDP has risen several percentage points since the institution of NAFTA is to obscure the fact that, since NAFTA, the poor have become very much poorer and the incredibly rich even richer.

While it may be true that other Latin American countries do not have quite the huge numbers of very rich elite, the same mechanisms of income and wealth distribution appear to exist in those countries also—and for some of the same reasons. Among the factors contributing to the dismal distribution of wealth and income are the rigid racial attitudes that persist in the form of denial of lower socio-economic people, especially the *indigenas*, the same opportunities in the economy as the upper classes (largely *criollos*) enjoy.

Other more recent factors include the biased model used by the IMF and World Bank and the even more biased "free" trade agreements. These biases, added to the already large gap between the rich and the poor, stress the societies of these countries to the breaking point. The United States' habit of throwing money toward the power elite in violent struggles like the one in Colombia has also contributed to the rich-poor gap and the ensuing conflicts.

Each community described in this chapter has devised somewhat different versions of cooperative economics. *Gaviotas* has developed a very tightly-knit community with an active council, participatory decision making, and a great deal of cooperation, using each individual's particular abilities in an effective way. The *silver artisans of Taxco* have worked together in a truly cooperative mode, actually writing the Rochdale principles into their bylaws. *Vicente Guerrero* has formed a council with farm owners as members. They share all common expenses, workloads, teaching or training responsibilities, and earnings. The *Maya* have worked together in truly cooperative fashion as was their tradition.

The concept of ownership of land varies from group to group. The Maya live on land set aside for them as indigenous peoples and share everything. The Taxco artisans and Vicente Guerrero farmers hold their workshops, training staff, materials, tools and products in common, but own their homes. Members of Gaviotas, although extremely cooperative in philosophy, work primarily as individual entrepreneurs and owned their own plots of land and workplaces. Water, power, and educational facilities are owned by the community and administered by a council. Decisions are made as a group with the charismatic founders holding a greater amount of influence.

Common themes in the stories of these four different enterprises are capitalization, legal orientation toward cooperativism, and training programs for workers.

The process of capitalization stretched out for many years before Gaviotas felt totally self-sufficient. Much capitalization in later years depended, as it did for a standard corporation, on satisfying and, in some cases, creating demand for their products outside of the community.

The artisans of Taxco will always be at the mercy of the Mexican legislature for a proper definition of their identity and at the mercy of changing demand for their products. Only the profit margin of their sales is available for capitalization.

Vicente Gerrero is probably the only one of these cooperatives that can count on fully capitalizing their enterprise through the proper use of their land. They can always maintain at least a subsistence level and usually have plenty left over for sale in the nearby urban markets of Puebla and Mexico City.

The Maya have been continually under pressure from the Mexican political establishment to sell their land to the corporate farms. In other countries where this has been the case, including the United States, the individual farmers have not fared very well—except where they could form cooperatives to free themselves from the uneven market pressures. The Maya, with their traditional bent for working cooperatively, and their ability to communicate with cooperatives elsewhere in the world, will probably survive their current bout with neo-liberal world economics.

All of the groups have somehow managed to survive within the legal system of their particular countries. Cooperatives in Mexico seem to have experienced more difficulty with their country's legal system than cooperatives in any other part of the world.

Most of the cooperative enterprises provide their own worker training. The silver artisans of Taxco have experienced some difficulty in retaining workers that they have trained. Vicente Guerrero actually markets its training model to other communities in the vicinity, a practice which not only ensures trained workers for everyone but increases the supply of working capital. Gaviotas depends on the Colombian higher education system, a university complex that is of very high standards and quality, for its engineers and scientists. The Maya will experience more and more difficulty in maintaining training and educational standards, due to racism and the virtual caste system in Mexican society. Most basic education in the Maya community comes from Mexican NGOs volunteering short-term teachers. These teachers are also likely to leave the area early because of threats from the right wing militias.

The overall impression of cooperatives in Latin America is that the movement thrives and holds promise for a more stable economy and more prosperous lives for those communities. Pressures to limit cooperative activity can come from several sources: (1) governments making laws and agreements like NAFTA that curtail the cooperatives' ability to offer their products to the world market, (2) capital markets throwing up barriers for the most effective applications of cooperation, (3) educational institutions failing to provide training needed for competence in the economies of the twenty-first century, and (4) overbearing neocolonial practices of transnational corporations. These pressures are being overcome in many creative ways by cooperative-minded people both in the so-called developing and developed world. The effect is that of a strong movement toward "globalization from below."

References

Banderas website (2003). www.banderas.com.mx/historia4.htm, "Breve Historia de Mexico."

Cockcroft, J. (1998). *Mexico's Hope: An Encounter with Politics and History.* Monthly Review Press, NY.

Flora Mex (2003). www.floramex.com, "The History of Silver in Taxco, Mexico."

Katz, F. (1998). *Life and Times of Pancho Villa*. Stanford University Press, Stanford, CA.

Sherman, J.W. (2000). *Latin America in Crisis*. Westview Press, NY.

Weisman, A. (1998). *Gaviotas: A Village to Reinvent the World*. Chelsea Green Publishing Company, White River Junction, Vermont.

Chapter 8

Puerto Rico's Cooperative Effort

Development! Not
Just a dam, nuclear plant,
And more Mickey D's   (Haiku by BL & BF)

The Caribbean islands are, in general, a kind of "melancholy" combination of cultures. There are remnants of the old Carib culture, the ancient natives who migrated north, perhaps from the northern regions of the South American continent, along the Antilles from island to island all the way to Cuba and Jamaica. The Taínos, by far the largest and most culturally advanced of all the early peoples, left a rich heritage. The descendents of the Spanish and French colonizers are prominent in the mix, as are the descendents of the hundreds of thousands of African slaves who were brought to the islands to work the sugar and fruit plantations in order to enrich the European traders and investors. There are scars of domination from the French, the Spanish, and more recently, the United States. In fact, economic dependency on the United States and the official political connection of the Commonwealth of Puerto Rico to the United States tend to keep the Puerto Rican people subservient to the exploitative economy.

Cultural histories of the Caribbean all report a pervading sense of solitude, a feeling of separation from the world, almost a cloistered life of the people. Literary and artistic pictures of the culture uniformly display a kind of romanticized, superficial view of the palm-tree lined beaches and smiling dark faces, as if the islands were some kind of utopian escape from the turmoil of the world. Some writers, catching the melancholy atmosphere of the Caribeños, paint a portrait of émigrés returning to a different planet, a picture of a homecoming without a home. Colonizers in the early 1800s often portrayed the islands in their journals as places definitely to shun. "The image occurs over and over of a hot, dangerous, and disgraced hell of exploitation on the face of the earth" (Rodriguez-Julia, 18; translation by author).

Rodriguez-Julia suspects that the image is not only a phenomenon of the colonizers but also of the colonized, because of the massive emigrations away from his native Puerto Rico, the experience of the "boat people" from Haiti during the 1980s and 1990s, and the huge exodus from Cuban communism. We can now see in homes of the poor, almost as shrines, pictures of family and friends who have left the Caribe. There is a kind of a religious devotion to those who have fled the cycles of neediness and desperation.

Puerto Rico, Sentinel in the Caribbean

Puerto Rico is the easternmost island of the Greater Antilles and the fourth largest island in the Caribbean, after Cuba, Hispañola (Haiti and Dominican Republic), and Jamaica. Its location at the crossroads of the trade routes both south and north has made Puerto Rico the "gem of the Caribbean" in the eyes of Europeans and North Americans. The United States, especially, claims Puerto Rico as a special "protectorate" as well as an area full of resources and people to be exploited.

With an area of 3,435 square miles, Puerto Rico is inhabited by 3.9 million people. Since 1917 the people of Puerto Rico have officially been citizens of the United States. In 1952 Puerto Rico's constitution established the island as an autonomous Commonwealth and territory of the United States. It has a governor, a bicameral legislature, a local judicial system, and participates in the US banking and postal systems. It forms a district in the Federal Judiciary with its own US district court. The legislature sends a non-voting representative to the US Congress, elected every four years. Most US federal agencies maintain offices in Puerto Rico; however, it has its own Internal Revenue system and is not subject to US federal taxes.

Early Peoples on the Island

The earliest archaeological evidence of human habitation on the island comes from a limestone cave at Loíza Aldea, a village on the north coast just east of San Juan. Hand-worked conch shells and hatchets trace the occupation of *Los Arcaicos* (The Ancients) from the first century CE. The evidence points to the same group that came across the Bering Strait into North America. Discoverers of the Loíza cache speculate that the group came to the island from present-day Florida on large rafts hewn from trees. Like most primitive nomadic tribes, *Los Arcaicos* created no permanent items such as pottery, canoes, or dwellings (Pfeffer, 1999).

From the first century on, there were migrations of various tribes. The Igneris, of the Arawakan linguistic group, traveled up the Lesser Antilles from the Orinoco basin about 300 CE, bringing with them well developed skills in pottery making, fishing, and canoe building. Settling along the coastal areas, they left behind them much evidence of their culture and language.

A second wave of peoples arrived about 600 CE, the Taínos. Like the Arawak, Taínos were descended from the *Arcaicos*—not from the Arawak themselves as formerly supposed because of the few observed linguistic commonalities. They were less skilled in pottery than the Igneris, but much more adept at agriculture. Archaeological evidence and reports from the first European explorers indicate that the Taínos had spread all through the West Indies, establishing villages everywhere they went and centering their civilization on the islands of Hispañola and present-day Puerto Rico, which they called Borinquén. The Taínos were small, dark-haired, and friendly people who, except for the *caciques* (tribal chieftains) and married women, wore no clothing. Their strong, cooperative society impressed all who took them seriously as human beings.

Some have estimated that there were over 400,000 Taínos on the island at the time of Admiral Christopher Columbus's "voyages of discovery." By the same estimates, there were at that time well over a million Taínos throughout the Caribbean Islands (Rouse, 1992, 7). Almost none survived for more than a few years after the European invasion.

Unfortunately, after Columbus "discovered" them, they served the Spanish as slaves for a short period. Again, unfortunately, the cargo of the 17 ships on the second voyage, in 1493, included a large number of European cattle and sheep, carriers of the smallpox virus. The Europeans had, by that time, become immune to the virus, but the natives in the Americas had never been exposed and had no defenses against the disease. Taínos who did not die of smallpox died from Spanish massacres or hardship.

By 1524, the Taínos had ceased to exist as a separate population group. Nevertheless, parts of their culture have survived, or have been revived, in the dominant Spanish culture of the area. European words coming directly from the Taíno language include *barbecue* (Spanish, *Barbacoa*), *batata* (sweet potato, Spanish, *patata*), *hurricane, savanna, jamaca* (hammock), and *cacique*. Although Cassava (*casabe*) made from yuca was their staple food crop, the Taíno were also responsible for introducing corn (*maiz*), beans, squash, peanuts (*mani*), and fruits like guava, mamey, and pineapple into the European diet. Ordinary potatoes and tomatoes were brought later, by the Spanish, from Central and South America.

The Taíno economy was collective. Private property was not recognized except for personal objects and decorations. The Taínos contributed mostly small fruits, grown in small portable pots (called *conucos*), to the Caribbean trade network. This trade was occasionally supplemented by limited hunting and fishing. They had a textile industry, cultivating cotton and intricate weaving for married females' skirts, belts for warriors, and hammocks for sleeping. These were introduced into the European economy, along with tobacco, during the few years the Taínos existed after the Spanish invasion.

At the time of Columbus, the Carib people were beginning to migrate up the chain of islands and had already established a small settlement on the eastern shore of Puerto Rico. They were a much more backward and violent people and were rumored to be cannibalistic. Those rumors were much overblown by the settlers, probably as a further excuse for the Spanish to enslave them (Rouse, 1992). It is curious that the area received its European name from these people rather than from the more populous, advanced, and long-term residents, the Taínos.

During Columbus's second visit, over a thousand male pilgrims brought by Columbus settled on the island, which the admiral renamed *San Juan Bautista* (St. John the Baptist). The city established on the north shore he named *Puerto Rico* (Rich Seaport). The switch in names took place some time after Ponce de Leon's governorship in the 1500s.

The Spanish Era

The Spanish ruled Puerto Rico for nearly four centuries. The road was not a smooth one, however, littered by attempted invasions by the Caribs, the Dutch, the French, the English, and a series of rebellions by the populace of the island. All these attempts failed, but damage was done to agricultural development and plans for European trade. Gold, the primary motivation for Columbus, Ponce de Leon, and the first Spanish settlers, soon ran out. Early hopes of immeasurable riches were dashed.

The earliest attempt at a cash crop was ginger. Trade promised to be brisk, but devastating hurricanes, disease, and boom-bust market cycles made profits from the spice nearly unattainable. A European mindset equating the West Indies with the East Indies hampered development of Puerto Rico's unique resources. Fleets of treasure ships passed Puerto Rico on the way to the Inca gold on the Isthmus of Panama (then part of present-day Colombia) or to the Silver at Veracruz, at the western end of the gulf.

French corsairs such as Francois LeClerc and English privateers such as John Hawkins and Francis Drake disrupted and nearly paralyzed Spanish shipping. El Morro, La Fortuleza, and Casa Blanca were constructed to defend the island and San Juan harbor from the pirate incursions. Colonizers particularly designed La Fortuleza as the seat of the Spanish government, and it still serves today as the residence of the governor of the Commonwealth of Puerto Rico, the oldest continuously occupied executive mansion in the Americas (Pfeffer, 1999).

In 1598 the English, under the leadership of the Earl of Cumberland, George Clifford, assaulted the beaches of Loíza and burned San Juan, driving the Spanish back to El Morro. Cumberland hammered the fortress until the walls began to crumble. The island's governor surrendered, but the English only stayed for 65 days. Dysentery wracked the troops and local guerillas harassed the invaders until Cumberland withdrew. The Dutch, having not read their history lessons very well, tried the same thing in 1625, only to retreat due to disease. In both cases, germs succeeded where guns failed.

Smuggling became the principal business of the seventeenth century, and the legitimate economy of the island deteriorated. The defeat of the Spanish Armada, political corruption, and the cost of defending Puerto Rico and all their other colonies around the world had virtually bankrupted Spain. For the next 150 years, Spain neglected its gem of the Caribbean.

During this period of neglect, the Puerto Ricans began to find their own feet. While Napoleon was ravaging Europe, further weakening the colonial powers, Puerto Rico could behave as if it were essentially independent. Farmers began to grow crops more suited to the climate, and the producers on the island began trading more freely with other Spanish colonies. At the same time, other Caribbean people began to flood the island. They became a large group of free non-white squatters on royal lands. The government began evicting these squatters in order to create a large landless peasantry who had no choice but to seek employment on the haciendas or accept low-percentage sharecropping arrangements in exchange for food and shelter.

The Haitian struggle for independence, at the end of the eighteenth century, sent a number of French and Spanish landowners packing. Many of these landowners came to Puerto Rico and brought with them important innovations in the cultivation of sugar. By this time, sugar had become the principle export for Puerto Rico, coffee production was on the increase, and for the first time in modern history, Puerto Rico prospered. The thriving economy, draconian laws, and the influx of so many conservative refugees loyal to the Crown dampened any revolutionary impulses.

The Spanish government abolished slavery in 1873, and the new Spanish Republican constitution granted Puerto Rican representation in Spain's parliament. A new movement for self-government began to grow in the 1880s, and finally, in 1897, largely through the efforts of Puerto Rican statesman, Luis Muñoz Rivera, Spain signed a charter granting the island some autonomy. The atmosphere was finally favorable for a long sought Puerto Rican independence (Pfeffer, 1999).

The Beginning of United States Domination

The new form of government in Puerto Rico had operated scarcely six months when the Spanish-American War erupted and US troops landed at Guánica in July, 1898, and occupied the island with little opposition. By December the Treaty of Paris ended the war and directed Spain to cede Puerto Rico to the United States. Puerto Rico remained under direct military rule for the next two years, beginning a new period of colonialism under their giant northern neighbor.

In 1900, the president of the United States appointed a governor, supreme court judges, and a state senate. A lower house of elected representatives was also formed, but all policies and proposals were reviewed by the state senate and the senate of the United States before they could be discussed. These domineering moves on the part of the United States came as a huge surprise to many people who regarded the Americans as their liberators.

American corporations moved in to buy out the haciendas and the tobacco industries. At the same time the army distributed food to the hungry after coffee production came to a halt as a result of the hurricane of 1899. The army engineers built roads. The medical corps virtually eliminated yellow fever by improving sanitation conditions and vaccinated the islanders against smallpox. But much of the freedom that Puerto Rico had won from the Spanish had disappeared. Island political leaders like Luis Muñoz Rivera kept the pressure on the US for more autonomy and political freedom.

After chafing under the US for the first three decades of the twentieth century, Puerto Ricans began again to improve their individual circumstances, though they were still not as well off as their Caribbean neighbors. Just as the economy was beginning to grow slowly but deliberately, two more hurricanes and the depression of the 1930s devastated the island. By 1933, only 35 percent of the population had jobs (Pfeffer, 25). Puerto Ricans tended to blame the US for its problems, and the freedom movement resumed strong protests.

In the 1940s, with the support of the president of the United States, Franklin Roosevelt, Puerto Rico began to shift its economic base from agriculture to industry and tourism. This project was popularly known as Operation Bootstrap. In 1947 the US returned to Puerto Rico the right to elect its own governor, Luis Muñoz Marín, founder of the Puerto Rican Popular Democratic Party and son of the deceased political leader, Luis Muñoz Rivera, was the first popularly elected governor.

The Commonwealth of Puerto Rico

In 1952, US President Harry Truman declared that Puerto Rico would henceforth be neither a state nor a free nation—*!Viva Puerto Rico Libre!* as in the famous Grito (shout) de Lares—but a Commonwealth. The 1868 uprising in the town of Lares, which is commonly called the Grito de Lares, was a pitched battle with the weakened Spanish forces that ensured the independence of Puerto Rico. The shout of Lares would be heard once again when a group of *independentes* opened fire on a session of the US House of Representatives in 1954, wounding five lawmakers. After this, the independence movement in Puerto Rico shrank further, for US citizens and Puerto Ricans alike are pragmatists and "know they must live as neighbors" (Pfeffer, 27).

As in many countries experiencing rapid industrialization, rural people began to migrate to the cities looking for factory jobs. Large numbers were unsuccessful in that search and signed up for migrant work in the United States, principally in New England. Compensation of 15 to 25 cents per hour, with 10 to15 cents withheld to the end of the season, were the typical earnings of migrants in the late 1950s. The practice of withholding kept the workers on the farm until the end of harvest in September or October. Most farms provided substandard shacks for their workers, and the workers themselves had to scratch for their own meals.

The 1990s brought another shock to the Puerto Rican economy. The transfer of the apparel industry from the island to Mexico created a large loss of low-wage jobs. This transfer was the direct result of the North American Free Trade Agreement (NAFTA). Balancing this shock somewhat, large demonstrations forced the US Navy to stop their fleet from using Vieques Island and its 10,000 residents as a target for bombing practice. The US followed closure of the base on Vieques by a radical reduction of all its heavy presence on the island, opening up Vieques and other areas of Puerto Rico for a more extensive, more profitable, and locally operated tourism industry.

The end of the twentieth century also has seen Puerto Rico struggling with overpopulation, the AIDS epidemic and persistent high unemployment. The push for statehood narrowly missed in 1993 (48.4 percent against and 46.2 percent in favor) and has waned steadily since. The movement for independence has become even weaker (less than two percent). Their present governor, Aníbal Acevedo Vilá, and his Popular Democratic Party favors remaining as a Commonwealth, as designated by the US Congress in 1952. Under Acevedo's very popular leadership, there is little likelihood that the statehood party will gain much more influence.

As official citizens of the commonwealth, Puerto Ricans can vote for their own local leaders but not for US congressional or presidential candidates. They pay no federal taxes but can join the US military. As economic conditions improve, it is likely that the push for independence will gradually disappear and the push for statehood will also diminish. In the rash of neo-colonialism, the US included a clause in the Internal Revenue Code, Section 936, exempting all US corporations from paying federal income tax on their operations in Puerto Rico. As Sila Calderón once said:

> Commonwealth status is perfect for us. It gives us a union with the United States and allows us to maintain US citizenship, which we cherish, but also allows us to maintain our own identity, our fiscal autonomy, our language and our Olympic team.   (Pfeffer, 28)

Cooperatives in Puerto Rico

Cooperatives in Puerto Rico are unique in several ways. Early in the 1950s, Puerto Rico established the only government department on the globe with the sole mission of encouraging and supporting the formation of cooperatives. The history and culture of Puerto Rico must also be taken into consideration when comparing the success and failures of cooperative enterprises. The Commonwealth of Puerto Rico has passed a series of laws prescribing the formal incorporation and monitoring of enterprises classified as cooperatives (Suarez, 1953).

The Interest of the Puerto Rican Government in Encouraging Cooperatives

Following World War II, the government of Puerto Rico became concerned that returning soldiers could not find jobs. They had sacrificed several years of their lives—or even their entire lives—but those returning found it almost impossible to make an adequate living in their home communities or to enjoy the freedom they fought for. The crisis was severe and the prospect bleak.

In the summer of 1945, the University of Puerto Rico invited a visiting professor from Nova Scotia's St. Francis Xavier University, who gave a series of courses and lectures describing the cooperative model that was gaining great popularity and thriving in Nova Scotia. The participants were so intrigued by this information that they persuaded the Puerto Rican Government to sponsor a delegation of professors, students, and business people to visit the cooperatives in Nova Scotia and bring back a report. As a result of that report, the legislature passed the 1946 General Cooperative Associations Act setting out several provisions:

- Only consumers and primary producers can form Cooperative Associations.
- The Associations must be structured along the Rochdale principles.
- Representatives of Associations will meet annually in a General Assembly to elect officers and provide for the selection and hiring of management.
- Members can serve only two-year terms on the board of their Association.
- Each Association must save 0.1 percent of its annual gross for education.

(Suarez, 1953)

In addition to the above provisions, the Act established a Department of Cooperatives for the Commonwealth of Puerto Rico. This department would supervise the activities of the Associations and work with the University Extension to provide training. Observing how the economy began to improve sharply after the formation of a large number of cooperatives, the legislature promptly passed laws providing further support and encouragement for cooperative associations and, notably, a law establishing a cooperative savings and loan institution (credit union) to provide capitalization for new cooperatives.

Current Legal Structures for Co-ops in Puerto Rico

Since 1946, the Puerto Rican legislature has proposed numerous amendments to the General Cooperative Association Act and to the Savings and Loan Act. Most of these amendments were designed to provide more support to cooperatives, including capitalization. The original law, officially Law Number 5, generated much discussion about similar provisions for savings and loan cooperatives (Suarez, 1953).

Law Number 6, passed on 15 January 1990, accomplished the same goals for Savings and Loan Cooperatives (Credit Unions). It was expanded and amended by Law Number 255, passed on 28 October 2002. On the next day, 29 October 2002, the legislature passed a special bill for the development of "Juvenile Cooperatives." The Puerto Rican people and their legislature recognized the importance of education in shaping economic understanding for the future. The bill specifically allowed youth to form legal cooperatives for actual commercial activity and provided funds for these enterprises and their formation within the curricula of public schools. In 2004 Juvenile Cooperatives based in the public schools in all five regions grossed $1.3 million (Ley Num. 239, 2004).

Law Number 50, passed by the legislature on 4 August 1994, titled the 1994 General Cooperative Association Act, included a much enlarged Administration for the Development of Cooperatives with even more funds for capitalization of new cooperatives. According to its successor, Law Number 239, a new act, proposed "to stimulate activities of production and services by way of a cooperative structure governing consumer, housing, agricultural, and transportation cooperatives—among others" (Fourteenth Legislative Assembly, First Ordinary Session, Law Number 239, passed on 1 September 2004 [translated by author]). The new law intended not only to encourage the formation of many different types of cooperatives but also to provide guidance, training, and increased amounts of startup capital.

What Has Cooperation Achieved in Puerto Rico?

Since the earliest laws establishing government support and encouragement for the formation of cooperatives in Puerto Rico, cooperative enterprises have grown and spread over the commonwealth surprisingly rapidly. In June, 2004, about 22 percent of Puerto Ricans were members of at least one cooperative, and the list of cooperatives included thriving concerns in almost every sector of the economy.

Sectors and types of cooperatives:

- *Consumer Sector*   32
  - Supermarkets   3
  - Gasoline Stations   7
  - Pharmacies   4
  - Cafeterias   16
  - Agricultural Stores   2
- *Commercial Sector*   7
- *Agricultural Sector*   16
  - Farms   6
  - Fishing   5
  - Agro-industrial   5
- *Insurance Sector*   2
- *Transportation Sector*   16
  - Buses/Vans   8
  - Taxis   5
  - Tourist Excursions   3
- *Home and Garden*   20
- *Banking Sector*   2
  - Savings/Credit Co-op   1
  - Cooperative Bank   1
- *Miscellaneous Types*   26

Source: Lista, 2004

In 2003, cooperatives netted more than $550 million in goods and services, and the new *Junta* (Cooperatives' Investment Fund—FIDECOOP) showed a balance of nearly $9.8 million (FideCoop, 2004).

At the publication of the last annual report on June 30, 2004, there were altogether 255 cooperatives formed under law #239. Another 31 co-ops not prescribed by Commonwealth law makes a total of 286 co-ops. The total number of member owners participating in cooperative in Puerto Rico was 851,252; non-member participants, another 360,706. Full time employees numbered 2,719 and part time workers, 242—less than 8 percent. A particularly interesting statistic, unique with Puerto Rico's cooperative system, is the large number of ATM machines established by the co-ops for use by members. In early 2005 there were 147 cooperative ATM machines in Puerto Rico (FideCoop, 2004).

In all cases, the individual members are in charge of the policy and operation of the enterprises. All members of local Associations confer in their annual meetings, make policy for the Association, elect officers, review the work of the senior managers, and approve all hiring. Delegates from each of the 255 Associations meet annually in the Regular Annual Meeting to coordinate policy for all its members. The entire cooperative system appears to be extraordinarily democratic and participatory.

In 2004 the Regular Annual Meeting established a statewide association of co-ops (Liga de Cooperativas de Puerto Rico). This is a service organization to consult with co-ops, assisting them with their ongoing operations. It is supported by the cooperatives, each contributing 10 percent of its income. The Liga conducts seminars on cooperativism in addition to training sessions for members and employees. Each member Association sends elected delegates to a regular annual meeting. Its services are all without charge.

Summary and Conclusions

Puerto Rico's easternmost position among the Caribbean islands of the Greater Antilles contributes to the importance of its resources and leadership in trade—both north-south and east-west. The island has been a favorite of colonists and pirates throughout the centuries.

Colonization by the Spanish in the late fifteenth and early sixteenth centuries completely destroyed the peaceful and content Taíno, by the sword and smallpox. Repeated attempts by the French, English, and Dutch to seize and dominate Puerto Rico failed. These failures have been attributed both to the strength of the armaments at La Fortuleza and to disabling disease.

When Spain's maritime strength slackened and finally died in the late nineteenth century, Puerto Rico finally attained its independence. Its freedom, however, lasted less than six months before the US Marines landed. The old freedom cry, Grito (shout) de Lares, "*!Viva Puerto Rico Libre!*" rang out again, but not for long. A slim majority of Puerto Ricans now favor keeping Puerto Rico as a Commonwealth of the United States; nearly all of the rest advocate statehood. Only a small militant margin still holds out for complete independence.

Following World War II, citizens and legislators became intrigued with the cooperative movement. The cooperative model, presented to the university community by a visiting professor from a Nova Scotia university in 1945, offered an alternative to the exploitative corporate model brought to Puerto Rico by large American companies.

The legislature, assisted by economists from the university, soon drafted a series of laws establishing a governmental department to encourage and support the formation of cooperatives. By January, 2005, cooperatives of all types, including savings and loan institutions (credit unions), numbered more than 268. New government funds for cooperatives were reserved strictly for new startup cooperatives.

In Puerto Rico, the capitalization problem was solved by funding from the commonwealth's general tax base. Capitalizing the cooperatives consisted of applying to the government for support and counsel. There was always some struggle in assuring the government that the need, the demand and the participation of the community were all high enough to warrant national support. In this system, there is always a danger that the government will apply undue pressure for control and decision making. The cooperative councils have established an Association of Cooperatives and a supporting group called FideCoop as watchdogs charged with the task of offsetting that danger. In any case, the cooperatives could probably never be totally free of government influence, which may not be a bad thing.

The movement is burgeoning and promises to bring Puerto Rico into an equitable economic system. The US Census Bureau reported a poverty rate for Puerto Rican children ages 5-11 of 68.3 percent in 1990 and a rate of 53.7 percent in 2000, a drop of 14.6 percent. It is very difficult to assign causation using raw data, but the drop is coincident with a sharp rise in the number of co-ops on the island, with about 20 percent of the total population as new cooperative members.

References

Administración de Fomento Cooperativos (2002). *Ley de Sociedades Cooperativas De Ahorro y Crédito de 2002*. Rio Piedras, PR.

FIDECOOP (2004). *Informe Anual, Asamblea Ordinaria, 11 Junio, 2004*. Rio Piedras, PR.

Ley Num. 239 (2004). *Ley Num. 239—14ta Asamblea, 7ma Sesión Ordinario, 1 Sept, 2004*. Rio Piedras, PR.

Ley Num. 255 (2002). *Ley Num. 255—14ta Asamblea, 4ta Sesión* Ordinario, *28 Oct, 2002*. Rio Piedras, PR.

Lista (2004). *Lista de Cooperatives Bajo La Ley 239, 2004*. AFC, Rio Piedras, PR.

Pfeffer, R. (1999). *Puerto Rico*. Lonely Planet Publications. Oakland, CA.

Rouse, I. (1992). *The Taínos: Rise and Decline of the People Who Greeted Columbus*. Yale University Press, New Haven, CT.

Rodriguez-Julia, E. (2002) *Caribeños*. Instituto de Cultura Puertorriqueña. San Juan, PR.

Suarez, L.A. (1953). Cooperatives in Puerto Rico: History, Problems, Research. *Rural Sociology Vol. 18:3*, University of Kentucky, Lexington, KY.

US Census Bureau (2000). *Small Area Income and Poverty Estimates: Estimates for States, Counties, and School Districts*. US Census Washington, DC.

PART III
Analysis and Implications
for the Future

The cooperative movement survives within a predominantly competitive global environment. The Standard Economic Model, driving most global enterprises, assumes that competition and not cooperation provides the most efficient means to distribute and utilize the world's resources. If freed from governmental and international regulatory constraints, its exponents claim, competition in the "free" market is the only fair way to reduce poverty and ensure a reasonable living for every person in the world. Therefore, motivated by self-interest, the competitive model, and the promise of higher standards of living, transnational corporations have exploited resources and spread a form of unbridled capitalism around the world. Still the cooperatives are flourishing. Chapter 9 tries to answer the question, "What makes a cooperative work?" The answers are based on interviews and direct observations summarized and analyzed in Appendix D.

But now it appears that the two major economic systems, socialism and capitalism, have failed. The fall of the Berlin wall signaled the collapse of totalitarian, government-owned and controlled socialism. An equally totalitarian and feudalistic form of "capitalism" (perhaps a 1984-type misnomer) is failing. Dominated by undemocratic and colonialist transnational firms, this system also shows definite signs of falling apart at its unethical and immoral seams. Can we draw up a workable blueprint for a more inclusive and cooperative economic system based on a truly free market? Can we offer the world a democratically motivated "globalization from below?" Could there be a kind of globalization with the common good and economic welfare of all of the people as its bottom line?

PART III
Analysis and Implications
for the Future

Chapter 9

What Makes a Cooperative Work?

But only if she
Moves behind the veil of glitz
To the birth of hope
(Haiku by BL & BF)

Regardless of legal strictures and scarcity of financial resources available to cooperatives around the world, a large proportion of these enterprises have worked—and many have worked phenomenally well. In spite of the large number and variety of cultural settings, members of cooperatives report surprisingly similar feelings and attitudes about their experiences with co-ops. Almost without exception, members of the community at large, where a cooperative has been functioning for several years, share positive impressions of cooperatives and can often cite specific instances of how co-ops have helped their community.

The National Cooperative Business Association has compiled lists of factors for failure and success of cooperatives.

Why Cooperatives Fail

- Poor selection of directors, especially those who fail to support their cooperative;
- Members who join but never use their cooperative and bypass it for a small gain elsewhere;
- Members who use cooperatives but fail to take responsibility. Each member must be ready to accept responsibility when asked, or as the need arises. Every member should have an equal opportunity to be president of the cooperative;
- Members who never ask questions and who let a few persons make policy;
- Members who don't attend annual meetings and directors who fail to attend board meetings;
- Lack of consistent membership education about the problems cooperatives face and the challenges they must meet;
- Not supporting the cooperative with enough money (risk capital) to get the job done;
- Low-cost management—it's the most expensive item for a cooperative. High-priced management is usually the least expensive item;
- Not closely watching the formation of cliques and special interest groups within the cooperative;
- Concealing facts about a cooperative. All facts, both good and bad, should be placed on-not-under-the table;

- Errors in financial policy, such as over-extension of credit, too little capital, poor accounting records, or lack of a financially sound and systematic program for reimbursement of equity;
- Errors in educational and social work. This begins by failing to teach cooperative ideals to members unfamiliar with how cooperatives function, neglecting general educational programs, failing to develop member loyalty or countering the development of factions within the association;
- Management errors, such as inadequate inventory, poor location, improper equipment, neglected appearance of physical facilities, employee dishonesty, ineffective management, incompetent directors, nepotism, poorly conducted meetings, or admittance of disloyal and dissatisfied members.

Why Cooperatives Thrive

- Providing only the goods and services members use;
- Financed by the members. The greater the financing (risk capital) supplied by the members, the more efficient the cooperative;
- Using all major fixed assets at the 75 percent level, or more;
- Members who do the majority of their business with the cooperative;
- Low administrative and overhead costs;
- More individualized and specialized services, particularly in the marketing area;
- Maintaining an open line of communication with members. Individual members will then become more influential;
- Selecting and developing a quality management team;
- Placing more emphasis on electing business-oriented directors;
- Developing and implementing a systematic method of cooperative education for members, employees, directors, and paid management;
- Aggressively positioning for changes in operations, markets, and member needs.

                                                                      (NCBA, online)

On-site Visits and Interviews

During January and February of 2005, 23 interviews with management and 38 interviews with worker-members of cooperative groups around the world were conducted and compiled. The results of these 61 interviews are summarized briefly in Appendix D. Failed cooperatives are hard to find (partly because they no longer exist), but some failures have been spectacular and the results of a few interviews with past members of these groups can also be found in Appendix D. This chapter will pull together these results in order to determine what factors, specifically, have contributed to success or failure.

To make a cooperative work, the factor most frequently cited as the most important is proper financing. If capitalization of the project is not solid and if sufficient cash flow cannot be established, nothing else can make it function properly. The need for full participation of members runs a close second. Related to these two factors are general community support, organizational structure (including competent management), legal problems, and the temptation to go public.

Some of these problem areas overlap. Member participation can certainly be affected by general community support, and both are related in some measure to organizational structure. A cooperative seldom spends a great deal on advertisement and tends to rely heavily on membership to communicate its needs and to participate in market planning. Co-ops see their mission as satisfying an existing market rather than creating one. Because of this orientation, the channels of communication between management and the membership are crucial. A cooperative market orientation is unfamiliar in US society and must be worked with for a period of time, three or possibly five years, before such an "upside-down" approach to the market can take a firm hold.

Because of the above considerations, the concept of "success" is difficult to define. In the Standard Economic Model, success is clearly defined in terms of growth and dollar bottom lines. As we saw in Chapter 3, expansion and control of the market have become the primary goals of capitalism as prescribed by this model. On the other hand, the cooperative model defines success by the answers to two very subjective questions:

1. Are the needs of the members being satisfied?
2. Are resources and goods being distributed sufficiently equitably across the membership?

Perhaps both of these questions can be answered, in part, by the level of participation. For either of these questions to be answered in the affirmative, cash flow must be maintained at reasonably high levels, which leads us to the first topic, finance.

Financing Cooperative Enterprises

Capital needed for starting cooperative enterprises, somewhat like other enterprises, can come from a number of sources. Initial financing can be provided by microfinance, government sponsorship, cooperative banking, partnerships with commercial banking, or simply a slow growth through profits from products in stable demand.

Microfinance

The Asian approach has largely been through microcredit. Bangladesh's Grameen (village) model and Indonesia's People's Bank have led the way in this sector. Although some bickering has marked the relationship between these two, they both follow some of the same initial steps. The large difference between Grameen and Indonesian capitalization was that the Indonesian government provided the bulk of start-up capital for the People's Bank, while the Grameen Bank began with about $20 out of Professor Yunus's pocket. Each began by empowering women in the villages with small business loans (totally unsecured in the case of Grameen Bank), and both grew within only a few years into large self-sustaining cooperative enterprises.

The Grameen Bank began by organizing small groups of women in the villages and training them to supervise and maintain their own financial health, following a set of strict rules of saving and daily lifestyles. Only much later did the bank open up its savings and loan program to the general public and redirect a portion of its retained earnings to loans for larger commercial enterprises. The People's Bank of Indonesia began with a large grant from the National Bank of Indonesia, and now directs its efforts through a few full-time staff people in each unit, which in turn serves the general public. Oversimplifying somewhat, the Grameen Bank uses a bottom-up flow of control and the People's Bank follows a top-down flow.

Government Sponsorship

The Indonesian People's Bank was started by the government of Indonesia through the Bank of Indonesia. Now its banking system is self-supporting through loan interest. The enterprise was entirely a cooperative system for financing small independent enterprises and cooperatives. In the Commonwealth of Puerto Rico, the government created a department to encourage and support the formation of cooperatives of all kinds. The government remains strict about subsidizing only new cooperatives for their first five years of operation. After that the cooperatives must become self-supporting.

In all other countries of the world, the government has provided support in a number of ways other than financial. In the United States and Europe, strong legislation has been provided to promote the formation of cooperatives, but direct grants or subsidies have never been used to encourage or support cooperative enterprises. In Mexico, the legislative climate has shuttled back and forth between indirect support for cooperatives and subtle forms of discouragement through incorporation fees and taxes. In Australia, the government climate has been frankly hostile to the formation of cooperatives.

These practices of receiving grants or loans from governments or governmental agencies, even to finance only start-up projects, raise questions of how much a cooperative enterprise should lay itself open to government influence. The genius of the cooperative movement is the strength of its grass-roots support. Some fear that the possibility of easy financing from government or corporate sources will dilute that cooperative spirit. However, whether the government encourages or discourages the formation and operation of cooperatives appears to make little difference in the long run. The vast majority of co-ops thrive anyway and become totally independent of outside support.

Cooperative Banking and Support of Cooperative Enterprises

Mondragón is unique in receiving initial capitalization from the Church and a door-to-door canvass. Its first task was to establish a technical school to provide more qualified engineering talent for the steel mill. Also the Mondragón Cooperatives have been a model for the world in establishing a cooperative Bank, the *Caja Laboral*, at the hub of its entire cooperative structure. This early move in the formation of Mondagón's approach to cooperation has resulted in a remarkably strong and resilient economic system for the entire Basque area. Central to the success of cooperation in Mondragón has been the focus of *Caja Laboral* on education, research, and development. Consequently, the excellence of its technical expertise and innovation has proven superior to those of many other enterprises in the world.

Partnerships with Commercial Banking

The ASP cooperatives in South-Central India provide our best example of successful partnerships with commercial banking firms in order to capitalize first a huge micro-credit program and then satellite cooperative enterprises of all kinds. The total of outstanding loans, however, has at all times been kept below annual earnings of the entire cooperative system.

Public Shares without Voting Privileges

Recently, there has been talk among management and governing boards of co-ops in the United States of floating shares to the public with a guarantee of dividend payment but without the voting privilege. The major criticism of this idea is that it could begin to lay the cooperatives open to pressure from outside its own membership and thus violate one of the important principles of cooperation. As an alternative, many cooperatives now offer additional shares to its own members carrying dividends but without conferring any additional control or voting privileges. Persons owning a large percentage of outstanding shares should have no more control or privilege than those owning only one share. However, temptation to award more power to large shareholders may become impossible to resist as time goes on. Fear of losing strong support may eventually erode resolve to maintain the essential cooperative principles.

The experience of the first Rochdale Cooperative should be kept in mind. Taking on external investors threatened to destroy the co-op, and the original owner-members were several years recuperating from that error. For all these reasons, the practice is not strongly recommended.

Taking on Wage Workers with Transferable Shares

Another serious mistake is illustrated by the story of Olympia Veneer Company, the first of the many plywood cooperatives in the Pacific Northwest, United States. Transferable shares were issued to the workers, and the efficiency of cooperative labor caused share values to skyrocket. And when more capital was needed to maintain an expanded production, instead of taking on more full owner-members, wage workers were hired to work on individually owned, transferable shares. Individual shares could be sold, so they began selling out as share values continued to increase. The company's viability was compromised, so in 1954 the remaining 23 full members calculated their individual worth—approximately $650,000 each—and voted to sell out. "Despite its egalitarian impulse, the seed of Olympia's demise was present at the start" (Bowman *et al.*, 2005, 4). Those seeds were planted when the company's charter was written to allow sale of workers' shares.

Capital Derived from Membership Fees and Ordinary Cash Sales

The Mondragón Cooperatives in Basque Country, Northern Spain, require rather large membership fees—on the order of one year's wages. They then make it possible to pay this one-time fee through a line of credit with the *Caja Laboral*. Most cooperatives could not set such a high membership fee, especially during the early years of an enterprise's career. Once the membership is built up, larger fees might be feasible, but who would want to raise the membership fees for long-time faithful members? In order to keep fees low, most retail co-ops offer a way of reducing the fee through volunteer activity. Most management specialists would advise cooperatives to base their planning on large cash flows through sales and not rely totally upon membership fees.

Unwise Use of Initial Financing, Starting Too Big

A series of fairly common mistakes in the original financing of cooperatives is illustrated by the experience of the Boulder Cooperative Market in Colorado, US. "Location, location, location" remain the three most important considerations in the success of retail ventures. Boulder Co-op Market chose an out-of-the-way location with little provision for parking for its market, and thus has suffered a great deal in trying to attract buyers. They also rented a building which was in many ways unsuitable for food retail activity, a building which had to be extensively and expensively renovated before moving in. A full year elapsed before normal activity could begin.

To make matters doubly difficult, the planners failed to negotiate for some kind of rent reduction to offset the large expense and attendant increase in value of the building due to the renovation. Now the co-op has a difficult time repaying large loans extended by members and local commercial banks. Business has been lost because of failure to keep shelves stocked with goods demanded. The co-op has been helped by the notable success of Café Prasad, a natural foods coffee shop, and a local craft sales department. These two portions of the enterprise substantially increase the co-op's cash flow.

To be fair, the land at the chosen location is comparatively inexpensive. The rent charged by the land owner is quite reasonable. Combining the monthly rent with the loan payment directly attributable to the renovation outlay, the property actually costs between $12 and $15 a square foot. This compares favorably with $20 to $30 a square foot ordinarily charged in other parts of Boulder.

Participation

No membership organization can last long without strong participation of its members. Most problems, both financial and social, experienced by cooperatives involve the level of participation. Among the cooperatives observed, six approaches to stimulating participation have been proposed. These six approaches are:

1. Carefully considering the concept of "critical fit" (David Korten, 1980);
2. Researching the demands and needs of the community;

3. Educating the community about the importance of cooperation;
4. Linking participation directly with members' livelihood;
5. Communicating effectively; and
6. Developing a sense of ownership among the members.

Critical fit refers to the match between the goals of the cooperative and goals of the community. One form of cooperation may fit beautifully within one cultural context but not in another. The appeal of cooperation among the Dalits in India is very strong. The Dalits want to participate and consider it an honor to have such an opportunity to develop the structures and outcomes of their own economy. There may not be such a draw for cooperatives among the lower socio-economic classes of the United States. Direct observation however, does not seem to bear out such a judgment. The appeal of coopertivism seems to be universal. Critical fit does not appear to be as important as earlier suggested.

Being able to *sense the demands and needs of a community* does help to increase membership and participation in a retail cooperative. Some food cooperatives have attracted people to a coffee house or natural food cafeteria. Again the attraction appears to be universal. The joy both of working in and of patronizing a small community coffee house feels much the same at a roadside cooperative funded by a micro-loan in South-Central India as it does at the *Café Prasad* in the Cooperative Market in Boulder, Colorado.

Education about the importance and socio-economic values of cooperative activity is crucial in building participation. The educational sector of the Mondragón cooperatives is a perfect illustration of that principle. Unique in the field is the elementary school curriculum on cooperative economics in Puerto Rico.

The close *link to the members' livelihood* in production cooperatives ensures almost 100 percent participation. The larger the cooperative and the closer it resembles a large corporation—as in the Mondragón cooperatives—the more difficult it becomes to experience this direct connection. On the other hand, with the Dalits in India the connection becomes starkly obvious, because this lowest caste is otherwise totally shut out of the economic system. Cooperatives are literally "the only game in town."

The artisans and the agricultural cooperatives in Mexico have succeeded in spite of all roadblocks. Most notably, the farmers of Vicente Guerrero in Tlaxcala, Mexico, have learned how to increase production in ecologically natural and sound ways. Word of their successes has spread across Central America, and there is no problem getting 100 percent participation and sharing in this kind of productivity. The farmers of Vicente Guerrero now are not only participating in actual farm production but teaching other farmers how to achieve a new level of agricultural technology.

Yellow Cab Cooperative Associations—a Tale of Two Cities

The experience of two Yellow Cab companies, one in Denver, Colorado, and one in San Francisco, California, both in the United States, illustrate the crucial importance of participation in the success and failure of cooperatives. Yellow Cab companies are typically operated by leasing fully equipped cabs to drivers for a set monthly rental fee. The driver keeps whatever fees are made, above the equipment rental fee. The companies are independent and urban based, some operated by closely held corporations and some owned by the drivers and operated cooperatively.

The Denver-Boulder Yellow Cab co-op has operated since the early 1970s. In 1993 they filed for Chapter 11 bankruptcy. A discussion with a former driver revealed that the drivers became tired of spending time on management and committee meetings. The drivers are not the kind of people who want to participate in any group processes. They prefer to drive their cars, collect fares, pay the monthly lease fees, and be done with it. Since the company sold to its new owners, the fees have gone up, but the drivers apparently still prefer just to drive and collect fares.

The San Francisco Yellow cab co-op is still operating as a cooperative and apparently doing very well. Its history is almost the exact reverse of the Denver-Boulder Yellow Cab co-op. The cab company was originally owned by San Diego's Westgate Corporation, which filed for bankruptcy in 1976 and ceased all of its operations, including the Yellow Cab subsidiary in San Francisco. After long negotiations with the bankruptcy courts in San Diego, a group of drivers, mechanics, dispatchers, and other local investors who had organized into a cooperative successfully concluded an agreement to purchase the San Francisco Yellow Cab company. Each of the members of the cooperative put in $5,000 for the down payment. Most of the original drivers of the company were back on the road by November of 1977.

Today the San Francisco Yellow Cab co-op is a completely independent, locally owned cooperative. The membership is very diverse, including women, gay, and minority shareholder/members. The manager does not necessarily have to be a member, but until 2002 no non-member was hired by the board of directors for any management position. The general manager has the power to hire, but the Board appoints a Safety Commission whose job it is to deal with accidents and any complaints brought against drivers. Any member whose behavior is considered a liability to the company can be dismissed only by a two-thirds vote of the entire membership. Due to the cooperative nature of the San Francisco Yellow Cab organization, the costs of management is considerably less than that of any private cab company. Partly because the drivers realize that they can earn more as members of the cooperative, the co-op has become very popular with its driver-members, who participate in its governance with enthusiasm.

Communication is undoubtedly a key to participation. Mondragón, in Spain, increased worker participation and solved worker conflicts by forming new Social Councils to increase influence over company decision making. The message to the worker-members was clear: Participation brings more results and more control by the individual workers over their own economic futures.

Finally, whatever will give the members a *sense of ownership* in a successful enterprise is sure to heighten their participation. This may be brought about by successfully fulfilling demands and needs of the community, by educating young students and adults about the values of cooperation, and by raising the level of communication among the members and between members and management. The consensus process for decision making has proved to be a significant contribution to the sense of ownership and to the ultimate success of the co-op.

Community support

Operating a cooperative enterprise without community support proves virtually impossible. Several methods cooperatives have employed to ensure community support have included the formation of advisory committees, community centers, and ordinary publicity.

Advisory committees have provided many cooperatives with a base of ideas and activities which involve the entire community. As soon as people in the community see the benefits of cooperation in providing goods, services and entertainment, members of the community will begin to take pride in their own cooperative efforts. For example, nothing could ever supplant or overshadow the pride felt by residents of Green Bay, Wisconsin, US, for their Packers (a unique sports fan's cooperative).

In forming advisory committees, care should be taken to include non-members in at least half of the committee. Advisory committees should be composed of prominent citizens who are representative of various segments of the community. These persons should also have demonstrated strong leadership abilities and substantive skills in their particular fields—especially in business management.

Several cooperatives have established *community centers* to promote participation, to attract new members, and to provide educational opportunities about how cooperatives work or about other services. The community center can house services such as massage, counseling, entertainment, or skill-sharing activities. The community center can also be the focus of a number of community support groups or youth activities. There is nothing like giving support to the community in order to get support from the community.

Publicity can take many forms. Establishing a community bulletin board is a minimum requirement to encourage the co-op to become a center of communication and information exchange. Word of mouth and other informal communication mechanisms can be the most effective form of advertisement. Also cooperatives should plan to announce special offerings of goods, services, and community activities regularly in local television, radio, and newspapers. Occasional human interest stories should be provided to all media on a regular basis. Above all, for the cooperative, publicity should be much more than advertisement of goods and services; it should be an educational experience for readers or viewers.

Organizational structure

Almost every cooperative has experienced a restructuring of its organization. As in all business enterprises, the skills, talents, and structures needed for establishing an organization may not be the best ones for moving the enterprise into the future. Promotional activities needed for organizing and setting up a cooperative are not the only ones needed for day to day operations. The three organizational components that have proven essential for ongoing success are (1) management qualifications and competence, (2) strong worker-member participation and sense of ownership, and (3) clear lines of communication within the membership and between management and worker-members.

An excellent example of organizational structure is the Mondragón Cooperative Corporation. It is amazing that they were able to operate satisfactorily for over 40 years before they needed a major organizational overhaul. They were able to provide ongoing management qualifications and competence through the early establishment of cooperative technical schools. As long as the cooperative was small and included the residents of only two or three Basque communities, the second and third components could be very informal. As they grew larger and spread over most of Basque country in northern Spain, the need for more solidarity among workers and, especially, better communications between management and the worker-members became critical.

The "Great Reorganization" of Mondragón came on the heels of the one and only strike experienced by the company since its inception. It became obvious that workers felt that they had little or no input into critical policy decisions. Several contentions were settled, and workers and management finally realized that the members literally and legally own the company and could hire and fire its management any day. The strike was seen as necessary, however, to call attention to the participation and communication problems.

Now composed of 218 companies distributed among 50 Basque communities and 21 countries around the world, new worker social councils were organized for direct input into management issues, and a newly constituted General Assembly of 650 worker-members convenes annually to review the work of all the councils and commissions of the company. Every small, medium-sized, and large sector of the company has a council of members governing it. Now the worker-members have direct input into every issue and activity from office to shop floor.

Whether a cooperative can ever foresee its future needs and organize for the long haul at the outset or must plod through every developmental phase, always modifying its structures and procedures to meet the needs of the hour, one thing is certain: The successful co-op must continually re-evaluate its organizational structure with the idea of always maximizing its member participation and its lines of communication. Co-ops must plan to maintain a training process for all worker-members, educating them in the principles and values of cooperation, ready to meet any challenge.

Legal Problems

From the outset, legal problems have plagued the cooperative movement in the United States. For production, retail, and distribution cooperatives, relevant law revolves around the Sherman Antitrust Act of 1890, the Clayton Act of 1914, and the Capper-Volstead Act of 1922.

The Sherman Act was passed to curtail attempts by the "Robber Barons" of the nineteenth century to form monopolies in order to control prices. That Act is still crucial today as large corporations attempt to corner larger and larger percentages of their markets. It would seem that runaway competition can easily destroy the free market and become overbearing to smaller businesses and cooperatives. The Act in its early form had the effect of dampening the growth of the cooperative movement and still prevents co-ops in the US from becoming multi-company or multi-sector enterprises, and prevents any one cooperative company from dominating the market.

To ease the pressure somewhat on agricultural cooperatives that were needed to save the family farms from total extinction, in 1914, Section 6 of the Clayton Act was passed to allow farmers to form cooperatives. The Act only covered some types of agricultural cooperatives, and was soon deemed to be inadequate.

The Capper-Volstead Act, named for its two most prominent champions, was passed in 1922 to remedy the flaws in the Clayton Act and to stop the abusive uses of the Sherman Antitrust Act to curtail cooperative activity. This Act is commonly referred to as the Magna Carta of cooperatives, because it freed the cooperative enterprises to match the activities of the large corporations. The Capper-Volstead Act greatly expands the definition of what cooperative activities should be considered legal.

There is continual pressure on the movement to conform to the standard corporate model. Every congressional session is peppered by proposals from the banking community to clip the wings of credit unions and cooperative banks. Fortunately the US legislature remains supportive of the cooperative movement and, at least at this point, tends to reject moves to curtail its activities.

In Mexico, laws defining legal activity for cooperatives change almost yearly. When the church, the *haciendas*, and *latifundios*, all holding exorbitant amounts of land in trust, were broken up into *ejidos* owned by the government, laws about the land's use became hopelessly confusing. At one point, it was possible for a cooperative group to take over (rent) the *ejido* land from the government; at another, the cooperatives were so outlandishly taxed that most of them dissolved their cooperative businesses and went private wherever possible—which may have been the intent of the law. In spite of all of these political machinations, some robust groups like the Silver Artisans of Old Taxco and the agricultural cooperative of Vicente Guerrero, Tlaxcala (both described in Chapter 7) were able to survive and even thrive. There still is no consistent corporate law in Mexico to allow development to proceed smoothly and in a cooperative fashion.

A study of the Puerto Rican cooperative system would be instructive at this point. Some developing nations have given one time grants or even supported specific cooperatives, but no other nation or state has ever established a governmental department to promote and support cooperatives. Not only has the Commonwealth of Puerto Rico established such a department, it has also facilitated the formation of a Liga de Cooperativas de Puerto Rico, an idea borrowed from the Italian LEGACOOP. The Liga, supported financially by 10 percent of the income of each member cooperative association, conducts seminars and training sessions. It also maintains a consultation staff for the support of cooperatives—all without direct charge to members.

Cooperative activities are protected by a series of laws complementing a rudimentary Cooperative Act of 1941. Following a seminar at the University of Puerto Rico led by a visiting professor from Nova Scotia, the Commonwealth legislature passed a remarkably comprehensive law, the General Cooperative Associations Act of 1946, including the establishment of the *Administración de Fomento Cooperativo*. Since then, numerous laws and amendments have been passed to strengthen the work of developing cooperatives. By June 2004, there were almost 300 cooperatives netting over a half-billion dollars in goods and services, with over 22 percent of the Puerto Rican population belonging to at least one cooperative.

Other countries around the world with fewer laws aiding or restricting the activities of cooperatives are also developing very rapidly partly because of the momentum of the cooperative movement.

Should We Go Public?

The huge California and Mexico avocado cooperative, Calavo, in spite of its inspiring success, has been a disappointment. After almost eight decades of highly successful operation, 90 percent of its members voted to go public. This vote came under the able leadership of Lee Cole, one of the largest avocado growers in California, and as a response to the pressure of NAFTA, the free trade agreement passed in 1994. The "free trade" agreements have universally restricted international activities of cooperatives by imposing unreasonably high tariffs on them. Calavo was at that time wanting to trade freely through its state of the art facility in Uruapan, Mexico, and we must remember that free trade agreements largely favor the transnationals. So however disappointing, it was no surprise that Calavo opted to join the ranks of the large transnationals.

Going public is a temptation both for the highly successful large multi-national cooperative and the small struggling co-op seeking large boluses of money in order to service overwhelming start-up loans. In both cases, the original members may still protect their majority ownership, but must now dilute their ownership and control by offering a portion (in dividends only or equity stock) of it to investors, whose bottom line is exclusively money, or worse yet to speculators.

Summary Discussion

What makes a cooperative work? The simple answer is: "a group of people who want it to work." In observing and interviewing such people, several factors became clear. Universally, the most important factors influencing success and failure are proper *capitalization* and a high rate of member *participation*.

The smoothest way to accumulate capital for a variety of production co-ops is through micro-finance or cooperative banking. Participation levels nearing 100 percent are virtually guaranteed in this way. Retail cooperatives can come later and should probably begin small and expand as cash flow permits.

Community support is, of course, essential. Little progress can be made without it. Successful cooperatives consistently find creative ways to involve the entire community in their programs. Some cooperative food markets have included a natural foods café or coffee shop within their stores. Others have featured community educational centers or craft shops.

Organizational structures change with the ongoing challenges to improve communications within the co-op, between the workers and management, and between the co-op and the community. Changes are often required by legal and political considerations, size and scope of the organization, and policy changes by the member councils.

Most flourishing cooperative ventures have resisted going public to solve their capitalization problems, or to compete successfully with other similar commercial companies. The future challenge most consistently reported by retail is working within the context of expanding national and international chains such as Whole Foods and Wal-Mart. What has been called "the Wal-Mart effect" will be dealt with in more detail in Chapter 10.

References

NCBA Online, National Cooperative Business Association (US). www.ncba.coop.
Direct Sources: Interviews and direct observations on fifteen cooperative sites. Jan-Feb 2005. See Appendix D.

Chapter 10

The Blueprint: Globalization from Below

Rich getting richer
And poor getting poorer
Can it ever change? (Haiku by BL & BF)

Anna used to work as a support person for a large professional group. The group was well known for its multi-cultural character and highly successful human services center near a large university campus. She describes the organization as "flat" in that it was very inclusive and showed few signs of a hierarchical structure. Staff meetings included support people as well as highly skilled and well educated professionals. In planning, problem solving, and evaluating, everyone's contribution was equally respected. Although the company was not owned by the workers, the director and professional staff firmly believed in a cooperative and non-hierarchical approach to their work and gave everyone a sense of "ownership" of the work. Their respectful attitudes toward each other and their clients, along with their multi-cultural approach, made them highly successful in their field.

Anna's original job title was "receptionist." The director, a highly skilled and seasoned professional, valued and respected Anna just as much as she did any of her other staff. After a few weeks on the job, the director sat down with Anna and went over her job description, making revisions according to Anna's suggestions and with attention to Anna's own strengths, preferences, and skills—particularly her artistic ability and training. She essentially designed her own job. Most managers and CEOs would consider this a "sissy" approach to management. The traditional management training teaches that a strong manager should maintain distance from her common workers and be clear about her expectations for them—a decided remnant of the *feudal* system.

Noticing Anna's computer skills and artistic flair in designing the company newsletter, the director procured a new, more powerful computer and top of the line professional desktop publishing software. The group began receiving favorable comments and inquiries from their professional associates about the newsletter Anna had developed. The director also noted Anna's people skills and asked Anna to accompany her and long-time staff members in presentations to public relations meetings. The group became even more well-regarded because of Anna's personable and artistic abilities to present the company's multicultural approach to the general public. Their services were more and more in demand and the director did not hesitate to give Anna full credit for their improved image and awarded her several raises in pay and upgrades to her job title.

As a result of her successes and positive reviews by the director, Anna happily continued to work with the company for eighteen years. Sadly, the director attained

the age of retirement, and a new director was hired. The new director's approach
to management was 180 degrees away from that of the recently retired one. His
attitudes and work style were much more traditional and definitely hierarchical. His
relationship with the support staff was condescending and distant. As time went on,
things were not going well, and the new director became more and more critical of
Anna's work and actually abusive in his attitude toward her. She eventually resigned,
mentally and physically ill. The entire staff is still miserable and far less productive.
The company is no longer well regarded by its public and potential clients.

Unfortunately, Anna's story is all too common. The usual workplace is becoming
less and less democratic and work itself more and more demeaning—labor a mere
commodity for the entrepreneur to employ as cheaply and with as little annoyance
as possible. The story illustrates the potential productive strength and the capacity
to inspire and empower workers using the cooperative model. The story illustrates
how cooperation works.

A Summary of What is Now Known About Cooperation

Earlier pages of this book presented the basics of the cooperative model, and how
cooperativism sprang from the needs of the grassroots of society and spread around
the world. To the traditional social scientist, the cooperative movement represented
an "alternative" theory of economic activity. To the members of such cooperative
enterprises, cooperativism seemed a more natural and a more democratic approach
to the distribution of resources and wealth. Traditional theories of political economy
were considered more conservative and "realistic" and have produced less active
participation of workers and consumers in political and economic decisions. This
reduction in political activity of the average citizen is reflected in low voter turnouts
and increasing disengagement from governmental processes. Cooperativism
proposes to reverse that trend.

Chapter 1 presented an overview of the history and theory of the cooperative
movement. Under favorable—and even unfavorable—political and legal conditions,
the movement has thrived and has even saved family farms in the United States
during the 1980s. At that time, expansion and power through competition were
seldom goals in agricultural mid-America; the central issue in that era was simply
survival. In the heart of the United States, under the pressure of the banking crisis,
people who did not consider cooperativism a subtle form of socialism were able to
work together for their common good.

Chapter 2 demonstrated how the cooperative model can operate quite successfully
in a multitude of social and economic situations. Where participants can see the
benefits of sharing power, profits, and outcomes, cooperation proves to be more
productive than competition or uncoordinated individual effort. Of the more than
1,500 studies comparing cooperation and competition, all of the carefully planned
studies agreed that, under a wide variety of circumstances and with outcomes
measured in a variety of ways, cooperation is by far the best method.

Chapter 3 showed how two totally different economic systems have been
operating—a cooperative one and a competitive one—side by side in the same social

space for a number of centuries. If both of these systems continue to grow, how will the system based largely on local cooperation fit in with a system based on global competition? How will a system based on equal shares and equal power survive next to a system based on unequal distributions of share ownership and power and how can each allow for the existence of the other?

Chapters 4 through 8 provided detailed, on-the-ground analyses of cooperative efforts around the world, in different cultures and in different political settings; Chapter 9 summarized the results of interviews both of management and members of cooperatives. The central questions in the interviews were: "What makes a cooperative succeed?" "What are the most obvious successes of your cooperative?" And, "What do you see as the greatest challenges for the future?" Direct observation and answers to the interview questions highlighted several challenges for the future: maintaining access to capital, increasing participation, remaining committed to cooperative principles, reaching the poorest of the poor, maintaining effective organization and competent management, and responding to the impacts of global business.

Unfortunately, we have not fully explored or understood the power of cooperation. Our social reflexes still pull us toward the competitive and the conservative model of economics. The American dream of the universal ability to acquire virtually unlimited wealth, or at least to be "comfortably well-off," is still very much alive. The fact is that, in two hundred years of standard economic development, large numbers of the world's people have never realized the dream and remain in abject poverty. These numbers continue to grow.

Even if most of us in the West have been awakened (rudely) by recent excesses of transnational capitalist corporations and absolutist governments, the dream still lingers, though dimly, before our eyes. Like frogs placed in cool water and slowly warmed, we have not yet realized that we are beginning to boil. Soon, jumping out of the hot water will become impossible. The elitist political economy of the West has been slowly warming up over the last century; soon our frog will be cooked!

Democracy and Inefficiency

Traditional economists will often insist that cooperatives or labor managed businesses are "unproductive and inefficient." Some even would claim that the most efficient system is essentially an autocratic one, where all the important decisions are made by a "benevolent dictator" in the form of a powerful, well-trained, and intelligent General Manager or CEO. Such managers, of course, do not take cooperatives seriously; they argue that democratic companies are unproductive and inefficient, and efficient companies win out in a competitive economy. There is no evidence to support such assumptions.

One can understand where this kind of assumption comes from when the century-long discussion about property rights and "commons" in the West is properly reviewed. We generally assume that everyone has a right to the air they breathe. It used to be assumed that every living being should have a right to clean water. Recent claims of private economic concerns to water rights have largely gone unnoticed, and from there on everyone's natural rights have been steadily eroded. Beginning in the fourteenth century, the Church and the aristocracy enclosed huge parcels of land with the excuse that resources can be more efficiently used that way.

Thus the Fable, "The Tragedy of the Commons," went: Once upon a time the pasture was held in common. Everyone was free to graze their cattle there. One day a certain farmer began to increase his herd beyond the size of all the others. Others increased their herd in an attempt to compete. Soon the pasture was overgrazed, became a mud hole, and everyone's cattle business was ruined. Moral to the story: The pasture should be privatized, so the best farmer could own it and control its use. The fable carefully omits the possibility that the smaller farmers who were then excluded fell into abject poverty, and their children all died of starvation.

The fable is exactly that: a fable. In fact, there is ample evidence that cooperatives can be much more effective and efficient than private ownership and traditional corporations. A study of 40 large cooperative plywood firms in the Northwest by economist John Pencavel reports that worker-owned industries are 6 to 14 percent more productive than their commercial counterparts (2002).

It could be amusing—and frightening—to carry the subject of rights to private ownership to its logical extreme. Recent debates over the ethics and legality of rights to common scientific knowledge, technical knowledge, or "intellectual property" grow more and more acute. A startling title appears on the cover of February, 2006, *Scientific American*, "Guess Who Owns Your Genes?" The article by Gary Stix, "Owning the Stuff of Life," informs the reader that nearly 20 percent of the genes in the human genome have one or more patents on them. For example, the gene in human cells that plays a key role in the early development of the spinal cord belongs to Harvard University. Incyte Corporation owns the purified form of a human gene controlling a receptor for histamine, the body's natural reaction to allergy. Merck Corporation holds exclusive patents on 365 different genes. Soon every human part and function will be exclusively owned by some large corporation.

Even more conservative economists like David I. Levine and Laura D'Andrea Tyson, economic advisors to President Clinton, in a study of worker-owned companies (Levine and Tyson, 1990), report a direct positive correlation between degree of worker ownership and productivity of the workers. The higher the level of worker ownership is, the more productive the workers are. This result echoed an even earlier study by Derek C. Jones and Jan Svenar reporting similar results (1982).

So why are more companies not taking the worker-ownership route? Is it only because management is loathe to share their power and relinquish domination over their workers? True worker-controlled businesses are relatively rare, because the dominant sources of capital—investors, lenders, and entrepreneurs—have little to gain from them. The reasons for this state of affairs are more a matter of competition and expansion of dog-eat-dog economic power than a matter of efficiency or productivity. In other words, the reasons why cooperatives and other worker-owned enterprises do not dominate the economic scene can be attributed to political and not economic factors.

Indeed, these cooperative and worker-directed firms are no longer as rare as they were in the 1980s and 1990s. In the 1990s, the cooperative sector in Italy, at that time the largest among industrialized nations, claimed only about 250,000 worker-members. At that time, Mondragón could account for only 30,000. By 2005 those numbers had increased to over 1 million and 70,000 respectively. Democratic practices are also being introduced to the more traditional, commercial sector as well, in order to achieve higher worker productivity and efficiency. Some perceptions of cooperative enterprises are beginning to change.

The Current Socio-political Matrix

A close examination of twentieth-century western political economy reveals a constant shift to the right, so that an appeal to equal economic, social, and political rights and opportunities for everyone in western society now sounds "leftist." In reality, such an appeal to more equitable distributions of wealth and natural rights demands a refocusing on the central values of enlightened democracy and thus is not left of center, but actually stands squarely in the middle of the democratic political tradition.

Modern capitalism was a reaction to concentrated wealth and exclusive rights to property and political influence in seventeenth and eighteenth century Europe. It was a reaction to aristocracy and its assumptions of ownership and power by virtue not of application and ability but solely of birth. Unfortunately, the twentieth century version of capitalism did not entirely rid itself of this aristocratic—or racist/classist—view of economic welfare. The inevitable result: concentration of wealth and intense poverty. This is certainly not a new phenomenon. An ancient teacher described his own "evil generation" as one in which: "For those who have, more is given, and from those who have nothing even what they have will be taken away" (D'Nazari, ca. 30 AD). The poverty experience has not changed much since then.

Such a state of oppression is again realized by so-called enlightened western capitalism. Neo-liberalism, reacting against and at the same time growing out of *feudalism*, actually brought with it *feudalism's* sense of exclusivity of ownership and political power. Along with the concept of domination and oppression came a strictly hierarchical corporate structure. In most corporations now, the President of the Board is also the CEO; even though ballots are circulated to shareholders, names chosen are members of a self-perpetuating power elite.

Understanding the current economic situation becomes easier if it is also understood that most classical economists were spokespersons for the elite classes and were therefore most concerned with protecting wealth and power. These economists hold that labor must be paid just enough to reproduce itself and that all wealth produced by technology should go to capital. Like the fable, all these theoretical ideas routinely ignored the fact that this accumulation of capital did not accrue to the common good but only to "grand castles and high living" (Smith, 2005b, 11; Perelman, 2000, 91).

An appeal to a more inclusive view of ownership and civil rights in no way advocates for government ownership of industry as socialism once did, but proposes equal access to the *wealth accumulation process* as originally propounded by Adam Smith. This equal access awards equal rights and opportunities to whoever wants to achieve a *democratic-cooperative-super-efficient capitalism* (Smith, 2005b). The cooperative movement can be seen to stand within this alternative democratic view of ownership and voting rights.

Unfortunately, neo-liberal economics has recently gained so much support from the elite and moneyed classes in Western society that the concerned citizen is almost afraid to criticize it. Voices of dissent have been muffled by the drum beat of dominance and power and the marching cadence of competitive empire—more riches for the rich and fewer opportunities for the *lazy and dirty* lower classes. Dictatorships would have crumbled long ago if they had not been put in power and kept in power by these neo-liberal forces of empire. Feudalism, together with an assumption of caste and class, remains alive and well in the twenty-first century. Ironically, this continuing unenlightened power system is often popularly called "liberal" and "democratic."

The Wal-Mart Effect

Probably the most blatant case of a neo-liberal/feudal assault on human decency in recent years has been Wal-Mart's corporate behavior. While the President/CEO of Wal-Mart instructed his "associates" to, "Tell the story..." and most importantly, "Stay the course!" the company was destroying smaller businesses (Greenwald's film, "Wal-Mart, the High Cost of Low Prices," 2005).

H & H Hunt's Ace Hardware in Middlefield, Ohio, part of the nation-wide Ace Hardware Cooperative, was known for its excellent service and knowledge of its products. Hunt's store was a real asset to the community. Its member-workers were well paid, with a share of the profits, plus generous medical insurance and other fringes. The Hunt family had run the store since 1960, done well, built a larger building, and increased its inventory. Then Wal-Mart moved in. Middlefield's city council awarded Wal-Mart a special tax break to build their huge store.

Mr Hunt learned about the special tax break and asked the council for a similar break for his large hardware store. The council refused this request. Within a year, the Hunts had to close Ace Hardware; the member-workers were all terminated. Some people were able to get jobs at Wal-Mart. The Wal-Mart management made it clear that, although they were called "associates," they were definitely not owners but "beginning level employees." Full time employment is defined by Wal-Mart at 28 hours per week, producing an annual income of less than $12,000, with no fringes whatsoever. Medical insurance is made available to "all who qualify," but no one on such a low pay scale can afford it. Wal-Mart's personnel department does assist its "associates" in using the public health systems like Medicaid and Social Security assistance. Wages for full time "associates" is low enough to qualify for various welfare programs. In this way, the US taxpayers are subsidizing Wal-Mart to the tune of over $1.5 billion dollars annually.

At the request of management, most Wal-Mart "associates" work as much as 30 hours per week overtime. This leaves little time for family or other activities, but they are afraid to refuse. In addition, with the low pay scales, they could use the extra money. At present there are 100,000 workers in 31 states suing for their overtime pay; the company never paid it. Apparently, Wal-Mart requires a lot of volunteer overtime. They call it "working off the clock."

Also Wal-Mart offers a very "generous" food and clothing charging program for its employees; they can charge as much as they like. With interest rates well over 20 percent, few workers who charge their necessities can afford to keep up the payments.

This is certainly reminiscent of the old company store game that plantation owners and other employers of poor farm workers used to play.

If He Hollers Let'm Go   When African American workers complained about the company, Wal-Mart simply relieved them of their jobs. When Anita Arana had not heard from the company for several weeks after her application for an open management position, her manager told her frankly, "We don't hire people like you for management positions." "What do you mean, 'People like me,' because I'm Black or because I'm a woman?" The reply, again frankly and openly, "Well, you got two out of two correct" (Greenwald, 2005).

Also if any worker spoke openly of organizing a union or even forming a grievance committee, a special force of management specialists would fly in to investigate. The errant workers were, again, simply relieved of their jobs (Greenwald, 2005).

In sum, documentation reveals that Wal-Mart destroys its competition with ridiculously low prices, at the expense of an equally ridiculous low pay for "associates." The citizens of Hearne, Texas, also learned that the advent of Wal-Mart introduced a sharp devaluation of business and residential property in their town. In contrast to the huge, shiny new Wal-Mart building, everything else looks old and delapidated. Main Street in Hearne's older downtown is now totally deserted. Offices and stores are closing right and left.

There is essentially no community left under the reign of Wal-Mart—only a *feudal* system for the benefit of the new Lords and Ladies of self-serving capitalism. There are also long lists of Wal-Mart's environmental violations in 22 states. They have already paid a few million dollars in fines for such violations, but they continue to break the law openly. Paying a couple of million in fines is cheaper for them than straightening out their relations with society and the environment.

Union-busting seems to be a favorite activity for Wal-Mart. The company hires investigators to fly in their corporate jet to a "trouble spot" at a moment's notice. If any "associate" happens to criticize the company or mention the possibility of organizing a union, the "Inquisitors" descend on them almost immediately. After a short debriefing in a private conference, these wayward "associates" are then *excommunicated*—let go without pay. Such accused and un-tried persons universally report that they were not even given a chance to recant. They are back on the streets with a "black eye," scratching somehow to feed their children (Greenwald, 2005).

To summarize the company's negative activities to date, we can list:

- ruthless and unfair competition in the market—small businesses destroyed;
- devaluation of property in their wake;
- racism;
- sexism;
- destruction of community and local culture;
- under-compensation of full-time (28 hrs/wk) "associates";
- stealing overtime by pressuring and failing to pay for "off the clock" work;
- putting needy workers on welfare and public health programs costing the taxpayers over $1.5 billion each year;
- multiple and uncorrected environmental violations;

- getting tax adjustments not available to smaller firms;
- union-busting and firing workers who complain about low pay and lack of fringes or talk about organizing.

Positive activities include providing jobs (low paying ones, but jobs nonetheless) and offering necessities to less affluent people at very low prices.

Radical Social Change Still Necessary

From a strictly theoretical perspective, a change toward real democracy in the workplace will require a radical redistribution of power and, in fact, a basic change in the culture. Worker-member co-ops are embedded in capitalism and find themselves "competing" with other sectors of the market while at the same time trying to preserve a totally cooperative approach. Thus co-ops defy the commonly accepted market "rationality" of self-centered grubbing for profit and power.

In a thoroughly capitalist economy, "...it just doesn't take much to stand in the way of even efficient cooperatives...The key obstacle is...access to capital. Businesses need money, often lots of it. And most people don't have the capital to risk in a speculative venture. Hence those who control the resources for investment can decide whether companies will be democratic or not" (Córdova, 1998, 46-7). The key decision makers in our modern economy are still mostly of the elite and moneyed classes, as was the case in feudal times.

The new cooperative paradigm demands a healing of the rift between capital and labor. In the Standard Economic Model, labor is treated as a cost of doing business, a cost which—like all other costs—must be minimized. In cooperative economics, labor is itself a major part of capital; the pooling of labor, rather than money and equipment, is the means for achieving the goal of a more equitable distribution of resources.

The Standard Model is about accumulation and concentration of wealth among owners and investors. The "Wal-Mart Effect" is still a large force in our Western economy and is rapidly spreading around the world—perhaps more rapidly than the cooperative movement. Cooperative economics is about the fair distribution of wealth among all producers and consumers.

Where Do We Want to Go?

The *blueprint* for a democratic economy, one based on the common good and on "labor as capital," is actually a form of capitalism, not communism or even socialism in its usual state-owned form. We have already had two economic disasters: the fall of state socialism and the feudalization of our current form of capitalism (the Wal-Mart Effect). We need something different. But what else is there? If a democratic approach to enterprise and cooperative business is the most productive and the most efficient, how do we work toward it?

Ethan Miller suggests that we can start by the stories we tell (Miller, 2005), stories about the way the world *really* works. This step might be a twenty-first century version of the 1960s "telling it like it is" to bring on the alternative to racism or classism. Our stories influence the way we see social reality; they tell us what is possible and what is impossible in the "real" world.

The dominant story up to now defines the economy as "The Free Market System." A version of that story has made globalization from above, as we know it, our only thinkable system. We see the capitalist market, driven and balanced by competition, as the great divine power (invisible hand), bringing the entire conflicting world together in a balanced economic co-dependency. According to that story, there is no alternative to huge, competitive transnational corporations driving labor down in a race to the bottom. This process, in fact, does not balance; it pushes well past the level where incomes of the lower half of society are sustainable.

In this story, capital and labor are both separate commodities, resources for the purpose of generating and accumulating more capital. These two resources, plus raw materials, must be exploited to the extent necessary to produce profits for the entrepreneurial owners and shareholders and to stimulate growth for the entire economy. The only real stakeholders to be considered in this story are the small class of owners and capital providers—banks, insurance companies, and shareholders. The workers and the environment are merely commodities, resources to be exploited to provide the private stakeholders, owners and shareholders, with the large profits of enterprise.

This story also tells us that any space not occupied by the market is occupied by the State. The State acts as both an accomplice to elitist formation of wealth and a regulator of this process. The State is thus the regulator, balancing the economy so that the resources, the environment and labor can all remain available to the top level stake-holders, so that the capitalist economy can thrive and expand. It is generally assumed that the pool of resources is infinite and cannot ever be exhausted by extraction or under-employment. At the other end of the production line, it is also assumed that the market can never be saturated by too much production. In fact, overproduction is necessary to maintain competition and lower prices. Thus, resources are bound to deplete rapidly.

> In this story, we the people are just worker-bees and consumers, making money and then spending it, always hoping for the opportunity of accumulating more. A community of creative and skilled people without money or capital (or the desire to *have* money or capital) is considered "unproductive," "backward," or "undeveloped."
>
> (Miller, 2005, 4-5)

But why should we tell such a story, a story that makes us feel small, only a cog in a great "free market" machine? Why not tell a story that makes us powerful and hopeful instead?

How Do We Get There?

Why should we remain subordinated to the will of transnational corporations, States, and international institutions that identify themselves with exclusionary interests, if together with our collective force, we can create public spaces, states, and new organizations that actually serve all of society? We must tell a new story of an economy "of the people, for the people, and by the people."

The new story is a tale of creative and satisfactory work, free from oppression and exploitation, and work that produces what is lacking in order to meet everyone's needs—cultural, physical, spiritual, emotional, and relational. The world conference of Latin American non-governmental organizations (NGOs) in Porto Alegre, Brazil, in August, 1998 made the following statement: "Our proposal is a socio-economy of solidarity as a way of life that encompasses the totality of the human being, that announces a new culture and a new form of producing to fulfill the needs of each human being and of the entire humanity" (Latin Meeting, 1998).

Is There a Viable *Blueprint* for Such a Socio-economy?

In order to change the paradigm of the neo-liberal Standard Model, or *residual-feudal exclusive* economics, to a *cooperative-super-efficient* capitalism, the following must be changed:

- privatization of the "commons";
- unconditional corporate charters;
- monopoly of capital and primitive accumulation;
- over-population and over-production;
- inequitable pay scales;
- global monopoly of food production;
- runaway militarism;
- unjust debts in the "developing" world;
- free trade among unequal regions: "trade by plunder";
- lack of "social cost" accounting;
- corrupt international development aid;
- corporate control of scientific information through patent monopolies, also known as protection of "intellectual property."

When mercantilism was urbanized, the aristocracy was supplanted by the princes of industry. Feudal Lords became the capitalist power elite, and the vassals and peasants were left behind—again. While the French aristocracy eschewed common work altogether, the English Lords were busy becoming scientists and industrial entrepreneurs. Whatever the details of the new capitalist economy across the "civilized" world, the classes formerly dominated by royalty were simply transferred as "property" to the moneyed upper classes. By taxes, rents, royalties, and other tricks of the economists' trade, the supply of working-class people was kept large in order to keep wages low.

At first, companies were chartered on the condition that profits were not simply pocketed by their owners, boards, and upper management, but were used for the "common good." The corporation was soon re-invented to protect the individual primitive accumulators (capitalists) from any legal challenges from the "untouchable" crowd. Thus was born the concept of private ownership and the status of the corporation as a "person." Over the years, private ownership and virtually unlimited capital accumulation by these corporate private owners became the power generators of Western economy.

For a few centuries, the domination system was supplemented by colonization to further increase the power and wealth of strong nations by exploiting the resources of weaker nations. Raw colonialism bred violent, and even more powerful non-violent, opposition that ultimately destroyed these huge empires. Soon the growing transnational corporations began assuming the power and wealth of the nation states and have, through capitalist globalization, begun a new colonialism.

In the early stages of colonial England, power and wealth was accumulated at home by "enclosures." Common lands, formerly used by farmers to graze their livestock and grow a few subsistence foods for their families, were *enclosed* by governments for the use of commercial farms and industries—"more efficient, more productive" activities. The common use was discontinued and the common people shut out of their accustomed informal cooperative economy. Modern corporations like Wal-Mart continue to *enclose* land and labor for their boxes and increase the poverty class by squeezing out their small community-based businesses. The name of the game now is to *enclose* larger and larger shares of the market. Leave the weak, the poor, the "lazy," and the "dirty mob" behind.

To reverse this trend, or at least to divert it into more civilized channels, the issues listed above must be addressed by taking the following ten steps:

Local and National Level

1. Re-establish the "Commons"

The air we breathe, the water we need, and life itself are certainly a part of the "commons." No individual or corporation should ever own these resources. Others would include land in this list of "commons" as well. Land is "social wealth" and should not be held under unconditional private ownership titles. All of society is entitled to its wealth (Smith, 2005b).

Henry George has proposed a kind of *conditional title* for the holding of land. "Resource rent" (for water rights, drilling rights, and so forth), currently collected by land monopolists, should be paid directly to society, that is, to an administrative agency or the government. The sum of such resource rents would be enough to pay for all the normal costs of government. Exclusive land ownership and monopolization would disappear as the use values are redistributed totally without pain or cost to anyone (George, 1981; Smith, 2005a, Chapter 24).

2. Governments should Reformulate Conditional Corporate Charters

Originally the British government and then the United States government would charter a corporation only conditionally. The principle condition was that the company's profits would not be used primarily to enrich the owners, the directors, the management, or even its shareholders. Corporations were founded to benefit the general public, the "common good." If the new company did not live up to these expectations, or if in any way the owners attempted to subvert this condition, the charter could be revoked (Bakan, 2004, 157ff.).

Later, the "common good" condition was watered down and the limited liability clause became the most important. In this clause, the corporation as a whole becomes legally equivalent to an individual in terms of rights, obligations, and liabilities. No single member of the corporation can be held responsible for breaches of the law or any kind of injury to other individuals. Corporations can be sued, but it is expensive and corporations are so rich and powerful that lawsuits are seldom effective. Moves toward tort reforms are further reducing liabilities of corporations and allowing them to be even more abusive and undemocratic.

The original "common good" clause should be restored and firmly enforced. Corporations would then be formed only for specific purposes that clearly improve the welfare of the general public and protect or increase the "common good." Small power elites could not dominate the market with impunity for the purpose of enriching themselves. The self-interest keystone of modern capitalism would be removed (Bakan, 2004, 140ff.). The "free market" would then be left open to cooperative, worker-owned, or consumer-owned enterprises.

3. Patent Laws should be Restructured to Limit Private Ownership of Intellectual Property

Along with conditional titles to land, there should be limited and conditional patents and copyrights on the world's resources, wealth, and intellectual property. Again it must be a part of the new cultural understanding that no single person or corporate entity, including Prometheus of Greek myth and the 2001 Genesis Space Mission, can personally own a piece of the sun. Awarding *exclusive patents* to ideas, natural organic compounds including DNA, and even important scientific discoveries is antithetical to a truly democratic society.

Reasonable royalties can be paid for the use of new ideas, manufacturing or management procedures, and inventions for a reasonable period of time. Originally this time period was 30 years, with the possibility of one patent or copyright renewal. Recently that period has been raised to 70 years after the inventor's death as a result of the famous Mickey Mouse law (Copyright Term Extension Act, 1998; for unsuccessful challenges and appeal for "free culture" see Lessig, 2004).

4. Start Cooperatives in Every Sector of the Economy, including the Financial Sector

Micro-finance can work to support every kind of cooperative enterprise, in the Western culture as well as in Asia and Southeast Asia. A cooperative bank might be a way to support cooperatives in every region and every sector of the economy.

The US National Cooperative Bank supports only expansions of existing co-ops, not new enterprises, and only in the agricultural sector. But local co-op banks could be formed with highly skilled business management advisors who could lead new cooperative projects to financial solvency and health. Many of the more successful cooperatives have started small, perhaps with a micro-finance component, and have energized people to commit time and resources to growth and success on a gradual timeline.

5. Limit Upper Management and Corporate Owners to Annual Stipends not to Exceed Six Times the Salary/Wage of the Average Low-Level Full-Time Worker

When Mondragón began its cooperative organization with the steel mill and the technical schools, the rule for compensating the CEO of the cooperative was that the highest compensation could not be more than three times the lowest paid fulltime worker. That rule has been extended to a factor of six. During the search for their last CEO, the General Assembly voted to allow the factor to expand considerably more, up to factors of 20 or 30, but the new CEO believed in the democratic principles of the cooperative and refused to take more than nine times more than the lowest-paid worker. Not only should we stop the "race to the bottom"—paying the laborers as little as possible, even below subsistence—but also the "race to the top"—being the corporation that pays their CEO the most. There are no data to support a perceived need to pay a general manager hundreds of millions of dollars. Anywhere in the world, we can find managers of co-ops getting the local median income or less, who are producing more than many highly paid CEOs of standard corporations.

6. All Primary Food Production and Distribution should be Kept at the Local Level as Much as Possible

With the improvement of transportation to and from distant parts of the globe and the increased demand for exotic agricultural products, food quality is not always what it ought to be and is difficult to guarantee. Essential nutrients are often lost in the processing and transporting of food products; attractive packaging for marketing (and ostensibly for the protection of the food) can add as much as 100 percent to its cost and often disguises the inferiority and deterioration of the product.

One of the most attractive aspects of a cooperative food store is the possibility of knowing how and where food is grown and exactly how fresh it is. Cooperative markets can ensure that food comes from organic, natural, and cooperative growers; members can personally verify that claim.

7. All Companies should Institute "Social Cost" Accounting

In The Standard Economic Model, social costs such as environmental degradation, resource depletion, and labor health and safety issues are traditionally considered "externalities." These external matters lie outside the Standard Model and therefore have not been of concern to the serious classical economist or to the corporations creating the costs. The result is that people outside the corporation must absorb these social costs. If the government must take up the slack in this standard model, then it is the taxpayer who must subsidize the corporation that accrues these social costs. If not the government, then the citizens, usually those at the low end of the economic scale, must pay the cost in terms of a much deteriorated life style—another manifestation of the "Wal-Mart Effect."

If corporate charters include the requirement that balance sheets and expense reports must include all social costs, they would more correctly reflect the true cost of doing business. Some have commented that, if such a practice were mandatory,

most corporations could not afford to do business. Certainly they could not afford
the "bubbles" of high returns on public shares or high salaries to top executives. How
the corporations pay these costs is very important. They can pay them by reducing
the extraordinarily high compensation to owners, shareholders, or executives or
by increasing prices to the consumer. A certain amount of reasonable regulation of
the process would certainly be in order. A cooperative, since it is answerable to no
shareholders except its members (in equal shares) and is governed by the members
themselves, would be more likely to spread social costs across the membership more
equitably—another great attraction of cooperatives.

International Level

*8. All Nations should Reduce their Military and Military Costs to the Minimum
Needed only to Maintain Internal Security*

Militarism has gotten out of control. A review of all extensive wars in the twentieth
century reveal a connection between military action and neo-colonial transnational
efforts to control the world economically. "All military weapons beyond that
necessary for internal security should be turned over to a democratically restructured
United Nations... and destroyed" (Smith, 2005b, 177). Recent actions of the United
States military in Iraq at a total cost exceeding $1 trillion has little, if anything, to
do with national security and was opposed by the vast majority of members of the
UN. Need we ask who will eventually pay for this military activity? Obviously, it
will be the lower echelons of society; Middle-eastern opponents of US policy pay
with their lives, while the citizens of the US pay through reduced or totally cut social
programs, inferior education, and non-existent healthcare.

9. Performance Contracts and Monitoring must be Required for Development Aid

Much government sponsored aid to developing countries has been diverted to
corrupt elite leadership in both developing and developed countries. To prevent this,
money and goods should not be distributed directly, but handled under stringent
performance contracts. Any industry or infrastructure built in developing countries
should be awarded by contract to local builders and suppliers and monitored by the
appropriate international agency. As soon as developing countries have their own
means of production, they should build their own industries and manage them under
cooperative models.

*10. Cancel All Unjust Developing World Debts, and Allow Free Trade only among
Equal Regions. Eliminate "Plunder by Trade"*

Honest social accounting will show that the "wealthy world is in enormous debt
to the developing world through centuries of imperialism, slavery, and structural
exploitation designed to create indebtedness" (Smith, 2005b, 177). All of these
unfairly accrued debts of weaker countries to stronger ones should be canceled. Free

trade should be established only between states that are economically approximately equal. Trade between countries where labor is unequally paid should be monitored closely to ensure that the weaker country is not exploited by the stronger one.

Observe that this 10-step program is mostly about sharing. Sharing is certainly part of our cultural story. In one of the classics of the twentieth century, Robert Fulghum's *All I Really Need to Know I Learned in Kindergarten* (1986), at the top of the list was, "SHARE EVERYTHING." If we could all write this law on our hearts and on our doorposts, so that we could touch it every time we enter or leave our homes and feel it in the midst of every social and economic relationship, the ten steps or "commandments" listed above would be unnecessary.

One last note needs to be sounded about monitoring and regulating economic activities in a climate of cooperative economics. The need to reinstate our "commons" and manage our resources collectively to prevent environmental depletion has spawned the emergence of over a half-million local resource management groups around the world. These groups are finding that, given proper conditions, they can collectively ensure sustainable use of local resources over the long term without inordinate amounts of governmental or corporate controls (Uphoff, 2002; Ostrom, 1990; Pretty, 2003).

Globalization from Below

What has been learned from all of the discussions outlined above is that *social capital is more important than material capital*. The solution involves the simple principle that social bonds and norms are of paramount importance for all people and communities. Furthermore, it is now known that cooperative social bonds can lower the cost of almost any economic activity (Pretty, 2003, 1913). Globalization based on a competitive form of capitalism fosters only a neo-colonial relationship with the developing world, marked by violent conflict and tribal reactionary behavior both in the developing and developed world. Cooperation, on the other hand, has made an environmentally and socially sustainable, and even global, economy feasible for thousands of communities. The Mondragón Cooperative Corporation and the Grameen Bank have not only provided viable local economies for their members but have provided models for global cooperation through their extensions and partnerships around the world. ASP in Secunderabad, India, will soon expand across the subcontinent and to other developing countries. The Anand Model for dairy cooperatives has now taken hold not only in Asia and southeast Asia but in Europe and the United States as well.

Brian Martin, in his analysis of the violence in current globalization processes, suggests five principles as a basis for this new kind of economics:

Principle 1: Cooperation, rather than competition, should be the foundation for all activity.

Principle 2: People with the greatest needs should have priority in the distribution of social production.

Principle 3: Satisfying work should be available to everyone who wants it.

Principle 4: The system should be designed and run by the people themselves, rather than by authorities or experts.

Principle 5: The system should be based on nonviolence. (Martin, 2001, 79)

Martin speaks as if such a system is entirely in the future and that we must construct it from scratch. The truth is that the system is already in play and has been for some time. All we need to do is the join it and make sure it stays on task. The cooperative movement is very popular because of its emphasis on workplace democracy, worker participation and even worker ownership. Thus, by its very nature, it is nonviolent. There is no need to reconstruct it from scratch. Martin thinks we must stop globalization. Rather, we should probably think of letting the natural democratic procedure of cooperativism transform the globalization process.

In fact, there are even some economists who warn against any form of de-globalization. Harold James, a Harvard history of economics professor, published a book *The End of Globalization* (James, 2001) in which he warned of the disastrous effects of attempting to decelerate the process of globalization. His study compared the current criticism of globalization to the events leading up to the Great Depression between the two world wars. On September 17, 2001, the prestigious *Economist* carried a full-page review of James' book, underlining James' warning. The twin factors of tightened immigration control and unwise monetary policy just before and after World War I, including the abandonment of the gold exchange standard, in central Europe and the United States, says James, led to mass closures of banks and widespread unemployment. The stage is now set, he warns, for a new disastrous de-globalization process.

Could the present rapid acceleration of international movement of goods and capital, especially since the fall of the Berlin wall, lead to a backlash that could end in an economic turmoil similar to the de-globalization of the interwar years? James argues that the progressive liberalization of trade and capital markets under the so-called Washington consensus have left many international organizations (such as the UN, IMF, World Bank, and WTO) fragile and insecure in their own missions. On the other hand, alternative visions and anti-globalization forces are also weak and disorganized. Both of these weakening processes have left the system wide open for radical change.

Cooperation must be initiated and operated on a local level by local people. It can spread just as far as its applications lead it—even to a global enterprise like Mondragón. Following all the steps of the *blueprint* outlined above, there would seem to be no reason that it could not encircle the globe, gradually supplanting—or, more likely, transforming—the kind of neo-colonial form of globalization we are currently experiencing.

The objective of this book has been to present an even simpler and naturally human form of globalization than the Standard Model, Brian Martin's five principles, or Harold James' catastrophic warnings envision. The grassroots cooperative movement is a straightforward and more humanistic way.

Looking at the present flourishing state of the cooperative movement, one can now see a buildup of strength and a growing international organization that perhaps was not evident to Harold James, and other sequestered scholars, even as recently as five years ago. Annual world conferences of NGOs and recent resolutions of the new United European organization have pointed the way toward a stronger and more cooperative globalization from below.

Doubtless current competitive power structures will soon realize what is going on and attempt to block the formation of more cooperatives. One can hope that they will be unsuccessful and that, through more cooperative and people-oriented economies around the world, the world will be made safe for real democracy.

Colander writes, "… in the debate about the possible future evolution of capitalism, the question of who controls business decisions is likely to take center stage" (1993, 77). In his discussion, he does not mention cooperatives as such, but he does predict that workers, consumers, and communities where the firm works could and should all have a say in how the firm operates. Will economic institutions actually evolve in this direction? This question immediately raises another and perhaps more basic question of why there are no more worker-controlled firms than currently exist. And this thought spawns a set of further questions. Why does capital continue to hire labor and not vice-versa? Why does labor continue to be regarded as a commodity and not as a form of social capital?

All of these questions suggest that a more desirable form of economy will not arise spontaneously from decentralized markets. Neither can they be established by centralized government fiat. Their probability of success, however, can be increased by national and international public education about the various alternatives to the present system, and can of course be sanctioned by favorable legislation (Hill, 2000).

It should be clear by now that there is sufficient cause to believe that a global network of cooperatives can sustain a reasonable lifestyle much more effectively than the Standard Model of self-interested runaway competitive capitalism. Furthermore, resources and wealth can be shared more equitably among members of such a society, and "untouchables" need no longer be excluded from vital economic activity anywhere in the world. Need for internal and border security can be at a minimum or can even be totally unnecessary. War and international violence can both be assigned to the scrap heap. And finally, we can all say goodbye to *feudalism* supported by colonial exploitation with its rich elite and poor masses separated by a shrinking middle class.

> The form of association…which if mankind continue to improve, must be expected in the end to predominate, is not that which can exist with capitalist as chief, and workpeople without a voice in the management, but the association of the labourers themselves on terms of equality, collectively owning the capital with which they carry on their operations, and working under managers elected and removable by themselves.
>
> (John Stuart Mills, *Principles of Political Economy*, 1848)

References

Bakan, J. (2004). *The Corporation: the Pathological Pursuit of Profit and Power*. NY: Free Press.

Bonin, J.P. and L. Putterman (1987). *Economics of Cooperation and the labor-managed economy*. Chur, Switzerland: Harwood.

Bonin, J.P., D.C. Jones, and L. Putterman (1993). "Theoretical and Empirical Studies of Producer Cooperatives: Will Ever the Twain Meet?" *Journal of Economic Literature* 31 (September), pp. 1290-320.

Colander, D.C. (1993). *Economics*. Boston: Irwin.

Copyright Term Extension Act of 1998, Public Law 105-298, Oct 27, 1998.

Córdova, R.V. (1998). "Why Economists are Wrong about Cooperatives," *GEO Dollars and Sense*, September/October, 1998, p. 44.

D'Nazari, Y. (ca. 30AD). Quoted in Mark 4:5 NRS version. Oxford, UK: Oxford University Press, 1989.

Fulghum, R. (1986). *All I Really Needed to Know I Learned in Kindergarten.* Ballentine Publishing Group (Random House).

George, H. (1981). *Progress and Poverty.* New York: Robert Schalkenbach Foundation (original edition, 1879).

Hill, R. (2000). "The Case of the Missing Organizations: Cooperatives and Textbooks." *Journal of Economic Education* (Summer), pp. 281-295.

James, H. (2001), *The End of Globalization: Lessons from the Great Depression.* Cambridge, MA: Harvard University Press.

Jones, D.C., and Svejnar, J. (1982). *Participatory and Self-Managed firms: Evaluating Economic Performance.* Lexington Press: Cambridge, MA.

Latin Meeting (1998). "Statement of the Latin Meeting," Porto Alegre, 1998.

Lessig, L. (2004). "How I Lost the Big One," *Legal Affairs*, March/April, 2004.

Levine, D.I. and Tyson, L. D'Andrea (1990). "Participation, Productivity and the Firm's Environment" in Alan Binder (ed.), *Paying for Productivity: A Look at the Evidence.* Brookings Institution, pp. 183-244.

Martin, B. (2001). *Nonviolent Alternatives to Capitalism.* London: War Resistors' International.

Meade, J.E., (1993). *Liberty, Equality, and Efficiency: Apologia pro agathotopia mea.* London: MacMillan.

Miller, E. (2005). "Solidarity Economics: Strategies for Building New Economics From the Bottom-Up and the Inside-Out," *Grassroots Economic Organizing*, February, 2004 (rev. June, 2005).

Mills, J.S. (1848). *Principles of Political Economy.* Recent edition by Augustus M. Kelley, Publisher, 1987.

Ostrom, E. (1990). *Governing the Commons.* NY: Cambridge University Press.

Pencavel, J. (2002). *Worker Participation: Lessons from the Worker Co-ops of the Pacific Northwest.* NY: Russell Sage Foundation.

Perelman, M. (2000). *The Invention of Capitalism: Classical Political Economy and the Secret History of Primitive Accumulation.* London: Duke University Press.

Pretty, J. (2003). "Social Capital and the Collective Management of Resources," *Science* Vol 302, 12 Dec, 2003, pp. 1912-1914.

Smith, J.W., (2005a). *Economic Democracy: The Political Struggle of the Twenty-first Century, 4th Ed.* Radford, VA: The Institute for Economic Democracy.

Smith, J.W., (2005b). *Cooperative Capitalism: A Blueprint for Global Peace and Prosperity.* Radford, VA: The Institute for Economic Democracy.

Uphoff, N., ed. (2002). *Agroecological Innovations.* London: Earthscan.

Appendices

Appendix A

Credit Union Statistics

Table A.1 United States State Credit Union Statistics

Year	# of CUs	# of Members	Savings ($)	Loans ($)	Reserves ($)*	Assets ($)
1939	4,771	1,420,143	119,376,358	109,657,053		143,585,577
1940	5,529	1,652,096	156,261,964	133,102,951		179,083,873
1941	6,203	1,859,916	176,522,002	148,119,414		216,357,800
1942	6,010	1,753,436				
1943	6,319	1,700,742				
1944	5,156	1,626,510	213,563,683	87,790,556	19,298,221	253,068,354
1945	5,061	1,617,863	237,407,249	92,575,717	19,499,633	262,132,455
1946	5,173	1,774,894	282,388,327	134,023,079		319,129,290
1947	5,277	1,900,794	330,618,496	191,978,049	24,806,689	380,066,826
1948	5,266	2,127,315	383,258,047	260,550,360	34,952,943	442,477,741
1949	5,569	2,283,886	432,843,652	318,542,943	33,252,473	510,726,464
1950	5,607	2,493,212	507,370,389	415,528,734	39,228,902	599,640,622
1951	5,885	2,744,768	604,388,735	446,328,252	43,214,595	693,613,295
1952	6,366	3,056,893	737,386,653	569,984,012	38,877,762	853,711,660
1953	7,125	3,372,539	903,989,076	738,338,980	48,897,431	1,043,836,040
1954	7,852	3,733,529	1,085,036,648	875,501,110	57,774,233	1,237,379,208
1955	8,397	4,100,833	1,286,540,095	1,072,450,790	68,280,945	1,476,014,249
1956	8,906	4,517,402	1,519,678,401	1,276,742,328	82,587,077	1,741,742,068
1957	9,466	4,913,346	1,766,732,200	1,520,987,859	96,604,038	2,021,144,712
1958	9,840	5,264,688	2,025,182,396	1,698,563,348		2,312,739,042
1959	10,076	5,632,392	2,362,264,039	2,043,685,363	131,130,626	2,671,666,116
1960	10,201	5,948,319	2,634,485,007	2,355,745,999	152,355,217	2,983,619,667
1961	10,344	6,340,190	2,962,315,287	2,572,411,786	179,467,785	3,354,224,000
1962	10,364	6,756,303	3,311,057,362	2,916,001,613	204,985,913	3,756,470,542
1963	10,420	7,087,300	3,716,313,965	3,260,248,115	231,993,155	4,217,688,785

Table A.1 Continued

Year	# of CUs	# of Members	Savings ($)	Loans ($)	Reserves ($)*	Assets ($)
1964	10,534	7,533,625	4,224,586,112	3,695,586,020	263,313,773	4,801,834,386
1965	10,579	8,111,902	4,708,102,386	4,225,533,247	299,566,249	5,383,462,323
1966	10,752	8,624,669	5,160,140,457	4,763,674,506	344,887,936	5,934,365,947
1967	10,833	9,195,498	5,682,863,387	5,192,316,461	388,773,037	6,545,194,804
1968	10,850	9,755,180	6,310,554,152	5,865,008,138	438,896,372	7,275,094,929
1969	10,961	10,302,956	6,983,308,226	6,598,049,451	490,280,420	8,073,830,335
1970	10,725	10,846,073	7,796,582,698	7,111,429,709	540,157,592	9,027,531,319
1971	10,564	11,390,590	9,044,542,109	8,051,301,802	597,828,463	10,437,943,004
1972	10,404	12,167,414	10,512,427,718	9,211,922,848	672,092,251	12,109,093,871
1973	10,308	12,830,127	11,941,998,827	10,611,659,876	754,655,014	13,652,623,202
1974	10,208	13,593,653	13,020,364,177	11,653,019,425	866,988,544	15,013,892,007
1975	9,958	14,267,399	15,348,876,245	13,287,237,238	987,344,219	17,439,362,056
1976	9,844	15,017,399	17,655,777,927	15,745,495,520	1,089,731,407	20,141,259,741
1977	9,655	16,275,622	20,792,579,987	18,835,070,961	1,223,836,540	23,831,192,482
1978	9,468	17,589,744	23,428,765,088	22,254,782,365	1,392,777,927	26,934,159,335
1979	9,266	18,552,892	24,909,112,984	23,513,280,945	1,511,944,522	28,641,183,461
1980	9,059	19,462,285	27,599,675,203	22,592,061,518	1,639,791,423	31,109,601,213
1981	8,841	19,782,935	29,254,207,421	23,290,756,040	1,718,989,992	32,939,317,652
1982	8,502	20,494,284	33,532,478,395	23,575,461,006	1,788,325,940	37,230,035,337
1983	8,143	20,693,784	39,833,684,075	27,345,243,568	1,946,054,830	43,881,851,130
1984	7,843	21,062,729	44,739,080,736	33,337,997,201	2,196,944,936	49,333,136,196
1985	7,544	22,362,727	54,307,741,823	36,914,337,532	2,425,295,691	59,293,760,858
1986	7,182	23,934,767	64,943,288,098	41,251,904,672	2,718,382,221	70,856,855,843
1987	6,889	24,434,933	69,715,114,211	46,674,776,027	3,109,901,899	76,595,182,809
1988	6,600	24,284,126	74,134,712,785	52,909,237,827	3,766,911,032	82,011,635,198

Table A.1 Continued

Year	# of CUs	# of Members	Savings ($)	Loans ($)	Reserves ($)*	Assets ($)
1989	6,333	24,878,053	76,966,037,433	56,528,602,948	4,778,595,655	84,778,102,176
1990	5,802	25,363,486	78,843,387,149	55,558,811,129	6,135,489,253	86,799,492,990
1991	5,757	25,173,520	89,182,054,402	57,919,136,822	7,483,417,550	98,195,877,777
1992	5,479	25,719,770	97,783,870,959	58,704,588,495	8,720,888,382	107,587,900,606
1993	5,255	26,241,752	102,108,710,084	63,182,427,705	10,241,550,120	113,683,746,171
1994	5,045	26,550,603	103,415,700,234	71,854,289,331	11,171,353,645	116,415,011,850
1995	4,881	27,129,662	108,533,479,748	77,864,151,174	12,633,696,378	122,400,032,247
1996	4,731	27,822,759	114,399,718,002	86,078,064,586	13,921,406,721	129,712,656,900
1997	4,681	29,972,494	127,863,635,330	98,551,179,889	15,968,887,350	145,480,151,714
1998	4,583	31,752,584	146,660,667,652	107,494,651,930	17,891,770,713	167,021,342,642
1999	4,453	33,586,238	160,218,114,707	124,435,490,368	19,812,843,566	184,188,083,802
2000	4,352	35,868,799	179,437,895,552	145,516,085,404	22,969,880,790	206,915,598,576
2001	4,237	37,770,399	213,811,704,462	160,567,795,671	25,976,774,870	244,568,137,860
2002	4,091	38,778,087	238,288,925,338	172,450,281,548	28,957,065,898	273,452,339,485
2003	3,935	38,690,844	253,989,865,155	184,742,727,998	30,804,323,229	292,549,042,296
2004	3,911	40,040,525	272,537,672,184	207,405,678,265	33,388,567,222	315,681,198,977

* Beginning 1990, Reserves includes undivided earnings.

Table A.2   United States Federal Credit Union Statistics

Year	# of CUs	# of Members	Savings ($)	Loans ($)	Reserves ($)*	Assets ($)
1939	3,265	831,323	42,042,382	36,577,718	1,107,571	46,418,275
1940	3,695	1,041,767	64,798,604	54,974,869		69,874,452
1941	4,115	1,386,847	96,048,376	68,650,127		102,822,560
1942	4,314	1,337,017	108,685,155	42,452,258	3,450,287	118,354,079
1943	3,842	1,293,255	116,166,173	34,965,084		
1944	3,774	1,293,452	132,619,718	34,133,279	4,100,850	143,227,631
1945	3,762	1,216,625	140,614,347	35,155,499	4,910,808	153,225,009
1946	3,771	1,302,062	159,718,040	56,800,937		173,166,459
1947	3,853	1,445,915	192,410,043	91,372,197	6,393,884	409,375,571
1948	4,054	1,627,874	235,004,540	137,640,859	7,928,899	258,326,594
1949	4,493	1,817,622	284,956,387	185,837,964	9,967,595	316,317,279
1950	4,979	2,123,874	361,841,659	263,677,086	12,917,522	405,748,661
1951	5,393	2,459,825	457,257,618	299,650,738	16,274,152	504,562,537
1952	5,914	2,847,736	597,135,507	414,889,585	20,553,576	662,157,248
1953	6,565	3,248,200	767,204,132	573,665,200	26,163,114	853,841,008
1954	7,215	3,592,782	931,025,577	681,768,457	33,400,307	1,032,770,041
1955	7,795	4,025,879	1,134,640,802	862,709,716	41,487,651	1,266,857,070
1956	8,340	4,495,717	1,365,470,528	1,048,655,864	53,115,035	1,528,332,874
1957	8,725	4,890,079	1,588,037,541	1,256,490,668	66,177,329	1,787,502,445
1958	9,020	5,201,767	1,810,496,653	1,378,688,715	80,687,301	2,033,204,683
1959	9,436	5,634,195	2,073,122,448	1,665,308,599	100,954,320	2,350,851,074
1960	9,893	6,077,074	2,341,843,855	2,020,046,221	121,917,300	2,666,998,847
1961	10,260	6,529,171	2,670,478,437	2,243,314,663	146,009,255	3,024,938,748
1962	10,620	6,992,353	3,016,790,364	2,558,413,842	174,094,539	3,425,850,569
1963	10,943	7,481,826	3,448,440,657	2,908,235,637	207,598,310	3,911,835,207

Table A.2 Continued

Year	# of CUs	# of Members	Savings ($)	Loans ($)	Reserves ($)*	Assets ($)
1964	11,266	8,073,723	4,012,216,000	3,345,491,000	246,011,000	4,553,584,000
1965	11,530	8,619,798	4,532,478,000	3,860,592,000	290,047,000	5,158,952,000
1966	11,928	9,247,601	4,937,127,000	4,319,535,000	338,385,000	5,661,044,000
1967	12,196	9,846,482	5,412,324,000	4,673,928,000	388,855,000	6,198,745,000
1968	12,570	10,476,910	5,976,080,000	5,389,569,000	446,596,072	6,890,698,000
1969	12,905	11,267,815	6,701,371,000	6,320,468,000	513,000,000	7,779,924,000
1970	12,962	11,929,438	7,614,296,000	6,956,137,000	583,997,000	8,844,388,000
1971	12,703	12,662,411	9,180,764,000	8,055,230,000	645,832,000	10,533,053,000
1972	12,694	13,529,983	10,934,658,000	9,404,260,000	723,862,000	12,490,065,000
1973	12,674	14,610,573	12,573,290,000	11,085,471,000	814,547,000	14,576,611,000
1974	12,732	15,856,346	14,320,401,000	12,691,654,000	911,148,000	16,646,562,000
1975	12,719	17,053,115	17,451,217,497	14,818,555,394	1,027,687,000	20,114,256,286
1976	12,737	18,567,133	20,906,649,000	18,179,434,000	1,177,442,000	24,159,455,000
1977	12,727	20,367,017	25,199,310,000	22,375,912,000	1,319,902,000	29,207,011,000
1978	12,735	23,166,604	29,292,721,000	27,177,010,000	1,358,194,000	34,081,705,000
1979	12,715	22,711,838	30,922,744,000	28,129,160,000	1,431,439,000	35,503,554,000
1980	12,406	24,468,284	34,124,197,000	26,110,471,000	1,477,701,000	37,864,586,000
1981	11,943	25,404,997	35,367,809,000	27,078,486,000	1,619,596,000	39,352,036,000
1982	11,395	26,074,241	41,314,861,000	27,913,317,000	1,771,765,000	45,450,310,000
1983	10,952	26,752,882	49,858,841,000	33,171,936,000	2,004,542,000	54,445,487,000
1984	10,532	28,147,548	57,829,008,761	42,103,714,431	2,448,701,329	63,626,714,979
1985	10,110	29,544,813	71,505,247,563	48,209,036,347	2,882,473,794	78,168,119,884
1986	9,746	31,012,913	87,916,498,983	55,266,272,850	3,309,891,970	95,441,724,909
1987	9,385	32,792,720	96,303,124,572	64,059,720,886	3,722,396,942	105,140,214,084
1988	9,109	34,403,664	104,375,878,137	73,709,982,456	4,819,657,902	114,500,421,971

Table A.2   Continued

Year	# of CUs	# of Members	Savings ($)	Loans ($)	Reserves ($)*	Assets ($)
1989	8,811	35,612,259	109,652,638,567	80,272,104,052	4,689,902,345	120,666,059,824
1990	8,747	36,247,473	117,893,346,668	83,030,259,565	9,752,382,405	130,074,630,761
1991	8,210	37,094,384	130,199,053,873	84,177,290,363	10,880,943,252	143,979,272,300
1992	7,899	38,125,997	145,637,012,236	87,350,142,951	12,936,347,159	162,066,337,159
1993	7,694	39,194,460	153,542,827,067	94,660,220,510	15,315,809,588	172,893,426,797
1994	7,495	40,839,245	160,225,898,896	110,089,691,287	17,205,354,059	182,533,510,393
1995	7,328	42,172,827	170,299,666,215	120,514,246,528	19,794,130,684	193,777,948,272
1996	7,149	43,559,006	180,959,971,854	134,117,375,250	22,080,805,675	206,679,573,911
1997	6,977	43,496,414	187,823,436,916	140,104,115,807	23,735,472,172	215,104,850,211
1998	6,809	43,864,033	202,650,620,786	144,849,091,060	25,357,796,318	231,904,074,423
1999	6,563	43,930,264	206,789,393,874	154,587,881,558	26,331,581,017	238,379,261,889
2000	6,332	43,883,074	210,187,430,252	163,850,998,610	28,109,020,668	242,883,220,814
2001	6,118	43,818,861	235,201,372,298	170,326,327,082	29,933,012,619	270,122,648,590
2002	5,950	44,567,060	261,816,657,203	182,782,554,621	33,080,970,114	301,234,912,785
2003	5,775	46,157,118	291,484,757,040	203,617,977,551	36,403,145,813	336,584,588,873
2004	5,572	46,856,085	308,317,947,302	224,556,960,534	39,393,880,340	358,700,824,824

* Beginning 1990, Reserves includes undivided earnings.

Table A.3 United States Credit Union Statistics

Year	# of CUs	# of Members	Savings ($)	Loans ($)	Reserves ($)*	Assets ($)
1939	8,036	2,251,466	161,418,740	146,234,771		190,003,852
1940	9,224	2,693,863	221,060,568	188,077,820		248,958,325
1941	10,318	3,246,763	272,570,378	216,769,541		319,180,360
1942	10,324	3,090,453				
1943	10,161	2,993,997				
1944	8,930	2,919,962	346,183,401	121,923,835	23,399,071	396,295,985
1945	8,823	2,834,488	378,021,596	127,731,216	24,410,441	415,357,464
1946	8,944	3,076,956	442,106,367	190,824,016		492,295,749
1947	9,130	3,346,709	523,028,539	283,350,246	31,200,573	789,442,397
1948	9,320	3,755,189	618,262,587	398,191,219	42,881,842	700,804,335
1949	10,062	4,101,508	717,800,039	504,380,907	43,220,068	827,043,743
1950	10,586	4,617,086	869,212,048	679,205,820	52,146,424	1,005,389,283
1951	11,278	5,204,593	1,061,646,353	745,978,990	59,488,747	1,198,175,832
1952	12,280	5,904,629	1,334,522,160	984,873,597	59,431,338	1,515,868,908
1953	13,690	6,620,739	1,671,193,208	1,312,004,180	75,060,545	1,897,677,048
1954	15,067	7,326,311	2,016,062,225	1,557,269,567	91,174,540	2,270,149,249
1955	16,192	8,126,712	2,421,180,897	1,935,160,506	109,768,596	2,742,871,319
1956	17,246	9,013,119	2,885,148,929	2,325,398,192	135,702,112	3,270,074,942
1957	18,191	9,803,425	3,354,769,741	2,777,478,527	162,781,367	3,808,647,157
1958	18,860	10,466,455	3,835,679,049	3,077,252,063		4,345,943,725
1959	19,512	11,266,587	4,435,386,487	3,708,993,962	232,084,946	5,022,517,190
1960	20,094	12,025,393	4,976,328,862	4,375,792,220	274,272,517	5,650,618,514
1961	20,604	12,869,361	5,632,793,724	4,815,726,449	325,477,040	6,379,162,748
1962	20,984	13,748,656	6,327,847,726	5,474,415,455	379,080,452	7,182,321,111
1963	21,363	14,569,126	7,164,754,622	6,168,483,752	439,591,465	8,129,523,992

Table A.3   Continued

Year	# of CUs	# of Members	Savings ($)	Loans ($)	Reserves ($)*	Assets ($)
1964	21,800	15,607,348	8,236,802,112	7,041,077,020	509,324,773	9,355,418,386
1965	22,109	16,731,700	9,240,580,386	8,086,125,247	589,613,249	10,542,414,323
1966	22,680	17,872,270	10,097,267,457	9,083,209,506	683,272,936	11,595,409,947
1967	23,029	19,041,980	11,095,187,387	9,866,244,461	777,628,037	12,743,939,804
1968	23,420	20,232,090	12,286,634,152	11,254,577,138	885,492,444	14,165,792,929
1969	23,866	21,570,771	13,684,679,226	12,918,517,451	1,003,280,420	15,853,754,335
1970	23,687	22,775,511	15,410,878,698	14,067,566,709	1,124,154,592	17,871,919,319
1971	23,267	24,053,001	18,225,306,109	16,106,531,802	1,243,660,463	20,970,996,004
1972	23,098	25,697,397	21,447,085,718	18,616,182,848	1,395,954,251	24,599,158,871
1973	22,982	27,440,700	24,515,288,827	21,697,130,876	1,569,202,014	28,229,234,202
1974	22,940	29,449,999	27,340,765,177	24,344,673,425	1,778,136,544	31,660,454,007
1975	22,677	31,320,514	32,800,093,742	28,105,792,632	2,015,031,219	37,553,618,342
1976	22,581	33,584,532	38,562,426,927	33,924,929,520	2,267,173,407	44,300,714,741
1977	22,382	36,642,639	45,991,889,987	41,210,982,961	2,543,738,540	53,038,203,482
1978	22,203	40,756,348	52,721,486,088	49,431,792,365	2,750,971,927	61,015,864,335
1979	21,981	41,264,730	55,831,856,984	51,642,440,945	2,943,383,522	64,144,737,461
1980	21,465	43,930,569	61,723,872,203	48,702,532,518	3,117,492,423	68,974,187,213
1981	20,784	45,187,932	64,622,016,421	50,369,242,040	3,338,585,992	72,291,353,652
1982	19,897	46,568,525	74,847,339,395	51,488,778,006	3,560,090,940	82,680,345,337
1983	19,095	47,446,666	89,692,525,075	60,517,179,568	3,950,596,830	98,327,338,130
1984	18,375	49,210,277	102,568,089,497	75,441,711,632	4,645,646,265	112,959,851,175
1985	17,654	51,907,540	125,812,989,386	85,123,373,879	5,307,769,485	137,461,880,742
1986	16,928	54,947,680	152,859,787,081	96,518,177,522	6,028,274,191	166,298,580,752
1987	16,274	57,227,653	166,018,238,783	110,734,496,913	6,832,298,841	181,735,396,893
1988	15,709	58,687,790	178,510,590,922	126,619,220,283	8,586,568,934	196,512,057,169

Table A.3   Continued

Year	# of CUs	# of Members	Savings ($)	Loans ($)	Reserves ($)*	Assets ($)
1989	15,144	60,490,312	186,618,676,000	136,800,707,000	9,468,498,000	205,444,162,000
1990	14,549	61,610,959	196,736,733,817	138,589,070,694	15,887,871,658	216,874,123,751
1991	13,967	62,267,904	219,381,108,275	142,096,427,185	18,364,360,802	242,175,150,077
1992	13,378	63,845,767	243,420,883,195	146,054,731,446	21,657,235,541	269,654,237,765
1993	12,949	65,436,212	255,651,537,151	157,842,648,215	25,557,359,708	286,577,172,968
1994	12,540	67,389,848	263,641,599,130	181,943,980,618	28,376,707,704	298,948,522,243
1995	12,209	69,302,489	278,833,145,963	198,378,397,702	32,427,827,062	316,177,980,519
1996	11,880	71,381,765	295,359,689,856	220,195,439,836	36,002,212,396	336,392,230,811
1997	11,658	73,468,908	315,687,072,246	238,655,295,696	39,704,359,522	360,585,001,925
1998	11,392	75,616,617	349,311,288,438	252,343,742,990	43,249,567,031	398,925,417,065
1999	11,016	77,516,502	367,007,508,581	279,023,371,926	46,144,424,583	422,567,345,691
2000	10,684	79,751,873	389,625,325,804	309,367,084,014	51,078,901,458	449,798,819,390
2001	10,355	81,589,260	449,013,076,760	330,894,122,753	55,909,787,489	514,690,786,450
2002	10,041	83,345,147	500,105,582,541	355,232,836,169	62,038,036,012	574,687,252,270
2003	9,710	84,847,962	545,474,622,195	388,360,705,549	67,207,469,042	629,133,631,169
2004	9,483	86,896,610	580,855,619,486	431,962,638,799	72,782,447,562	674,382,023,801

* *Beginning 1990, Reserves includes undivided earnings.*

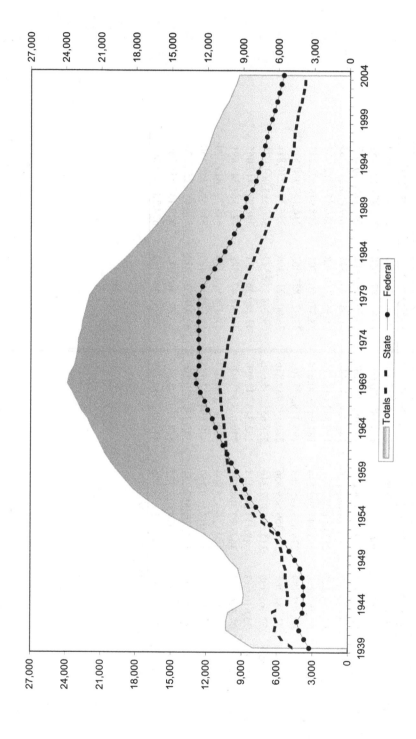

Figure A.1   Number of US Credit Unions, 1939-2004

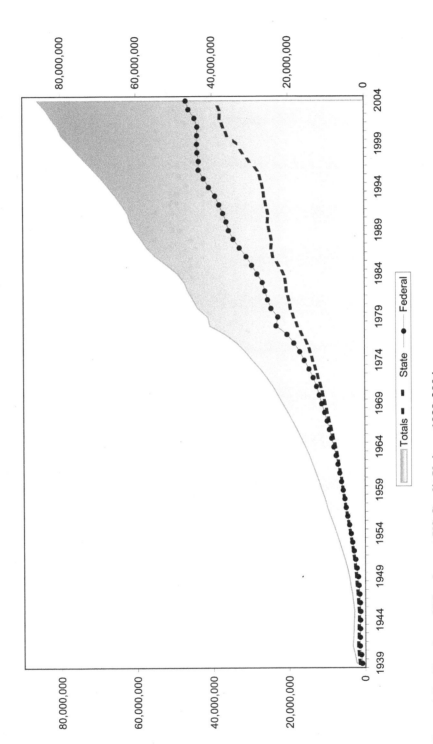

Figure A.2   Number of Members at US Credit Unions, 1939-2004

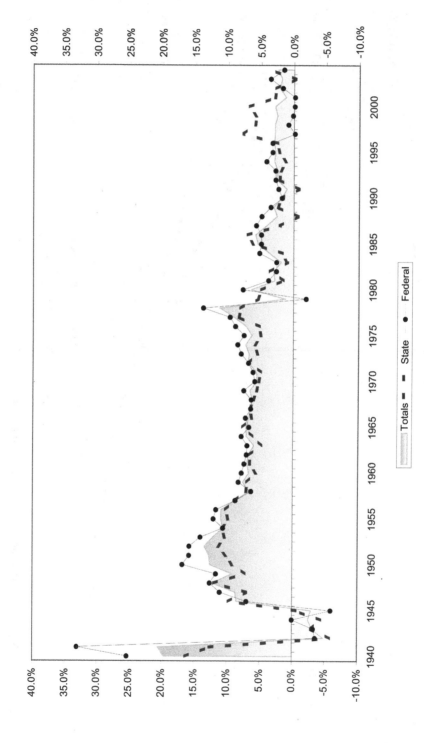

Figure A.3   Membership Growth at US Credit Unions, 1940-2004

Totals ▨   State ▬   Federal ●

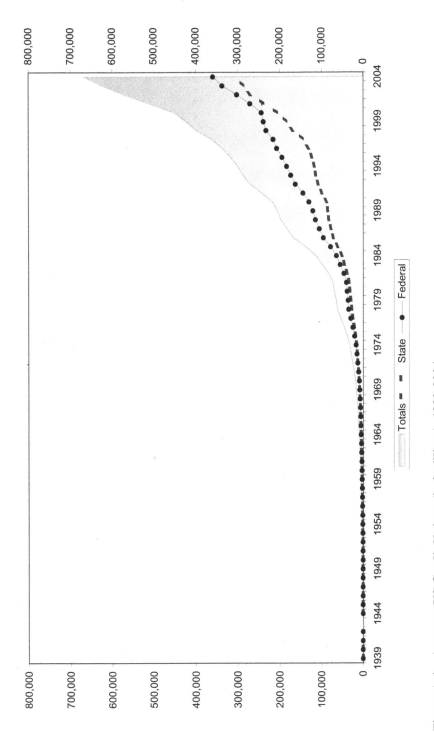

Figure A.4   Assets at US Credit Unions (in $millions), 1939-2004

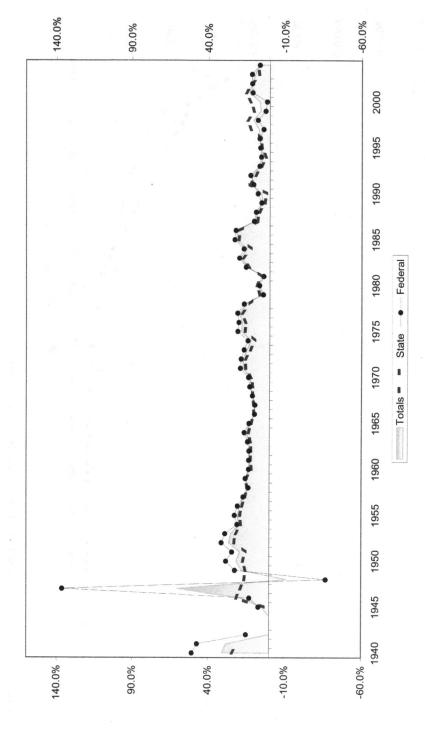

Figure A.5   Asset Growth at US Credit Unions, 1940-2004

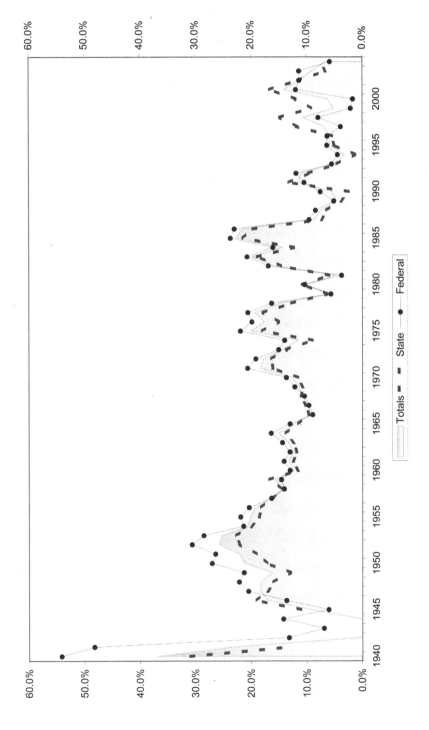

Figure A.6   Savings Growth at US Credit Unions, 1940-2004

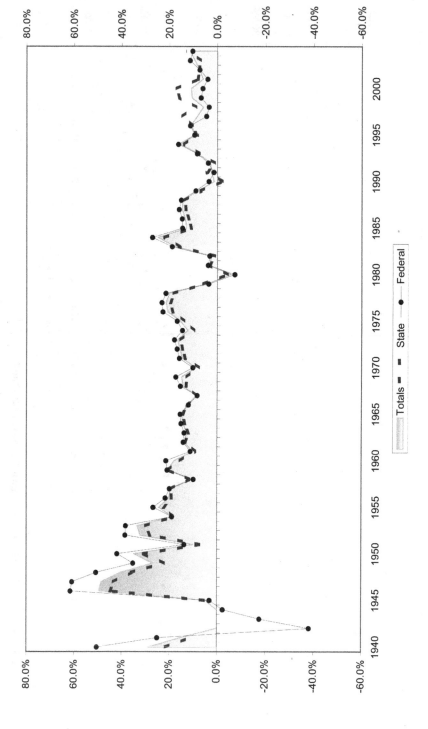

Figure A.7 Loan Growth at US Credit Unions, 1940–2004

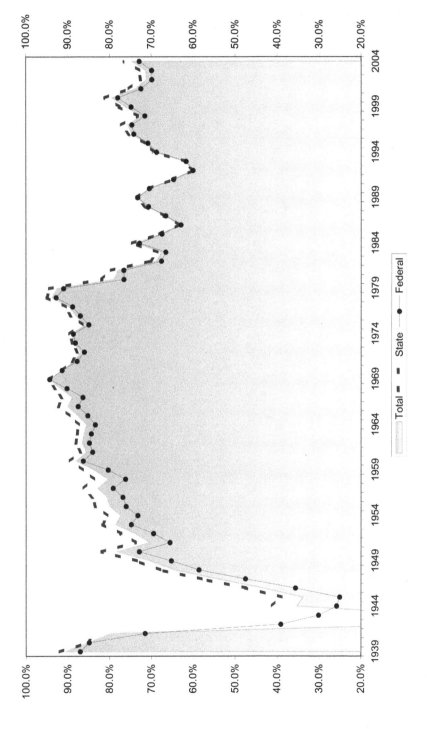

Figure A.8   Loans to Savings Ratio at US Credit Unions, 1939-2004

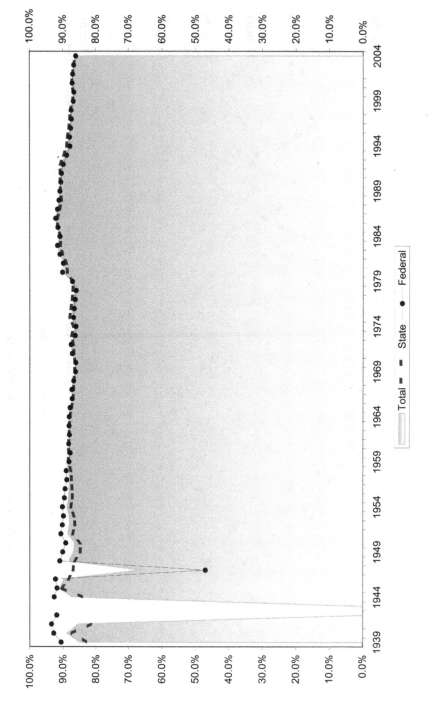

Figure A.9 Savings to Assets at US Credit Unions, 1939-2004

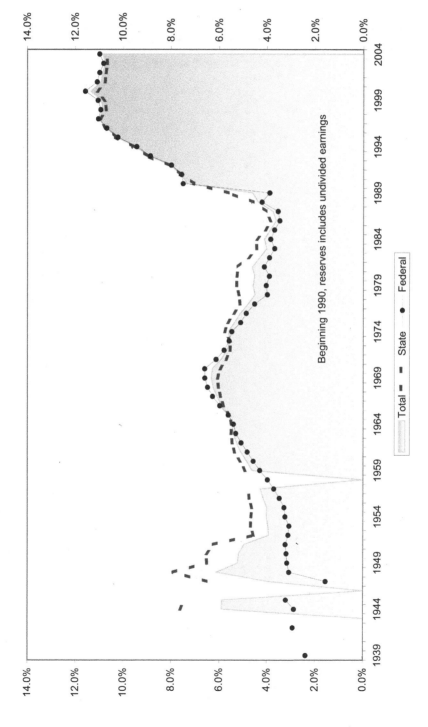

Figure A.10 Reserves to Assets at US Credit Unions, 1939-2004

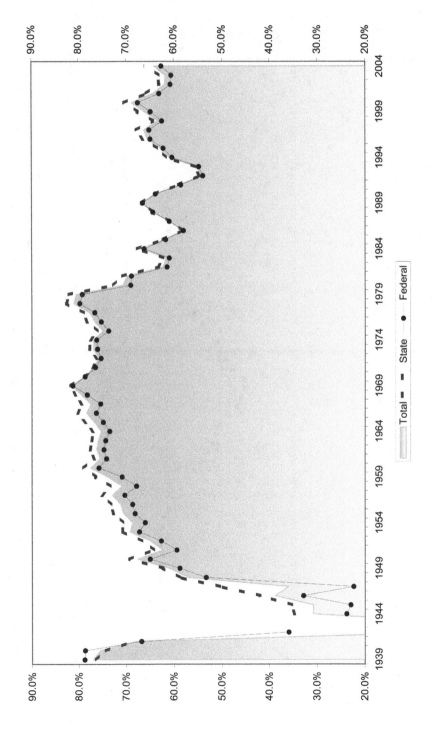

Figure A.11 Loans to Assets at US Credit Unions, 1939-2004

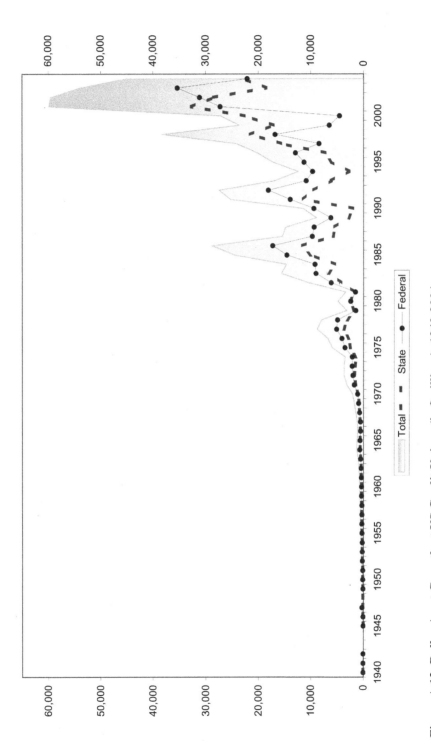

Figure A.12 Dollar Asset Growth at US Credit Unions (in $millions), 1940-2004

Appendix B

Measuring Effect Size

In a meta-analysis, researchers compare a number of studies about a common theoretical hypothesis and common operational definitions. Studies may differ on a number of points, such as size of sample, actual statistical measures used, and methods of computing probabilities. In order to obtain a clear and quantitative picture of what the studies, taken together, actually show, a common metric is needed. The common metric used in these cases is called *effect size* and is defined as the "standard mean difference" between a pair of procedures being compared. All the differences, expressed by the same measure, in this case *z-scores*, are summed and divided by a "within group standard deviation."

To summarize, in case memory fails, a standard deviation is calculated by first finding the *mean (m)* of a set of scores, X(capital X). This is done by dividing the sum of scores by the total number of scores (N). Then the mean is subtracted from each score to get a series of (x – m). Each (x – m) is then squared, and all the squares are summed to get the *sum of squares*. Then the *mean sum of squares* (or *variance*) is found by dividing the *sum of squares* by N. If the series of n's is a sample, then the *sum of squares* is divided by (n-1). Otherwise the sample variance will be too small.

Finally, the *mean sum of squares* is brought to the original scale of the scores by taking its square root. This final result is called the *standard deviation*. Of course a computer can do all of this in a flash! But, in order to understand what kind of numbers result from this procedure, everyone should go though this procedure by hand at least once with a small number (10 or 11) of scores. Nowadays many hand calculators can do the procedure fairly quickly. Try dividing the *sum of squares* both by n and by (n-1) to give a sense of the size of bias you might get by using n with your sample. Note: *n* (not *n-1*) is still used to arrive at the mean (m) in the first step of the procedure.

For people who like to "speak" math, the formula for the *standard deviation* is given below:

$$\sigma = \sqrt{\frac{\sum(X_i - \mu)^2}{N}} \text{, where } \sigma \text{ is standard deviation of a total } population, \quad \text{(1)}$$

X_i is each X from 1 to n,
μ is the mean of n Xs, and
N is the total number of Xs.

or

$$s.d. = \sqrt{\frac{\sum(X_i - m)^2}{n-1}} \text{ , where } s.d. \text{ is the standard deviation,} \qquad (2)$$

$$m \text{ is the mean of a sample, and}$$
$$n \text{ is the number in the sample.}$$

The Greek upper case Σ indicates summation; therefore, the numerators in formulas (1) and (2) are the *sums of squares*. The entire expression under the radical sign (sign for square root) is then *mean sum of squares* or variance. Take its square root to find the *standard deviation*.

A *population* is a distribution of a complete set of scores, e.g., everyone in the United States or the world. A *sample* is a small set of scores usually selected randomly from a *population*. How to get a truly random sample is a topic for an entire field of research and study called "sampling theory." Some people devote their entire careers to "sampling theory." Note the use of the Greek letter σ (lower case sigma) to represent the standard deviation of a population, and *s.d.* or simply "s" denotes the standard deviation of a sample. Similarly, the Greek letter μ represents the mean of a population, and *m* denotes the mean of a sample.

Now a word about what is meant by a few technical terms. The original set of raw scores is called a *distribution*. A *standard normal distribution* is a set of scores with a mean of zero and a standard deviation of one. The word "standard" is used to make it clear that all the statistical measures used—whether the original scores are in single digits, hundreds, thousands, dollars, percentages, inches, metric units, or whatever—are comparable, that is, on the same scale. A raw score expressed in terms of how many *standard deviations* away from the mean it is, is called a *z-score* or a *standard score*. A very interesting property of a random sample is that as its size (n) increases, and a large number of samples are taken from the same population, the distribution of the sample means (*the sampling distribution*) always approaches a normal distribution—regardless of the distribution of the population. This result is called "the central limits theorem."

The mathematical formula for a *z-score* is:

$$z = \frac{X - m}{\sigma} \text{ , where X is the raw score,} \qquad (3)$$

$$m \text{ is the mean of the distribution,}$$
$$\sigma \text{ is the standard deviation.}$$

Another important term used by researchers is the *p-value*. It represents the probability that the associated result is not true—or could have been found by chance. It is computed by several different methods depending on the type of distribution. The principle behind the *p-value* is a proof called the "central limits theorem" mentioned above—i.e. that all sample means will approach a normal distribution as the number of samples gets larger. A normal distribution is often represented by the familiar "bell curve." A random sample of 100 or more cases (n > 100) has essentially all the properties of a normal distribution; with such a large n, the function representing the "bell-curve" distribution is a smooth one, and the function, called the normal probability density function is given as:

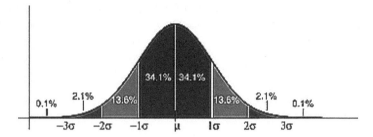

Figure B.1   The Standard Normal Distribution

$$f(x; \mu, \sigma) = \frac{1}{\sigma \sqrt{2\pi}} \exp\left(-\frac{(x-\mu)^2}{2\sigma^2}\right). \tag{4}$$

where the second term, beginning with "exp", indicates that the quantity between the parentheses is actually an exponent of the base of natural logarithms, e, which is a constant (like π)with a value $\cong 2.718\ldots$ The question of where e comes from and why it is used here is beyond the scope of this discussion. Again the formula is reprinted here for those who like to speak math.

The famous "bell curve" that represents the above density function is shown in Figure B.1.

In Figure B.1 above, *p-values* are expressed in percentages. These percentages represent the areas below the curve between the particular points marked by the number of standard deviations (σ) away from the mean (μ). The *p-values* of the greatest interest are the small ones out in the tails. The chance of being at least 2 standard deviations away from the mean of a normal distribution is about 2.15 percent or *p-value* = .0215. Since 99.7 percent of cases will fall between -3 and +3 standard deviations around the mean, the chance of being above the upper 3 standard deviations would be about 0.15 percent or a *p-value* of .0015. The usual *p-value* for statistical significance in the behavioral and social sciences is set at 0.05. Consulting a table of *the density function* (how a *probability-p-value* is distributed across all possible values) or computing directly, that would correspond to a *z-score* (number of standard deviations) of +1.96.

The mathematical formula for *probability* (area under the curve) is the integral of the *density function* defined above:

$$P(\mathbf{x}) = \frac{1}{2\pi} \int_{-\infty}^{x} \exp\left(-\frac{u^2}{2}\right) du, \tag{5}$$

Where "u" takes on values between -∞ and "x" (the *z-score* being used).

Tests of Significant Differences

The *z-score* and its associated *p-value* can be used to test the significance of differences between the means between two populations or large samples. If the *z-score* difference is sufficiently large to produce a *p-value* below a certain level (called the alpha-level), usually p=0.05, but for a more stringent test p=0.01 can be used. Calculations on the differences between smaller samples (with n less than 100) will use a *standard error of the mean* calculated from the standard deviation by dividing by the square root of "n-1":

$$se = \frac{s.d.}{\sqrt{n}}, \text{ where "se" stands for "standard error."}$$

Then the *p-value* is found on a *t-distribution* rather than a normal distribution, because the smaller n biases the probabilities, especially at the extremes (tails) of the curve. The density function of the *t-distribution* looks much like the bell-curve of a normal distribution, except that its tails are fatter. The *t-ratio* is computed similarly to the *z-score*:

$$t = \frac{m_1 - m_2}{se}, \text{ where } m_1 \text{ and } m_2 \text{ are the means of two samples and}$$
$$se \text{ is the standard error.}$$

If there are more than two group means to compare, the test statistic is the *F-ratio*. This is quite easy to compute. It is the ratio between the *within-variance* and the *between-variance*. The *within-variance* is the mean sum of squares of the distances between all data points and their group means. The *between-variance* is the mean sum of squared differences between the means of each group and the grand mean.

$$F = \frac{BetweenVar.}{WithinVar.}$$

When there are only two groups, "F" turns out to be equal to "t^2".

The Stouffer z-score as Effect Size

The *Stouffer z-score* is very interesting (see Stouffer, 1949) in that, instead of using a raw score from a single distribution as its unit **X**, it uses the overall outcome of a given study, in whatever form it was computed. It is found by following the following 4 steps:

1. Compute the exact *p-value* of whatever statistic is used by the author. If no statistic, such as t, F or X^2, is available assume *p-value* = 0.05.
2. Compute the exact *z-score* corresponding to the *p-value*.
3. Find the average of all the authors' *z-scores*:

$$Sz = \frac{\sum_{i=1}^{n} z_i}{\sqrt{n}}, \text{ where "Sz" is } Stouffer\ z\text{-score,} \qquad (6)$$

z_i is the vector of all authors' *z-scores*, and
n is the total number of authors.

4. Refer to table or use formula (5) above to find the *p-value* of the resulting
Stouffer *z-score*.

Note that the assumed use of *p-value* = 0.05 in step 1 may overestimate the probability of the Stouffer *z-score*. Thus the results of the meta-analysis will be understated. The resulting Stouffer *z-score* is then the overall *effect size* and its associated *p-value* is the probability of finding such an overall effect by pure chance. A procedure adjusting the Stouffer *z-score* for varying sample sizes across all the studies in the meta-analysis is given in Hedges and Olkin (1986).

Now in the Stouffer *z-score* we have a measure of *effect size* that gives both direction and magnitude of differences between "cooperation" and "competition" or "individual effort." As a bonus, it is possible to compute from the Stouffer *z-score* a probability that our results are in error. Fortunately the large effect sizes reported in Chapter 2 allow for only a tiny probability of error.

References

Hedges, L. and I. Olkin (1985). *Statistical Methods for Meta-Analysis.* New York: Academic Press.
Stouffer, S. (1949). *The American Soldier: Vol I. Adjustment During Army Life.* Princeton, NJ: Princeton University Press.

Appendix C

The IMF "Merged Model"

Target Variables

Δy	Growth measured by GDP
ΔR	Change in Reserves
ΔP_D	Change in domestic price levels

Instrumental Variables

T	Taxes
G	Government expenditures
ΔE	Change in exchange rate
ΔL^g	Change in credit to government

Mediating Variables

ΔF	Change in net foreign assets
Y	National income
Y_{-1}	Last year's income
ΔY	Change in national income
E_{-1}	Last year's exchange rate
X	Total exports
J_{-1}	Last year's imports
Q_{J-1}	Price of last year's imports
y_{-1}	Last year's GDP

Parameters to be Estimated

σ, τ, α, η, δ, and s.

Simultaneous Equations

$$\Delta P_D = \frac{-\kappa + (\sigma - \tau)\Delta y}{\delta \tau y_{-1}} - (1-\delta)\delta^{-1}\Delta E \tag{1}$$

where: $\kappa = sY_{-1} + (1-s)T - G + \Delta F + \Delta L^g$

$$\Delta R = X - J_{-1} - \left(Q_{J-1} - \eta E_{-1}\right)\Delta E - E_{-1}\left(\alpha\Delta y + \eta\Delta P_D\right) + \Delta F \tag{2}$$

$$\Delta R = \tau y_{-1}\left(1-\delta\right)\Delta E - \Delta L_g - \tau(y_{-1}\delta\Delta P_D + \Delta y) \tag{3}$$

$$\Delta y = \frac{\kappa + \tau y_{-1}\Delta P_D}{\left(\sigma - \tau\right)} \tag{4}$$

where: κ = as in equation (1) above.

Comments

- Growth, reserves, and domestic price levels are targets of a simulation based on the above four equations.
- Mediating variables are all supplied by the subject country's own economic data.
- The six parameters are estimated from the country's economic data to provide the nearest possible match to the country's economic experience.
- Instrumental variables are manipulated to arrive at optimum values of the target variables.
- The simple linear functional forms are derived from economic studies on how the operational variables affect each other.

Notes

- Although the major goal of the IMF is to eliminate poverty around the world, no variable expressing poverty levels or rates and no parameters or variables defining income or wealth distribution appear anywhere in the model!
- It is curious, given the IMF's interest in eliminating poverty, that the three targets of their model are economic growth, monetary reserves, and price levels.
- The model is strictly a monetary one and allows for no general human welfare variables of any kind, assuming that if the monetary problems are solved, the economy will adjust to the "free market" and human welfare will take care of itself. This is the basis for all efforts at stabilization and structural adjustment.
- The model is totally simultaneous and allows for no time lags.

Appendix D

Interviews: Protocol and Summary Data

Interview protocol

Questions for Management, PR Persons, or Worker-members

Organization
1. What is your basic cooperative unit?
   (Producer, consumer, distributor, individual, family, co-op, all of above, other)
2. Are you a manager or a worker-member?
3. If you are a manager, what is your position in the company?
4. Member qualification (member fee, occupation, saver, borrower, both)
5. How many co-ops (working units) in your group?
6. How many member total?
7. How is the CEO hired?
8. How are other top management hired?
9. How is central support staff hired (supervisory, if more than one local group)?
10. How is local group staff hired?
11. How are long-term policy decisions made?

Financial
1. How was original capital secured?
2. If by loan or grant, what was source?
3. What is indebtedness, if external loans are outstanding?
4. What are your coop's total annual earnings?
(From 3 and 4, a debt/earnings ratio can be calculated: DEBT = total debt/earnings.)

Labor
1. Is there some kind of labor council?
2. What percent of workers are members?
3. Is there a union organization?
4. Do workers seem to have a sense of ownership in the group?
5. Is participation high or low?
6. Do important policy decisions include input from worker-members?
7. Is there non-participation or low productiveness of worker-members?
8. Is the size of your organization a problem (too small or large), is the size okay?

Open-Ended Questions
1. What works best in your coop?
2. What is not working so well?

Interview Codebook

VARIABLE	TYPE	RESPONSE
ENTRY	Integer	Numbers 1 through 58
COOP	Alpha	
GROUP	Integer	1 = staff, 2 = worker/member
POSITION	Alpha	
UNIT	Integer	1 = producer, 2 = consumer, 3 = distributor, 4 = individual, 5 = family, 6 = co-op, 7 = all of the above, 9 = other
QUAL	Integer	1 = member fee, 2 = occupation, 3 = saver, 4 = borrower, 5 = both
NO. COOPS	Integer	Number of co-ops or work units
NO. MEMBERS	Integer	Total number of members
CEO HIRE	Integer	1 = board, 2 = member vote, 3 = local group
MGMT HIRE	Integer	1 = board, 2 = member vote, 3 = local group
CENT STAFF	Integer	1 = board, 2 = member vote, 3 = local group
LOC STAFF	Integer	1 = board, 2 = member vote, 3 = local group
DECISION	Integer	0 = mgmt fiat, 1 = plurality, 2 = majority, 3 = consensus
WHO DEC?	Integer	1 = membership, 2 = council/board, 3 = mgmt, 4 = all
ORIG CAPITAL	Integer	1 = member shares, 2 = memb loans, 3 = outside loan, 4 = grant
LOAN/GRANT	Integer	1 = government, 2 = corporation, 3 = foundation, 4 = commercial bank
LOANS OUT	Numeric	Total amount of loans from outside
D/E RATIO	Numeric	Ratio of external debt to earnings in percent
LAB COUNC	Integer	1 = yes, 2 = no
%WORK-MEM	Numeric	Percent of total workers who are members
UNION	Integer	1 = yes, 2 = no
OWNER SENSE	Integer	1 = yes, 2 = no
PARTIC	Integer	1 = high, 2 = low
INCLUSIVE	Integer	1 = yes, 2 = no
LAZY WORK	Integer	0 = none, 1 = few, 2 = many
SIZE PROB	Integer	0 = just right, 1 = too small, 2 = too large

Note: Perceptions of "Successes" and "Challenges" are enumerated and grouped separately.

Variable Definitions

ENTRY	Respondent's numeric order
COOP	Name of cooperative of respondent being interviewed
GROUP	Whether the respondent is a manager or a worker-member
POSITION	Alphanumeric designation of respondent's position
UNIT	Type of cooperative unit: producer, consumer, etc.
QUAL	Qualification of membership
NO. COOPS	Number of Co-op or working units
NO. MEMBERS	Total number of members

CEO HIRE	Who hires the CEO/GEN MANAGER?
MGMT HIRE	Who hires the upper managers?
CENT STAFF	Who hires the central staff (all levels)?
LOC STAFF	Who hires a local group of district staff?
DECISION	How are long-term policy decisions made?
WHO DEC?	Who makes these policy decisions?
ORIG CAP	Source of original capitalization
LOAN/GRANT	If original capitalization is a loan or grant, what source?
LOANS OUT	Total amount of loans to the co-op from outside
D/E RATIO	Total amount of debt divided by total earnings (in percent "X100")
LAB COUNC	Is there some type of labor council or worker input group?
%WORK-MEM	Percent of workers that are members of the co-op
UNION	Is there a local union?
OWNER SENSE	Do the workers/members seem to have a sense of ownership?
PARTIC	Is the worker-member participation high or low?
INCLUSIVE	Do important policy decisions include input from worker-members?
LAZY WORK	Is there non-participation or low productiveness of worker-members?
SIZE PROB	Is the size of the organization a problem (to small or too large) or is size ok?

Summary and Analysis of Interview Data

Data were collected by interviews with 23 managers and support staff and 38 member workers in 15 different cooperative groups around the world. The answers given by the interview subjects were of three types: numeric, multiple-choice and open-ended. The multiple-choice responses could be coded numerically according to the codebook presented on page 216 above. Some of these data did not vary, such as the variable UNION, because none of the cooperatives had organized unions. The staff hiring was almost uniformly done by elected boards and councils. The only exception was the Puerto Rico Department to Form cooperatives. There the management and staff hiring is all done by local group boards and councils, because the department is only an association of cooperatives. With these variables omitted, a summary of the multi-choice answers was compiled.

The number before the equal sign is the value as coded and the number after, the tally of subjects giving that answer. For example in the first variable, UNIT (type of membership), two were producers, one was a consumer, none were distributors, six were individual, four were family, and two were "all of the above" (meaning all forms of membership were available in their co-op). In the second, QUAL (How do you qualify to be a member?), eight qualified by membership fee, two by virtue of their occupation, none by simply being a saver, one by being a borrower, three by being both a saver and a borrower, and none designated "other" type, and so on.

Multiple Choice Questions

UNIT (type of membership): 1=2, 2=1, 3=0, 4=6, 5=4, 7=2
QUAL (member qualification): 1=8, 2=2, 3=0, 4=1, 5=3, 9=0
DECISION (how decisions made): 0=0, 1=0, 2=3, 3=12 (most by consensus)
WHO DEC? (who decides): 1=7, 2=5, 3=1, 4=1
ORIG CAPITAL (how obtain orig. capital): 1=8, 2=1. 3=1, 4=5
LAB COUNCIL (Is there a worker council?): 1(yes)=3, 2(no)=12
PARTIC (Is worker partic. high or low?): 1(high)=10, 2(low)=5
INCLUSIVE (All policy decisions include workers?): 1(yes)=12, 2(no)=3
LAZY WORK (Any non-productive workers?): 0=9, 1=6, 2=0
SIZE PROB (Is there a size problem?): 0(just right)=10, 1(too small)=4, 2(too large)=1

Open-ended Questions

The two open-ended questions, "What have been your successes?" and "What do you consider your greatest challenges right now?" were simply listed by key words or phrases. Notice that there are far more successes than challenges listed by the interviewees. Considerably more thought was required to answer the question about challenges for the future; the shortness of the challenge list should not be an indicator of their lesser importance.

List of Successes

(from both managers and worker-members)

Easy loans and fair rates
Easy payback if problems arise
Team work democratic; management staff help workers
Good working conditions
Good space to work in
Good community relations
Good training opportunities
Values obvious within group
Women are empowered (especially Muslim women in Bangladesh and Indonesia
    and all women in India)
Larger income for workers
Meetings productive
Eliminated "middle-man"
Better support for disasters (viz. Tsunami victims)
Rapid growth
Workers have consciousness of ownership
Make better products (especially Kerala and Mondragón)
The café and craft shop (ASP and Boulder)

List of Challenges

(General agreement between management and worker-members. Numbers indicate the number of times the particular challenge is espressed.)

Maintaining cash flow and continuing to obtain necessary capital 5
High interest rates on micro-finance (Indonesia) 2
Need more volunteers 1
Need more training time 1
Need more work orders (Bangladesh Weavers) 3
Staff too small (Bangladesh Children's Home) 1
Low participation rates 4
Not reaching the very poor (urban poor) 3
Supervision sometimes not good; management competence (ASP-India, US) 3
Slow communication responses from management 2
Low level workers hard to find (MILMA-Kerala) 1
More people demanding ATM services [competition with transnationals] 3
Need more community support (US) 3
Management competence (US)

Quantitative Analyses

The major research question that motivated the interview-based study was to get a clearer idea of what helps cooperatives to succeed. In order to approach that question quantitatively, several concepts need to be defined operationally. One certain way to get an outcome measure would have been to interview a number of people who had experienced failed co-ops. Not having access to such persons prevents us from getting definite outcome information of that sort. Another problem with that method is that if we did interview persons who experience a co-op failure, they would undoubtedly have already formed an opinion of what made the co-op fail, and we would not be able to get accurate, unbiased data about the actual operational causal factors themselves.

What can be done from the data available is to construct a tentative outcome score by counting the number of successes reported by the management and members of a given co-op and subtracting the number of problems reported:

SCORE = #SUCCESSES – #NUMBER OF PROBLEMS

This process could imply that the co-op with the most problems is most likely to fail. That may not necessarily be so, but it could be true that factors that generate the most problems would also be those that would probably cause a co-op to fail. A co-op reporting no particular successes and a number of problems would achieve a large negative score and perhaps be on the brink of failure. Only one co-op in the list could report no great successes, but did report multiple problems. Although organized as a co-op, it is a program that depends entirely upon goodwill contributions; without those contributions every year, the group will certainly fail; the group is not a self-sustaining co-op. Another of the co-ops in the original list of 15 was unable to provide useful outcome information about successes and problems. That co-op was eliminated for the purpose of quantitative analysis. The resulting N = 14, very small for a definitive analysis, but some correlations are interesting and make theoretical sense.

A correlation study revealed several factors which correlated, not highly, but significantly with the SCORE outcome variable:

Variable	Pearson r
#MEMB (Number of Members)	-0.288
ORIGCAP (Original Capital source)	-0.375
DECIS (Decision making)	0.545
DEBT (Debt ratio)	-0.354
PARTIC (Participation)	0.238
INCLUS (Inclusion of Workers)	0.252

There are also several strong correlations among the factors. The largest ones involved the size of membership's negative correlation with democratic decision making (-0.543), inclusion of workers in policy decisions (-0.616), and general participation of workers (-0.328). Consensus (democratic) decision making was positively correlated with the number of successes reported (0.495) and negatively correlated with number of problems (-0.440). These last two correlations can be interpreted as: The more nearly in consensus the co-op members are the more successes and the fewer problems they will report.

A study of these correlations leads to a regression analysis—trying to create a reliable predictive instrument. Using the outcome SCORE and regressing against it against the factors listed in the table above, a backward stepwise regression was performed. This method begins by estimating the regression with all of the possible causal factors included, and begins backing out factors that do not meet sufficient predictive levels. This process ends when the R-square value and the coefficients of the factors are all "significant" at the 0.05 level.

Given the small size of the sample, there was little hope of finding any significant predictive variables. However, one factor did stand out and is a significant predictor of the outcome variable, SCORE, with a confidence of 95 percent (a *p-value* < 0.05). That factor was DECIS, the degree of democratic decision making. Recall that this factor was scaled as follows: 0=management fiat, 1=plurality vote, 2=majority vote, 3=consensus. The regression or prediction equation was estimated to be as follows:

SCORE = .545 DECIS, with both SCORE and DECIS standardized.

The F-ratio was a significant 5.083, and p-value for DECIS of 0.044. The R-square value, indicating the strength of the relationship or prediction, was 0.298. This means that the decision mode used can explain nearly 30 percent of the success of a co-op. The simple single-factor equation above can be used to predict success with only a 4.4 percent likelihood of error.

Suspecting the existence of interaction terms, two more analyses were tried with (1) interactions between #MEMB (number of members in coop) and DECIS (democratic decision making) and (2) interactions between PARTIC (whether participation is a problem) and INCLUS (including workers in decision making). Neither analysis added anything significant to the above conclusion. Given the small size of the sample, more complex analyses would not be likely to produce significant results.

It is interesting that how the original capital was found, size of the cooperative membership, or even the debt ratio were all eliminated early in the analysis. Again, given the size of the sample, their effects, although theoretically in the right direction, were too small to be statistically significant. Perhaps if larger samples and more precise variable definitions were used, future research could construct a more complex quantitative model of success. The preliminary result obtained above, however, shows the deep importance of democratic, consensus decision making in the effectiveness of cooperative organizations.

Note: For all statistical calculations, SYSTAT 8.0 was used on Microsoft's Windows XT system software on COMPAQ high speed hardware.

Index

Ability (as it affects cooperation), 45-48, **49**, 52, 54
Ace Hardware, 170
    See also Cooperatives, distribution
Agnew, Spiro, 37
Alinsky, Saul, 83
Ambedkar, Dr. BR, 97-99
Americas, **125-138**
Anand, 14, 108-109, 129
Anand Pattern Cooperative Society (APCOS), 109
Andes, 126
Andhra Pradesh, 4, 5, **99**, 103, 106
Ankuram-Sangamam-Poram (ASP), **99-110**
    See also ASP
Antonio Gramsci, 19
Apartheid, 75
Arizmendi (Fr José Maria Arizmendiarrietta), 114-115
Artisanal Boat, *See* SIFFS
ASP, 99, 100-104
    Ford Foundation, 103
    GramPhone, 103
    MACS, 101-103
    Natural Fibre, 103
Assumptions about cooperation, 167
Australia, 91-94
Autonomous Communities (Basque), 113
Avestan, *See* Persia, language
Aztec, 128

Babasaheb, 98
    See also Ambedkar
Bangladesh, 84-87
    Rural Agricultural Center (BRAC), 84
Bank Crisis of 1980s, 8, 23
Bank for Reconstruction and Development, *See* World Bank
Baroda, India, 97
Basque Country (Euskadi), 11, 113, 114, 123, 156
    Araba, 113, 114
    autonomous communities, 113, 114
    Bizcaia, 113, 114

Gipuskoa, 113, 114
Navarra, 113, 114
Rioja, 113
See also Spain
Basque Nationalist Party, 114
BBKA, 119
Beck, John, 10
Belgium, 11, 68, 76, 89
Benevolent Dictator, 69, **70**, 167
Blueprint for cooperative globalization, 6, 149, 165-181
Boom, 21, 58, 63, 141
Borda, José de la, 130
Brahma, 96
Brazil, 120, 174
Bretton Woods (NH), 60
Britain, 10, 11, 68, 84, 99, 125

Cacaxtla, Tlaxcala, Mexico, 132
Cádiz Conference
    autonomous communities, 113
    See also Basque Country (Euskadi)
Calavo, 22, 23, 34, 162
Canadian Parliament, 26
Capital, 39, 181
Capitalism
    competition, 57, 181
    entrepreneurial, 71
    externalities, 62, 78, 177
    free market, 3, 4, 31, **57**, 58, 61, 72, 74, 78, 107, 149, 173, 176, Appendix C-214
    growth, 60, 61, 65, 92, 94
    market forces, 59
    military costs, 178
    monetarism, 74
    resources, 59
    technology, 59, 168
    upper management, 177
Capper-Volstead Act of 1922, 4, 16, 32-34, 60, 160
Cárdenas, Lázaro, 129
Carib culture, 139, 141
    Igneris, 140
    Taíno culture, 5, 139, 140, 141, 147

Caribbean, 139-143, 147, 148
    African slaves, 139
    Arawakan, 140
Carlist Wars, Spain, 114
Carpenter's Cooperative, 21
Carranza, 128
Cartagena Protocol, 75
Casa Blanca, 142
Caste system, 96-99, 110
    Brahmins, 96, 97
    Dalits, 96, 99, 100, 110, 157
    Kshatriyas, 96
    Shudras, 96
    Vysyas, 96
Castillian presence in Euskadi, 113
Cheese cooperatives, 10
Chennai (Madras), 108
Chiapas, 4, 9, 134, 135
    See also Maya Coffee Cooperatives
Chocó, 126, 127
Chowdar Tank demonstration, 98
Christian Missionaries, 95
Christians in India, 98
Civil rights, 21, 169
Civil Society, 95, 99, 135
Civil War, 20
Clifford, George, 142
Coady, The Rev. Dr Moses, 27
CoBank, 15
    See also Cooperatives, financial
Collateral, 27, 85, 90, 91, 94, 100
Colonialism, 125, 129
Columbia University, 97
Columbus, Christopher, 140, 141
Common Good, 52, 70, 88, 149, 166, 169,
    172, 174, 175, 176
Commons, The, 168, 175
Communes, Utopian Communities, 1, 10,
    125, 126
    See also Gaviotas
Communication, 73, 111, 152, 153, 158-
    160, 162
Competition, 3, 7, 17, 34, 37, **38**, 39, 40, **41**,
    43-57, 71-75, 149, 166-181
    win-lose, 38
    zero-sum games, 38
Concentration of wealth, 169
Conditional corporate charters, 175
Confcooperative, 19
    See also Italy

Conquest, 125, 129
    See also Colonialism; Neo-Colonialism
Conquistadores, 125, 128, 129
Consumer Index, 61
Consumerism, 92
Coolidge, 21, 128
Co-op Group, 9, 18
.Coop online, 13
Cooper, David, 44
Cooperation, 38, 39, 41, 43, 45, 47, 49, 51,
    53, 54
    effectiveness, 20, 39, 42, 44, 46, 122
    partnerships with Commercial Banking,
        155
    productivity, 11, 39, 42, 43, 44, 45, 46,
        50, 52, 53, 54, 157, 168, 169
    win-win games, solutions, 38
Cooperative Associations
    Alaska native corporations, 28
    ASA ("hope"), 84
    ASP (India), 99, 101-104, 111
    California Avocado Commission, 23
    community associations, 13
    Congress of Cooperatives, 10
    Cooperative Associations Act, *See*
        Puerto Rico
    DAPPU, 100-102
    DOWCALM (India), 100
    Grange, 20
    ICA *See* International Cooperative
        Alliance
    Massachusetts Credit Union
        Association, 27
Cooperative capitalism, 174
Cooperative corporation, 13, 26, 116, 124
Cooperative Model, 4, 5, 17, 45, 78, 100,
    101, 106, 119, 145, 153, 166
Cooperative Principles
    autonomy, 13
    independence, 4, 13
    new social order, 115
    one share-one membership-one vote, 12,
        33, 88, 131, 155
Cooperatives
    agricultural, 9, 14, 22
    Andhra Pradesh, 99
    artisan, 15, 131
    bookstores, 93
    community advancement, 93
    distribution, 14
    education, 11, 88, 145, 157

electric co-ops, 21, 29
and environment, 12, 14, 30, 75, 86, 127
financial, 15, 26, 145, 162
fire insurance, 10
gambling, 93
housing, 11, 15, 18
medical, 11
networks, 13
producer, 14
quasi-cooperatives, 30
retail, 15, 33
service, 15
trading co-ops, 93
value-added, 14
volunteer labor, 14
Cooperativa Colonia Mexicana, 22
Cordilleras, 126
Corporate inventory, 62
Corporate Welfare, 77
Corporations, 13, 16, 23, 74, 115, 119, 120,
   131, 168, 174-177
worker-ownership, 168
Corsairs, 142
Cortez, Hernán, 129
Credit Unions, 15, 17, 26, 27, 28, 145, 148
Raiffeisen, Friederich, 25-26
Schulze-Delitzsch, 25, 26
See also Finance
Criollos, 128, 129, 136
See also Mexican culture
Cuban communism, 139
Cumberland, Earl of, 142

Dalit NGOs, 100
Dalitbahujan, 96, 99, 100
See also Caste system
DAPPU, *See* Cooperatives Associations
Davis, James H, 44
de Boyve, Edouard, 11
Decision making by consensus, 3, 101, 109,
   116, 131, 158
Democracy, 66, 77, 113, 121, 123, 124, 169,
   172, 180, 181
Department of cooperatives (Puerto Rico),
   145
Dependent variables, 40, 42, 54
Desjardins, Dorimene, 26
Alphonse, 26
Deutsch, Morton, 40
Development, 11, 125
Díaz, Porfirio (Mexican President), 128, 129

Directory of French Cooperators, 18
See also France
Distribution of income, 31, 62
Domination paradigm, 61, 69, 71
See also Imperialism
Don Carlos, 113
DOWCALM (India), 100-102
Dowry system, 85, 86
Drake, Francis (privateer), 142
Dutch colonies, 87

East Bengal, 84
See also Bangladesh
Eastern Europe
Czech/Slovak, 16
Hungary, 16
Poland, 16
Soviet model, 16
Ecole Nimes, 11
Economic revolution, 84, 85
Economics, supply side, 25, 74
Effect size, 40, **41**, 43, 44, 48, 49, 50, 51, 54
Ejido system, 128, 129
elkartason (Sp. solidaridad), 120
See also Spain, Mondragón
Cooperatives, Ten Principles
Elphinshire School, 97
Employee Stock Ownership Plans, ESOP,
   28, 31, 78, 90
Energy Information Administration
Electric co-ops, 30
See also Cooperatives
Environment, 12, 62, 75, 77, 78, 177
European elites, 114
European influence in India, 96
European Union (EU), 108, 115
Euskara (Basque language), 113

Fabre, August, 11
Failed cooperatives
Calavo, 162
Lee Cole, 162
New England Protective Union, 10
Why Co-ops Fail, 151
Failure, 9, 52, 53, 68, 151
Failure of cooperation, 9, 52, 53, 151
going public, 162
See also Calavo
legal problems, 160
starting too big, 156
take-overs, 92

Fair Trade, 18, 77
Fair Trade Assitance (FTA), 131
Fernando VII (of Spain), 114
FIDECOOP (Puerto Rico), 147, 148
Filene, Edward, 27
Finance
    banking, 11, 26, 162
    cash flow, 153, 156, 162
    investment, 12, 13, 66, 172
    micro-finance, 85, 90, 91, 94, 153
        default rates, 90
    resources, 151
    venture capital, 87
Financial Credit for the Poor, 84
    See also Grameen (Village) Model
First World, 125
France, 1, 10, 11, 14, 18, 19, 67, 68, 76, 89,
    113, 125
F-ratio, 48, 55, 210
Free-market fundamentalism, 74
Free rider effect, 52
Free trade, 23, 60, 61, 64, 65, 66, 105, 126,
    162, 174, 178
Friendly societies (Australia), 92, 94
Fueros, *See* Basque Country (Euskadi),
    autonomous communities

G-8, Group of eight nations, 74, 76
Gandhi, Mohandas, 84, 95
GATT, 64
    See also North American Free Trade
        Agreement
Gaviotas, 4, 5, 126, 127, 136, 137, 138
GDP, Gross Domestic Product, 61- 63, 69,
    92, 136
Gender, 12, 39, 47, 51, 54, 70, 103
Genetic factors, 52, 53
Germany, 1, 10, 11, 17, 24, 25, 69, 76, 89,
    114
Gernika, 114
GESPA, 119
Gide, Charles, 1, 11
Globalization, **72**, 110, 117, 180
    corporate, 92, 111
Globalization from above, 73, 75, 77, 110,
    123, 124, 173
Globalization from below, 34, 74, 75, 76,
    78, 124, 137, 149, 165-181
    blueprint, 6, 149, 172, 174, 180
    Porto Alegre, Brazil, 174

Gloucester Co-op, 18
    See also United Kingdom
GNP, Gross National Product, 61, 69
Government Intervention, 88
    See also Political intervention
Grameen (village) model, 83-87, 90, 91, 93,
    94, 100, 101, 153, 154, 179
Grameen Bank, *See* Grameen Village Model
Grange Movement, 20
    See also Cooperative Associations
Grito de Lares, 143
Gross World Product (GWP), 63
Growth, *See* Capitalism, growth
Guánica, 143
Guatemala, 133, 134, 135
Gund Institue, Univ. of Vermont, 63, 79

Hacienda system, 128, 129, 143, 161
    Latifundios, 129, 161
Haiti, 139
Harding, 128
Harrapan civilization, 96
Hawkins, John (privateer), 142
Healthcare, 28, 95, 178
Hegemony, 69, 96
Hero mythology, 71, 72
    See also Imperialism
Hidden hand, *See* Invisible hand
Hierarchical model, 1, 3, 21, 22, 47, 69, **70**,
    71, 121, 128, 165, 166, 169
Hindu Society and culture, 84, **96**
Hispañola, 139
Hoover, Herbert, 21
Hostility toward cooperatives, 92

IMF, International Monetary Fund, 2, 60,
    63, 64, 73, 74, 76-78
Imperialism, 61, 64, 67, 68, 74, 75, 178
    classical, 66, 68, 74
    economic, 66
Income, 19, 33, 58, 60, 62, 63, 66, 68, 71,
    76, 77, 83, 85, 86, 105, 108, 110,
    118, 125, 131, 136, 144, 147, 161,
    170, 177
Independence (Puerto Rico), 143
Independent variables, 40, 41
India, 12, 83, 84, **95-111**
    AMUL, 14, **108**
    Aryans, 96
    Constitution, 99

gender equity, 103
independence, 95, 105
Kerala, 5, 14, 19, **105-110**
  Communist Party, 105
  dairy cooperative (MILMA), 109, 110
  fisher cooperative (SIFFS), 104,
   106-107
  Trivandrum, 108, 109
  village of Mottum, 106
  Society Registration Act, 106
  urban beggars, 104
Indian "society", 106
Indigenas, 128, 136
  See also Mexican culture
Individual Effort, 37-55
Indonesia, 87-91
  Bank (BRI), 89, 90, 153
  Ministry of Cooperatives, 88
International Cooperative Alliance (ICA),
  10, 11, 12, 13, 17, 20, 35, 93, 120
Interviews, *See* Appendix D-215ff.
Investors, 11
Invisible hand, 3, 72, 173
Italy, 19

Jamaica, 139
Jay, Pierre, 26, 27
Jogins or Dedasis, temple prostitutes, 100
Johnson, David and Roger, 39-56
Juarez, Benito (Mexican President), 128

Kagel, John, 44
Kanda, Dr Mohan, 101
Kaulback, John
  New England Protective Union, 20
  See also Failure; Failed cooperatives
Knights of Labor, 20, 21
Kohlberg, L., 42, 45, 56
Kolkata (Calcutta), 84, 108
Kreuger, Ivar, 71, 72
Kurian, Dr, 99, 108

La Fortuleza, 142, 147
Labor
  organized, 2, 16-17
  retirement, 17
  strikes, 16
  support, 16-17
  training, 17
  unemployment insurance, 17
Land O'Lakes, 9, 14, 22

Land reform, 129
Las Abejas (Worker Bees), 135
Latin America, 135, 136, 137, 138
Lebret, Fr Louis, 126
LeClerc, Francois (privateer), 142
Legal
  intellectual property, 168
  restrictions, 16, 23
  support, 106
   Massachusetts Bank, 27
  systems, 15, 16, 26, 32, 33, 34, 130,
   137, 144, 145, 146, 148, 161
Lerdo Law, 129
llanos, 126, 127
Lodges (Austalia), 92
Loiza Aldea, 140
London Times, 72
Los Arcaicos, 140
Low Quality Studies, 49

Maharaja of Baroda, 97
Manu, 96, 98
Marshall Plan, 60
Martin, Brian, 179, 180
Martin's Five Principles, 179, 180
Maya Coffee Cooperatives, 134
Maya, 40, 128, 132, 134, 135, 136, 137
  See also Mexican culture
McKay, Paul and Mary, 133
Membership, 12, 13, 14, 17, 23, 27, 53, 78,
  86, 88, 89, 93, 107, 109, 117, 121,
  127, 129, 131, 151, 153, 155, 156,
  157, 158, 178
  youth participation, 13, 114, 145, 159
Membership fees, 156
Mennonite Central Committee (MCC), 131,
  133
Mennonites, 19
Mercantilism, 174
Merged Model, *See* Standard Economic
  Model
Mestizos, 128
  See also Mexican culture
Meta-analysis, 39, 41, 43, 46, 49, 52, 53, 54,
  55, 56
Meta-cognitive strategies, 42, **45**
Mexican culture, 128, 129, 136
Mexico, 5, 9, 15, 19, 23, 64, 120, 125-137,
  144, 154, 157, 161, 162
Migrants, 144
Militarism, 68, 75, 174, 178

Military costs, 178
   See also Capitalism, military costs
Mills, John Stuart, 9, 181
Moctezuma, 132
   See also Mexican culture
Models, 2, 37, **58**, 59, 60, 71, 72, 75, 76,
   105, 111, 179
Modern monopoly capitalism, 34
   See also Capitalism, free market
Mohammad Hatta, Indonesia, 87
Mondragón Cooperative Corporation
   (MCC), 116, 123, 160, 179
Mondragón, *See* Spain, Mondragón
   Cooperatives
Morelos, 128
Moreno, 132
   See also Mexican culture
Motivation, 39, 44, 47, 48, 54, 56, 71
Multi-sector Cooperation, 18
Mumbai (Bombay), 14, 97, 98, 108
Muslims, 98
Myth of competition, 61
   See also Imperialism

Nahuatl (language, Mexico), 132
Napoleon, 113
Narmada Dam Project, India, 75
National Cooperative Bank (NCB), 28
National Cooperative Business Association
   (NCBA), 13, 151
National Development Board, 109
   See also Operation Flood
Near East, 13
Neocolonialism, 125, 129
Neocorporate economics, 16, 17
Neo-liberalism, 74, 92, 105, 110, 137, 169,
   170, 174
Netherlands, 11, 68, 76, 78
New Cooperative Network, India, 101
New World, *See* Americas
Nonviolence, 75, 76, 84, 179, 180
Normans in Italy, 67
North American Free Trade Agreement,
   NAFTA, xi, 64, 131, 134-137, 144
North American Indigenous, 125
Nova Scotia, 27

Obregón, Álvaro (O'Brian), 128
Ocean Spray, 9, 14, 22
Oil crisis, 16
Old guard effect, 52

Old Taxco, Mexico, **130-132**, 161
Olmec, *See* Mexican Culture
ONCE, Spain, 119
Operation Bootstrap, Puerto Rico, 143
Operation Flood
   dairy cooperative (Anand), 108
   (MILMA), 109
   See also India, Kerala
Other Backward Communities, *See* Caste
   system
Outboard motors (OMBs), 106
Outcome evaluation, 73
Overproduction, 67, 68, 173
   See also Capitalism, overproduction

Pacific Rim, 64, 91
   See also Australia
Panama, 142
Parity dollars (PPP), 92
Patent laws, 176
   See also Legal restrictions
Paulo Lugari, 127
Pencavel, John, 168
Pension Savings Plan for Depositors, 87
Peoples Bank of Indonesia, 89, 90, 94
Perestroika, 20
   See also Russia
Performance contracts, 178
Persia
   language, 96
   Caspian, 96
Philippines, 84, 126
Piaget, J., 42
Picasso, Pablo, 114
Political
   constraints, 12, 16, 20, 31, 33, 129, 137,
     160, 161
   world debt, 178
   intervention, 12, 33, 87, 88, 92
     See also Political, constraints
   parties, 1, 11, 17, 19, 20, 24, 77, 105, 106
   support (United Europe), 11, 17, 78, 180
Ponce de Leon, First Governor of Puerto
   Rico, 141
Portugal, 68
Portuguese traders in India, 105
Poverty, 2, 5, 9, 20, 24, 25, 27, 58-66, 73,
   75-87, 90, 93-95, 99-101, 105, 106,
   110, 111, 125, 128, 129, 134-139,
   148-149, 167-172, 175, 181
Poverty index, 76

Poverty line, 20, 64, 94
 See also Poverty index
Poverty Reduction Strategy Paper (PRSP),
 73, 79
PRI party, Mexico, 134-135
privateers, 142
Private property (property ownership), 85, 141
Process gain/loss, 43, **46**
Public School curriculum, 88
Public School Teachers cooperative,
 Indonesia, 88
Public shares without voting privilege, 155
Puerto Rico, **139-148**
 ATM machines, 147
 Cooperative Associations Act, 145
 Cooperatives, 144
 Juvenile Cooperatives, 145, 146
 University, 145
p-value, 41, 43, 44, 46, 48, 50

Quaker, 133
 See also MacKay, Paul and Mary
Quality of life, 9, 34, 73, 90, 94, 95, 105
Quality of Reasoning, 42, **44**
Quebec, 26

Racism, 75, 91, 92, 99, 137, 171, 172
Recession, 58, 63
Reliability, 41, 50, 53
Relocalization, 177, 181
Rhine Valley, 25
Rich-get-richer effect, 52
Rivera
 Luis Muñoz, 143
 Luis Muñoz Marín, 143
Robber barons, 31, 72, 160
Rochdale, 10, 12, 16, 20, 30, 31, 34, 80, 92,
 155
Roosevelt, F.D., 21, 24, 143
Rural Electrification, REA, 21, 29
Russia, 20

Saint Francis Xavier University, 145
Salinas, President of Mexico, 135
San Juan Bautista (Puerto Rico), 141
Sanskrit, 96, 97
Santa Prisca Church, Taxco, Mexico, 130
Scandinavia, 24
 Norway, 13, 76, 78
 Sweden, 13, 68, 72, 76, 78

Scheduled Castes, 96, 101
 See also Caste system
Scheduled Tribes (ST), 101
 See also Scheduled Castes
Schumpeter, Joseph, 57, 67, 79
Seattle, 75, 76
Second World, 125
Secondary cooperatives, 121
Secunderabad, 99, 179
selvas, 126, 134
SERRV, 131
Shakespeare, 97
Sherman Antitrust Act, US, 4, 31, 34, 68, 160
SIFFS, 106, 107
 See India, Kerala, fisher cooperative
 (SIFFS)
Silver Artisans Cooperative, 130
Smith, Adam, xiii, 3, 38, 66-67, 169
Smith, J.W., 169, 175, 182
Social capital, 179, 181
Social justice for workers, 120, 123
Social Organization, 69, 70
Southeast Asia, 4, 83-94
Soviet Union, 61, 125
Spain, 4, 5, 11, 13, 68, 76, 81, 113-116, 120,
 124, 128, 129, 142, 143, 147, 156,
 158, 160
 Civil War
  Franco, 114-115, 120, 123
 Mondragón Cooperatives, 11, **113-124**
  Caja Laboral Popular, 115, 116, 117,
   119, 121, 122, 123, 154, 155, 156
  challenges for future, 122
  communication, 118, 121, 122, 123,
   153, 158, 160
  Councils, 116, 117, 118, 121, 122
  Directorate, 119
  EROSKI, 117, 122
  external corporations, 119
  General Manager, 117, 167
  Ikerlan (insurance), 115, 116
  interest groups, 118, 122
  management salaries, 118
  New organizational structure, 119, 120
  profit sharing, 118
  research groups, 117, 118, 122
  role of Catholic Church, 115, 120
  schools of technology, 114
  shop floor relations, 117, 160
  steel mill, 115, 118, 154

strike of 1974, 115
temporary and part-time workers, 115
Ten Principles, 120
Spanish Armada, 142
Spanish Civil War *See* Spain, Civil War
Spencer, Herbert, 38
Spratling, William, 130, 132
Standard Economic Model, 3, **57-80**, 111,
        153, 172, 174, 177, 180
Standard Model
        See also Standard Economic Model
Statehood (Puerto Rico), 144, 147
Structural Adjustment Program (SAP), 60,
        64, 65, 77, 214
Subsidies, 64, 65, 77, 135, 154
Success of cooperatives, 7, 20, 25, 93, 123
        Café Prasad, 157
        Calavo, 22, 23, 34, 162
        communication, 159
        community, 156, 158, 159, 162
        interviews, Appendix D
        Mondragón, 122, 123
        organization, 159
        participation, 122, 153, 157
        Why Co-ops Succeed, 152
        Yellow Cab, 15, 157, 158
Sucker effect, 52
Sunkist, 9, 14, 22
Supply-side economics, 74
Sustainable development, 12
Suzuki method, 46
Symmetry of Trade, 60, 61, 64

Telugu (Language), 100
Tennessee Valley Authority (TVA), 29
Thin World, *See* Development
Third World, *See* Development
Toltec, 128, 132
        See also Mexican culture
Trade balance, 60, 69, 91
Transfer of learning, 43
Transferable shares, 155
Transnational Corporations, 21, 23, 34, 64, 66,
        72, 74, 75, 88-90, 94, 105, 110, 125,
        135, 137, 149, 162, 167, 173, 175
Treaty of Paris, 143
t-ratio, 50, 51, Appendix B-210
Truman, Harry, 143
Tsotsil, 134
        See also Maya Coffee Cooperatives

Tsunami of 2004, 94, 107, 111
Tulane University, 130

Unemployment, 17, 29, 61, 65, 77, 92, 114,
        128, 144, 180
Union-busting, 171
Unión Progresista Artisanal, Old Taxco,
        130-132
United Kingdom (UK), 9, 10, 11 14, 15, 18,
        76, 84
Universidad Nacional, Colombia, 126
Universidad Nacional, El Salvador, 11
University Cooperative Bookshop
        (Australia), 93
University of London, 97
Utopian communities, 1, 10, 127, 139
        See also Communes

Vedic Hinduism, 84
Veracruz, 142
Vertical model, 61, 69, 70, 71
        See also Hierarchical model;
        Imperialism
Vicente Guerrero Cooperative, 132 ff.
Villa, Francisco (Pancho), 128
Volunteer labor, 14
Voting method (in Meta-analysis), 43

Wage Equity, 118, 120
Wal-Mart, 16, 64, 89, 163, 170-177
Washington Consensus, 57, 58
        See also Standard Economic Model
Wealth, 21, 24, 31, 34, 60-76, 98, 105, 125,
        126, 129, 130, 136, 166, 167, 169-
        176, 181
Weavers, 10
        See also Rochdale
World Bank, 2, 60-80, 105, 125, 180
World Trade Organization (WTO), xv, 73,
        76-78, 180
World War II, 11, 16, 21, 60, 68, 84, 87,
        115, 125, 145

Yunus, Muhammad, 83, 84, 85, 93

Zamagni, Stefano, 19
Zapata, Emilio, 128
Zero-sum games, 38
z-scores, 40, 41, 42, 43, 46, 48, 53, 54,
        Appendix B